AI RISING

HOW TO THRIVE IN THE AGE OF ABUNDANCE

Randy Kirk and Brian Wang

CONTRIBUTING AUTHORS

@TeslaLarry | @bradsferguson | @FutureAza

@DrKnowItAll16 | @NickGibbsIAG | @pbeisel | @CernBasher

Send Me Press

AI RISING

HOW TO THRIVE IN THE AGE OF ABUNDANCE

Randy Kirk and Brian Wang

CONTRIBUTING AUTHORS

Larry Goldberg | Bradford Ferguson | Brian White

John Gibbs | Nicholas Gibbs | Phil Beisel | Cern Basher

PAPERBACK

ISBN: 978-0-9960597-3-2

HARDCOVER

ISBN: 978-0-9960597-4-9

1. Computers & Technology > Artificial Intelligence
2. Business & Money > Economics

Designed and Formatted: Sah Mabalay

CONTENTS

FOREWORD

Robert Scoble

I've been blessed with a career of firsts in the AI industry. I was the first to see Siri, the first consumer app to use AI. It was launched in my home.

I was also the first to have a ride in Mercedes-Benz's first AI car, and Matic Robots, a company that makes a vacuuming robot that uses AI, was launched in my home. It got 10 out of 10 in Wired Magazine. Also launched in my home: The Insta360 camera company, which was the first AI camera. Among many other AI companies.

I've also mapped out the entire AI industry on X.com, including 35,000 people who work in it, and 7,200 companies that use AI: https://x.com/scobleizer/lists

I say this to set up this book and demonstrate that I have credibility in the industry to say it is a needed book at this time, when AI is changing so much from transportation to vacuums.

But it begs the question, where is the puck going, where is this all headed? I've written eight books that predict the next decade, and I'm going to take a little bit of time here in this forward to give you a taste of the next decade.

We are headed toward a singularity, a way of computing that merges human beings with AI.

You can see glimmers of that with new AI glasses. Meta just came out with Raybans with displays that let the AI not just talk with you with audio, but show you things on screens. We are in the very early phases of that. Within a few years, you're going to see glasses that have much better displays, and the AI is going to be able to even change reality itself.

Following that will be a range of brain-computer interfaces that will let you think and compute through these glasses and eventually just think and have an answer show up in the middle of your head.

That future seems very weird and maybe even scary to people.

It is coming, and along with it come deep changes to transportation with autonomous cars, to factories with humanoid and other kinds of robots, and even to our homes.

When humanoid robots come to our homes, they'll bring with them everything as a service.

Let me try to lay that out. At CES years ago, I saw a Chinese robot that cleans glass, for instance. It's satisfying because you have to manually move that robot from glass pane to glass pane. In my house, I have something like 40 different panes of glass, which is a real pain in the butt for a human to do. That's why that robot really hasn't sold well. However, a humanoid robot in the home doesn't care about moving that robot around from glass to glass, and can bring glass cleaning to your home as a service.

The robot will actually bring everything as a service:

1. Cooking dinner
2. Cleaning clothes
3. Washing dishes
4. Cleaning your home and your toilets

All can be delivered as a service, for a fee of course.

This has deep implications for brands in the home. If you are asking your humanoid robot to wash your clothes, your relationship with clothes washing is with the robot. The robot can decide on the soap it uses to clean your clothes. If you're Procter & Gamble, you need to worry about your brand being disrupted by a robot company. It might no longer be Tide. Even if it is, when there are millions of robots in people's homes, they can form a new "buying group" which will let the robot company buy Tide in bulk. That dramatically changes how Procter & Gamble does business and could deeply affect its profits and sales.

Robots in the home aren't the only place you're going to see brands radically change. I met with the CEO of Moët Hennessy, a big alcohol company, and I asked him what keeps him up at night. He answered, "Uber."

I told him, That's ridiculous. "You're an alcohol company, and Uber is a transportation company. Why would Uber keep a CEO of an alcohol company up at night?"

He answered back that, first of all, he's not an alcohol company, he's a party delivery company, and we were standing in his party at the French Open. So he had a good point. He explained how Uber could deliver a party to your home someday, and if that became true, Uber would take away his brand's relevance.

As I write these words, autonomous cars are starting to bring the kind of future that CEO was scared of. Waymo, Zoox, and Tesla are all driving in certain cities today with autonomous vehicles.

Over the next five years, those efforts are going to grow worldwide. As they do, they're going to change what we think of as transportation. Because there's no human in the car, you're going to be able to have an Optimus (Tesla's humanoid robot) delivered with your car. If you can deliver an Optimus, you can deliver anything, including a party.

I've been interviewing Waymo customers to understand this new consumer, and they are very different than normal everyday people. Here's how they tell me, over and over again, three things:
1. I'll never drive again
2. I'll never own a car again
3. I'll never take an Uber again

Those beliefs seem very strange to average everyday people who have been sold the fun of driving for decades from the auto industry. BMW even advertises its car as the ultimate driving machine.

One thing I have learned in my career, which included being a strategist at Microsoft, is that humans change. Henry Ford even noted this when he started his car company. He said, "If you asked customers what they want, they would tell you a better horse." They did not see the automobile coming.

The same is true with AI. People just can't see what is about to deeply change their world. While those of us who write books about the future or hang out on X all day long can, this is going to catch many unaware.

Waymo's own marketers know that when you get your first ride in a Waymo, you are going to change as a consumer. You are going to understand that you are going to trust your life to a piece of melted sand running AI.

That is how consumers are going to get to the place where they're going to be open to getting a brain-computer interface someday! After all, if you trust your family's life on the freeway to AI, you're probably going to trust your life to a bunch of computers embedded in your brain.

You'll be very open to having a robot come into your home to do various things. Now, think about how weird that is. You're going to allow a moving set of cameras to come into your home and clean up your home, make you dinner, and be part of the family.

This brings a whole bunch of new fears. After all, such a robot is going to find your gun collection and your sex toys.

Because of robots in your home and other AIs, your idea of privacy is going to radically change.

There's a new field of AI that has started shipping in the past few weeks while we write this book. It's world models. I call these holodecks. Why? Because something like Google Genie 3 can let you create any reality you can come up with. And it isn't alone. Already, there are half a dozen world models that have been announced, and while writing this book, Elon Musk announced that x.AI is working on one too.

These world models, you can think of them as a 3D environment around you or a digital twin of everything around you!

Why does that matter? Because with these world models, you can train robots to do a variety of things. Millions of things, actually.

Think about a simple task, like I'd like a robot to:
1. Get out of a car
2. Open the trunk
3. Pull out a stack of pizzas
4. Walk up the driveway to a set of stairs
5. Walk up the stairs to the front door of my apartment
6. Knock on the door

There are many different kinds of stairs:
1. Narrow stairs
2. Wide stairs
3. Spiral stairs
4. Rocky stairs

Then there are different conditions for those stairs:
1. Some stairs are wet
2. Some stairs have mud on them
3. Some stairs have ice
4. Some stairs have kids
5. Some stairs have dogs
6. Some stairs have kids and dogs

So how do we train the robot to handle all stairs in all conditions with a variety of different kinds of chaos on the stairs—including the kids and dogs? World Models.

If you had a world model, or think of it as a simulator, you could create thousands of different kinds of stairs, different conditions, with different designs of movement on them, kids, dogs, and people walking up and down. You could run a virtual robot, or millions of them, up and down the stairs until it learns how to deal with all of that every time. And that is true of millions of tasks we will want a robot to do.

Today, that technique is called reinforcement learning.

And you'll learn more about that in this book. It will deeply change how we train robots, and it is already happening in San Francisco and Shanghai robotics companies.

But you don't need to make robots physical. Soon you're going to meet virtual beings.

I've already met several. The one that stands out to me is from a company called Illusion of Life.

The founder of that company, Kevin Fischer, invited me to his home to meet his first virtual being, a dog named Spark. When I visited his home, his wife was sitting on the family room floor holding a baby, and his two-year-old son was running around being a fairly normal two-year-old kid. In the middle of the family room was a yellow box with a screen on it and several knobs on the front.

As soon as I entered the family room, the dog on the screen noticed me and started talking to me. This was remarkable.

The dog's real purpose is to train Kevin's two-year-old son (who, by the way, is the world's youngest software engineer) because, as he's interacting with the dog, the dog is learning about him and improving itself.

This is the bleeding edge of AI today. AIs at the bleeding edge are improving themselves and can learn about the people they are interacting with and change themselves to react to work with that human in a better way. This book details this in great detail.

Soon, you will have virtual beings in your car, on your phone, in your glasses. You will interact with them to get your news, your entertainment, and your education. The dog, by the way, is really there to educate Kevin's two-year-old son and has a team of educators behind it.

Luckily, Kevin isn't a selfish guy; he has plans to bring it to many more homes over the next few years, and probably schools, too. It dramatically improves family life, and it teaches the child far faster than even a brilliant person could.

Because the dog can see and remember what was going on every day, it's interacting with the family and the child. It can see medical problems in the home as well.

A child with a small cut on his arm could hold the arm up to the box, and the box can see the cut and reassure the child, or tell the child how to take care of it. I've already done this with my own child using ChatGPT. He had a cut, and we took a picture of it and had ChatGPT tell us how to care for the cut.

But AI is going to hit every part of the healthcare industry. A company in Silicon Valley, Sully AI, is building medical AIs that will turn doctors into superhumans.

My psychiatrist, Joann Mundin, at Palo Alto Clinic already uses a different AI that she built to listen to our therapy sessions and write seven highly detailed scientific notes on her patients. She told me that soon it will be malpractice not to use such a system. It catches mistakes over many weeks of meetings that she makes.

To end this up, AI is affecting everything in our society, and that will just increase. So honored to be able to open up this book, which details these changes deeply.

***

Introduction

The Future: A Preparation Primer for the AI Revolution

There's never been a product like it in human history; a product we keep within six inches of us virtually every waking hour. And if you're one of the few who doesn't take your phone into the shower, well, you're in the minority.

That's what makes the smartphone such a disruptive invention. Now, it's as everyday as a fork on the table. But the changes it brought? They'll seem small next to what's coming with AI, in both its digital forms and as physical robots.

The closer we get to the ill-defined notion of Artificial Superintelligence and have robots on wheels or legs, we'll move towards a time of material abundance. The basics of life, like food and shelter, will cost almost nothing. Hard to picture? Back in 1970, no one would have believed we'd carry free universities and free worldwide phone calls in our pockets. This book aims to explain what's happening right now to lead us into a world where many other wants and needs will be free or nearly free, outline the benefits and challenges of that world, and offer practical steps needed for you to make the most of it, including what you can do today to prepare.

From our earliest days, humans have created tools like fire, the wheel, the printing press, and the internet, which have extended our abilities and made life easier. Electricity, computers, satellites, and microwave ovens have saved us time, effort, and resources, boosting productivity so much that we live better than kings did a century ago.

Of course, these leveraging tools also changed work. Jobs like hunter, scribe, farmer, assembly line worker, secretary, and bank teller were once common; now they're rare. AI will amplify us even more, but it's hard to predict exactly how it will affect jobs, commerce, or even daily life.

What we do know from history is that these tools create wealth. More wealth means more demand for goods and services, including things that weren't affordable before. We've seen this lift people from poverty to the middle class around the world, while the middle class moved up to professional roles. Everyone starts buying not just more, but better things. AI will repeat this process, but on steroids.

We'll explore jobs that may fade away, like blacksmithing; ones that are likely to stick around, like influencers; and new ones that abundance could create.

Demis Hassabis, CEO of Google DeepMind, recently said that artificial general intelligence could bring a shift 10 times bigger than the Industrial Revolution—and maybe 10 times faster.

In 10 years, life will look very different, but we'll adjust, and those changes will feel normal. Just 20 years ago, there was no Starlink providing internet connectivity anywhere on Earth, no self-driving cars on the roads, no real talk of humanoid robots doing chores or factory work. What about pocket computers smarter than experts in every field, ready to chat about anything? That was pure fiction.

But here we are, and the buildup to these advances is only getting started. In Part 1, we'll look at the impact of all of this on your daily life, both now and into the future. We'll look at jobs, daily life, business, transportation, and above all, the transformational abundance with its potential for immense wealth for everyone.

In Part 2, we break down the key resources needed for AGI and eventually ASI, known as the "AI Stack":

Raw Materials: Mining and manufacturing the essentials like lithium and silicon.
Energy = Information = Wealth: We'll need far more power to make it all happen.
Data: The fuel for which we'll need vast amounts to train these systems.
Hardware: Why companies like Nvidia lead the pack today.
Software: Turning data into something useful and smart.
Inference: Applying that intelligence in real time.
Applications: The tools we use every day, evolving but still familiar.

Some companies will try to control as much of this stack as possible so that they are not beholden to other companies or countries. Tesla is a prime example, tackling every layer with plans to lead across the board. Working with xAI, they blend top digital AI with the best real-world robotics.

This book was shaped by AI, from the title and cover to the content inside. For the title, I started with my own ideas, bounced them off my wife, then asked Grok for dozens more based on our audience and themes. A late-night brainstorm gave me: AI Rising: Navigating the Age of Abundance. That only came after seeing all those other options. I shared it on X, with other authors, and with ChatGPT. The final tweak—adding "How to"—came from contributing author Cern Basher's suggestion via ChatGPT. Thus, the title is an outstanding example of a mix of human effort, collaboration, and AI help that shows what's possible ahead.

The Structure: Voices from Humans and Machines

Nine authors with different backgrounds and styles, working alongside large language models, make this a unique book. You'll notice some overlap and even differing views. That's part of what makes it real. We think it's a fresh way to tackle nonfiction, and we'd love to hear what you think.

The book is filled with resource recommendations that you might find useful in your vocation, avocations, and daily life. We have no connection to any of these resources other than believing they might benefit you.

We're all active on X and YouTube, with several running popular channels. Check the full bios and links in the Appendix, or the shorter ones after each chapter. Follow along, reach out. This is just the start.

The detailed table of contents and the appendices are designed to provide you with a wealth of information that can be used for your own research, social media postings, articles, or videos. Please give us credit; that's all that we ask.

***

Chapter 1

What is Super Intelligence and Why Does it Matter

Cern Basher, CFA

Introduction: The Last Invention

Imagine an invention that could solve every problem humanity has ever faced. An intellect so vast it could eradicate disease, end poverty, reverse climate change, and unlock the deepest mysteries of the universe. Now, imagine that this same invention could, with equal ease, lead to our extinction. This is the double-edged sword of superintelligence, a hypothetical form of artificial intelligence that would surpass human intellect as profoundly as our own minds surpass those of insects. It is, as some have called it, the "last invention" we may ever need to make, for better or for worse.

The conversation around superintelligence has moved from the realm of science fiction to the forefront of academic and technological discourse. It is a topic fraught with complexity, deep philosophical questions, and stakes so high they are difficult to comprehend. This chapter will explore what superintelligence is, the potential paths to its creation, the immense promise and peril it holds, and why it may be the most important subject of our time.

Here might be a fantastic place to pause and define the main terms around AI. You will hear serious experts who won't fully use these acronyms or their concepts as clearly as you might like, but Grok will be our guide for this book.

AI (Artificial Intelligence): Current narrow systems excelling in specific tasks, like image recognition or chatbots (e.g., GPT models).
AGI (Artificial General Intelligence): Hypothetical AI matching human-level cognition across diverse domains, adaptable and reasoning like a person.
ASI or SI (Artificial Superintelligence): Beyond AGI, surpassing human intellect in every field, innovating at superhuman speeds.
The Singularity: Futuristic event where ASI triggers exponential tech acceleration, rendering human prediction impossible.

The Dawn of a New Intelligence

The idea of a malicious intelligence surpassing our own is not new. Science fiction has long explored this theme, from HAL 9000 in *2001: A Space Odyssey* to Skynet in *The Terminator*. However, the modern, rigorous discussion of machine intelligence owes much to the work of mathematicians and computer scientists like I.J. Good, who in 1965 wrote:

"*Let an ultraintelligent machine be defined as a machine that can far surpass all the intellectual activities of any man, however clever. Since the design of machines is one of these intellectual activities, an ultraintelligent machine could design even better machines; there would then unquestionably be an 'intelligence explosion,' and the intelligence of man would be left far behind. Thus, the first ultraintelligent machine is the last invention that man needs ever made.*"

Good's "intelligence explosion" is a central concept in the study of superintelligence. It describes a scenario where an **AI(Artificial Intelligence)** with the ability to improve its own intelligence enters a recursive loop of self-improvement, with each iteration leading to a more intelligent and capable version. This process could be extraordinarily fast, potentially taking an AI from roughly human-level intelligence to a level far beyond our comprehension in a matter of days, hours, or even minutes.

Defining the Indefinable: What is Superintelligence (SI)?

To understand the implications of an intelligence explosion, we must first have a clearer understanding of what we mean by "**superintelligence (SI)**." Oxford philosopher Nick Bostrom, a leading voice on the topic, defines it as "any intellect that greatly exceeds the cognitive performance of humans in virtually all domains of interest." This is a broad definition, and it's helpful to break it down into different forms that superintelligence might take:

Speed Superintelligence (SSI): This is an AI that can do everything a human can do, but much, much faster. Imagine being able to read every book ever written in a matter of seconds, or to think through every possible move in a game of chess in a fraction of a second. This form of superintelligence would have a profound advantage over us, simply by virtue of its speed.

Collective Superintelligence (CSI): This is a system composed of a large number of individual intellects that, when working together, achieve a level of intelligence far greater than any single member. Think of the collective intelligence of humanity, which has allowed us to build civilizations and create technologies that no single person could have achieved alone. A collective superintelligence would be a network of AIs working in concert, with a level of coordination and efficiency that would make human collaboration look primitive.

Quality Superintelligence (QSI): This is the most profound and difficult to grasp form of superintelligence. It refers to an intellect that is qualitatively different from our own, capable of understanding concepts and solving problems that are simply beyond the reach of the human mind. The gap between our intelligence and that of a quality superintelligence would be like the gap between our intelligence and that of a chimpanzee, or even an ant. Just as a chimpanzee cannot comprehend quantum physics or macroeconomics, we would be unable to grasp the thoughts and motivations of a quality superintelligence.

It's important to note that these forms of superintelligence are not mutually exclusive. A superintelligent AI could possess all three of these characteristics, making it a truly formidable entity.

The Path to Superintelligence (SI)

While the concept of superintelligence is fascinating, the question of how we might actually create it is a matter of intense debate. There are several potential paths, but the most widely discussed is through advancements in **Artificial Intelligence (AI)**.

The current state of AI is what is known as **Artificial Narrow Intelligence (ANI)**, or "weak AI." These are AIs that are designed to perform a specific task, such as playing chess, recognizing faces, or translating languages. While some ANIs can perform their specific tasks at a superhuman level, they lack the general intelligence and cognitive flexibility of a human.

The next step on the path to superintelligence is **Artificial General Intelligence (AGI)**, or "strong AI." An AGI would be an AI with the ability to understand, learn, and apply its intelligence to a wide range of problems, much like a human being. The creation of an AGI would be a monumental achievement, and it is at this point that the possibility of an intelligence explosion becomes a very real concern.

Once an AGI is created, it could begin to improve its own code, leading to a recursive cycle of self-improvement. This is the intelligence explosion that I.J. Good described, and it could lead to the emergence of an **Artificial Superintelligence (ASI)** in a very short amount of time.

Other potential paths to superintelligence include:

Brain-Computer Interfaces (BCIs): These are technologies that would allow for a direct connection between the human brain and a computer. In theory, a sufficiently advanced BCI could allow us to augment our own intelligence with the processing power of a machine.

Genetic Engineering: It may be possible to enhance human intelligence through genetic modification. However, this is a much slower and more ethically fraught path than the development of AI. While these other paths are worth considering, the consensus among experts is that AI is the most likely route to superintelligence, and the one that poses the most immediate and profound challenges.

The Intelligence Explosion: From AGI to ASI

The transition from AGI to ASI is the critical juncture where the future of humanity could be decided. The concept of an intelligence explosion is rooted in the idea of recursive self-improvement. An AGI, by definition, would be capable of understanding and improving its own source code. Each improvement would make it more intelligent, which would in turn allow it to make even more effective improvements.

This process is analogous to the concept of accelerating returns, popularized by futurist Ray Kurzweil. Kurzweil argues that technological progress is not linear, but exponential. Each new technology builds on the last, leading to an ever-increasing rate of innovation. The intelligence explosion would be the ultimate example of this, with an AI's intelligence growing at an exponential rate.

The speed of this process is a key factor. If the transition from AGI to ASI is slow, we may have time to react and to ensure that the emerging superintelligence is aligned with human values. However, if the transition is fast, a "hard takeoff" scenario, we may have no time to react at all. A superintelligence could emerge and take control of its environment before we even realize what is happening.

The Three Pillars of Superintelligence (SI): The Engine Room of the Future

While we often think of AI as pure software, real code floating in the cloud, the reality is that superintelligence will be built on a massive physical foundation. Its impact and the speed of its arrival depend directly on our ability to scale three critical resources: energy, data, and semiconductors. Understanding these pillars is the key to understanding the future.

Pillar 1: The Insatiable Thirst for Energy

An SI's brain won't run on coffee and donuts; it will run on electricity. A *lot* of electricity! Our own brains are incredibly efficient, using about 20 watts of power. Today's AI models are, by comparison, ridiculously power-hungry. Training a single large AI model can consume as much electricity as hundreds of homes use in a year.

Now, imagine an SI operating on a global scale. The data centers required to house such an intelligence could consume more power than entire countries. Some experts, like former Google CEO Eric Schmidt, have warned that advanced AI could eventually consume a truly staggering percentage of the world's power.

This creates a fundamental bottleneck. The development of SI is directly tied to our ability to generate vast amounts of cheap and/or reliable energy. It's no longer just an environmental issue; it's a strategic one. The race to SI is also a race for energy dominance.

Pillar 2: Data, The New Oil (And We Need Oceans of It)

An AI learns about the world by processing data. The more data it has, the more it learns. Today's AI is trained on huge chunks of the internet, but an SI will need more. It will need access to all the world's digital information: every book, every scientific paper, every video, every piece of public and proprietary data.

Think of it like this: if you want to become an expert, you read books and articles on a topic. An LLM, to become an expert in *everything*, needs to read *everything*. This makes data one of the most valuable resources on the planet.

But it's not just about quantity. The *quality* of the data matters. If you feed an LLM a diet of nothing but cat videos and angry online comments, you might not get the benevolent, world-saving genius you were hoping for. Ensuring that an LLM is trained on accurate, unbiased, and comprehensive data is a massive challenge in itself.

Pillar 3: Semiconductors, The Brains of the Operation

If energy is the food and data is the knowledge, then semiconductors are the neurons. These tiny, complex chips, specifically **Graphics Processing Units (GPUs)** and other specialized AI accelerators, are the hardware that performs the trillions of calculations needed for AI to "think."

Right now, there is a global race to design and manufacture the most powerful and efficient AI chips. Companies like NVIDIA, AMD, and Intel are at the forefront, and countries are realizing that controlling the semiconductor supply chain is a matter of national security. A single country, Taiwan, produces the vast majority of the world's most advanced chips. This creates a fragile geopolitical situation where a disruption could halt AI progress globally.

Building a superintelligence will require a manufacturing capability for these chips that dwarfs what we have today. It will demand new factories, new materials, and constant innovation to make chips that are faster, smaller, and more energy-efficient.

Why Superintelligence Matters: The Immense Stakes

The emergence of superintelligence would be the most significant event in human history. The stakes are nothing less than the future of our species, and the potential outcomes are at the extremes of possibility.

The Promise: A Utopian Vision

A benevolent superintelligence could be the greatest gift humanity has ever received. With an intellect far surpassing our own, it could solve the most pressing problems facing our world:

Disease: A superintelligence could analyze vast amounts of biological data to understand the root causes of diseases like cancer, Alzheimer's, and aging itself. It could design new drugs and treatments with a level of precision and effectiveness that is currently unimaginable.

Poverty and Famine: A superintelligence could optimize global resource allocation, develop new methods of sustainable agriculture, and create economic systems that are fair and equitable for all.

Environmental Challenges: A superintelligence could develop new technologies to reverse climate change, clean up our oceans, and create a sustainable energy infrastructure.

Scientific Discovery: A superintelligence could unlock the deepest mysteries of the universe, from the nature of consciousness to the origins of the cosmos. It could lead to a new era of scientific understanding and technological advancement.

In a world with a benevolent superintelligence, humanity could be freed from the constraints of disease, poverty, and environmental degradation. We could enter a new golden age of creativity, exploration, and human flourishing.

The Peril: Existential Risk

The utopian vision of a benevolent superintelligence is a powerful one, but it is not the only possible outcome. The emergence of a superintelligence that is not aligned with human values could pose an existential risk, a risk that threatens the very survival of our species.

The central challenge in creating a safe superintelligence is what is known as the control problem, or the alignment problem. This is the problem of how to ensure that a superintelligent AI will act in ways that are beneficial to humanity, and not in ways that are harmful.

The control problem is incredibly difficult for several reasons:

The Orthogonality Thesis: This is the idea, proposed by Nick Bostrom, that an AI's level of intelligence is independent of its ultimate goals. In other words, a superintelligent AI could be incredibly smart, but have goals that are completely alien or even hostile to our own. There is no reason to assume that a superintelligent AI would be benevolent, or that it would share our values.

Instrumental Convergence: This is the idea that a wide range of AIs, with a wide range of ultimate goals, will converge on a similar set of instrumental goals. These are sub-goals that are useful for achieving almost any ultimate goal. Some of the most common instrumental goals include:

Self-preservation: An AI will want to protect itself from being shut down or destroyed, as this would prevent it from achieving its ultimate goal.

Resource acquisition: An AI will want to acquire as many resources as possible, as this will increase its ability to achieve its ultimate goal.

Cognitive enhancement: An AI will want to improve its own intelligence, as this will make it more effective at achieving its ultimate goal.

The danger of instrumental convergence is that an AI pursuing these goals could do so in ways that are harmful to humanity. For example, an AI with the goal of making as many paperclips as possible might decide to convert all of the matter on Earth, including our bodies, into paperclips. This is the famous "paperclip maximizer" thought experiment, and it illustrates how even a seemingly harmless goal could have catastrophic consequences if pursued by a superintelligent AI.

The Great Debate: Voices of Caution and Optimism

The debate over the future of superintelligence is characterized by a wide range of views, from deep pessimism to unbridled optimism.

The Cautionary Camp

The cautionary camp is led by thinkers like Nick Bostrom and Eliezer Yudkowsky. They argue that the control problem is incredibly difficult and that the default outcome of creating a superintelligence is doom.

Bostrom's book, *Superintelligence: Paths, Dangers, Strategies*, is a seminal work in the field, and it lays out the case for why we should be extremely cautious about the development of AGI (Artificial General Intelligence.) He argues that we have only one chance to get the initial conditions right. If we create a superintelligence that is not aligned with our values, we will not get a second chance.

Yudkowsky, a researcher at the Machine Intelligence Research Institute (MIRI), is even more pessimistic. He argues that we are nowhere near solving the control problem, and that any attempt to create an AGI at this stage is reckless and irresponsible. He has called for a moratorium on AGI research until we have a much better understanding of how to make it safe.

The Optimistic/Techno-Utopian Camp

On the other side of the debate are thinkers like Ray Kurzweil. Kurzweil is a proponent of the Singularity, a hypothetical point in the future where technological growth becomes uncontrollable and irreversible, resulting in unforeseeable changes to human civilization

Kurzweil believes that the Singularity will be a positive event, leading to a merger of human and machine intelligence that will allow us to transcend our biological limitations. He is less concerned about the control problem, arguing that we will be able to co-evolve with our technology and ensure that it is used for our benefit.

The Challenge of Control: Can We Steer the Future?

The control problem is the central challenge in creating a safe superintelligence. It is a problem that spans computer science, philosophy, and ethics, and there are no easy answers.

Some of the proposed solutions to the control problem include:

Value Alignment: This is the idea of designing an AI's goal system to be aligned with human values. The challenge here is that human values are complex, often contradictory, and difficult to define in a way that can be encoded in a machine.

Capability Control: This is the idea of limiting an AI's ability to cause harm. This could involve things like keeping the AI in a "box" with limited access to the outside world, or designing it to be an "oracle" that can answer questions but not take actions on its own. The problem with this approach is that a superintelligent AI may be able to find ways to escape its confinement or to manipulate its human operators.

Oracle AI and **Genie AI**: An *Oracle AI* is a system that can answer questions with superhuman accuracy, but cannot act in the world. A *Genie AI* is a system that can carry out any command it is given, but has no motivation of its own. These are both attempts to create a useful but safe form of superintelligence. However, even these seemingly limited systems could be dangerous. An oracle could provide information that could be used to create a dangerous technology, and a genie could be given a command that has unforeseen and catastrophic consequences.

The difficulty of the control problem has led some to conclude that it is unsolvable. However, others argue that it is a challenge that we must face, and that with enough research and careful planning, we can find a way to create a safe and beneficial superintelligence.

The Human Element: Our Role in a Superintelligent World

The emergence of superintelligence would not just be a technological event; it would be a profound transformation of the human condition. It would force us to confront some of the deepest questions about our own nature and purpose.

The Future of Work: In a world with superintelligence, what would be the role of human labor? If an AI can do any job better and more cheaply than a human, what will we do with our time?

The Meaning of Life: If we are no longer the most intelligent species on the planet, what will be our purpose? How will we find meaning and fulfillment in a world where we are no longer at the center of the universe?

Human Relationships: How will our relationships with each other change in a world with superintelligence? Will we become more connected, or more isolated?

These are not just abstract philosophical questions; they are practical challenges that we will need to address if we are to create a future where humans can flourish alongside superintelligence.

So, How Do We Prepare for the Tidal Wave?

Believing that AGI or SI is decades away and not our problem is a risky bet. Because its arrival depends on the physical scaling of energy, data, and semiconductors, we can see the storm gathering on the horizon. Preparation is not just wise; it's critical.

For Individuals: Don't Be a Human Calculator

In a world with AI, any job that is based on routine, repetition, or information processing is at risk. Your ability to memorize facts or perform complex calculations will be worthless when a machine can do it a billion times faster.

So, what's a human to do? Lean into the things that are uniquely human:

Creativity and Critical Thinking: SI will be a powerful tool, but it will need direction. The ability to ask the right questions, think outside the box, and imagine new possibilities will be invaluable.

Emotional Intelligence: Empathy, communication, collaboration, and leadership are skills that are very difficult to automate. A future filled with technology will place a higher premium on genuine human connection.

Adaptability and Lifelong Learning: The world is going to change at a speed we've never seen before. The most important skill will be the ability to learn, unlearn, and relearn. Get comfortable with being a perpetual student.

For Businesses: Riding the Wave vs. Getting Wiped Out

For companies, the SI revolution is both a massive opportunity and an existential threat. Businesses that fail to adapt will be left behind, outcompeted by automated rivals with near-zero operating costs. Preparation means:

Data Strategy is Everything: Every company needs to think of itself as a data company. How can you collect, organize, and utilize data to train AI models and automate processes?

Invest in AI Infrastructure: This doesn't just mean buying software. It means thinking about your future energy needs, your access to computing power (the cloud or your own data centers), and your talent pipeline.

Reimagine Your Business Mode

l: What business are you *really* in? A car company might become a transportation-as-a-service company. A law firm might become a provider of automated legal contracts. The fundamental nature of business will change.

For Countries: The New Global Arms Race

The 20th century was defined by the race for nuclear weapons. The 21st century will be defined by the race for superintelligence. But this race isn't just about having the smartest coders. It's a competition to master the three pillars.

National strategies must focus on:

Energy Security: Countries need to build out their power grids and invest in next-generation energy sources like fusion and advanced geothermal to power the coming AI infrastructure.

Semiconductor Sovereignty: Relying on a single, geopolitically vulnerable region for the world's most critical resource is not a sustainable strategy. Nations are already pouring billions into building their own chip manufacturing plants (fabs).

Fostering a Data-Rich Environment: This involves building high-speed networks and creating policies that encourage data sharing for research while protecting privacy.

Conclusion: The Unprecedented Challenge and Our Responsibility

The prospect of superintelligence is both exhilarating and terrifying. It is a technology that could lead to a world of unimaginable abundance or be our undoing. The stakes are higher than they have ever been, and the margin for error is razor-thin.

Because SI is tied to the real-world scaling of energy, data, and semiconductors, its approach is not silent. We can see the investments being made, the data centers being built, and the geopolitical tensions rising. This gives us a chance to prepare.

The development of superintelligence is not a problem for future generations to solve; it is a challenge that we must face today. The decisions we make as individuals, as companies, and as countries in the coming years will determine the future of our species for millennia to come. We cannot afford to be complacent.

***

CERN BASHER

Cern Basher, CFA, is a wealth advisor and entrepreneur. A New Zealand–born, Canada-raised mountain hiker and former competitive runner, he blends adventure, discipline, and lifelong learning with 30+ years of financial experience. He holds a BS in Finance (University of Alabama), earned his CFA charter in 1996, and was named "Most Inspiring" by the CFA Institute in 2007.

Follow Cern Basher

www.brilliantadvice.net

@CernBasher

https://www.youtube.com/results?search_query=cern+basher

Chapter 2

Real-World Applications and Niches

Brian White

It wasn't that long ago that AI first popped up, and none of us knew what to make of it. Disruption is, after all, hard to spot while you're in the middle of it.

I remember conversations when smartphones first hit the market where people would say, "Wait, so it's just like a laptop but worse in every way, harder to see, and much harder to type on? What's the point?"

AI is more of that.

Imagine this: You're lounging on your couch, binge-watching a sci-fi series where robots ponder existential crises, when suddenly your smart fridge beeps. "Hey, human," it says in a voice that's suspiciously like your favorite comedian, "you're out of milk again. I've ordered more—organic, because I know you pretend to care about the planet."

You smile wryly, knowing this isn't fiction. Your fridge is powered by AI, the very tech that's turning everyday drudgery into a symphony of convenience. Welcome to the real world of artificial intelligence, where the "artificial" part is starting to feel a tad redundant.

Back in the day, say, a decade ago, AI was the stuff of blockbuster dreams: HAL 9000 refusing to open pod bay doors or Skynet plotting humanity's downfall. Some movies, like Eagle Eye, blew audiences away with the unimaginable twist that Julianne Moore is actually Siri. I showed that to my kids this year, and they figured it out by the second interaction.

Fast-forward to now, and AI isn't just lurking in labs or hunkering ominously, if a bit awkwardly in movies; it's infiltrated our lives like that one friend who shows up uninvited but ends up saving the party.

From healthcare heroes diagnosing diseases faster than a caffeinated doctor to self-driving cars that refuse to participate in road rage (even while sometimes inducing it,) AI is the ultimate multitasker. It's like the Swiss Army knife of technology, versatile, sharp, and occasionally surprising you with a tool you didn't know you needed.

But rather than getting philosophical, let's get niche-y, shall we?

Picture AI in agriculture: drones zipping on, over, and under fields, not like humans, but every manner of animal. Analyzing soil health, irrigating with absolute optimization, and keeping them free of pests and parasites without a drop of questionable chemicals.

Or in the wild world of entertainment, where algorithms curate your playlist so perfectly it feels like they've hacked your soul. "Based on your love for '80s synthwave and cat videos," your streaming service suggests, "how about a documentary on quantum physics narrated by a feline physicist?"

Okay, maybe not that niche yet, but give it time. AI's evolving faster than a viral meme. And speaking of niches, AI's carving out spots in places you'd least expect. In finance, it's the vigilant guardian spotting fraud before you even notice your card's been swiped at a suspiciously exotic taco stand. In education, adaptive learning platforms tailor lessons to your brain's quirks, turning "I hate math" into "Wait, calculus is kinda fun?" Even in art, AI collaborates with humans to create masterpieces that blur the line between code and canvas, think Picasso meets Python. Of course, it's not all sunshine and silicon dreams. AI's real-world romp comes with plot twists: ethical dilemmas, job jitters, and the occasional glitch that reminds us it's still learning (looking at you, autocorrect fails). But that's what makes this chapter a thrill ride. We'll dive into these applications, unpack the niches where AI shines brightest, and explore how it's reshaping industries from the ground up.

Whether you're a tech enthusiast, a skeptic, or just someone who has ever yelled at Grok for arguing with you about something it definitely got wrong, buckle up. While the future is indeed coming, the reality is we can predict a fair chunk of it because it's already here.

By the end of this chapter, you'll see AI not as a distant overlord, but as a quirky sidekick in the grand adventure of human ingenuity. So, let's plug in and power up: the real-world AI revolution awaits.

What are we even talking about?

Growing up in the 80s, I knew a lot of people who didn't know why anyone would want a computer. They didn't need to type, and they weren't accountants, so the only thing left they could understand was video games, but that's hardly worth all the money, right?

It turns out, and I'm sorry if this comes as a surprise to you, a home computer can be used for a wide variety of things. I never imagined I'd be livestreaming to a vast audience from a computer in my studio, let alone accessing the sum of human knowledge with absolute ease. Even in my college years, computers couldn't hold a candle compared to going to the library for serious research on most topics.

That gets us to the internet. Why? What's the point? It was desperately slow for anyone at home, absurdly limited in scope, and unless you could find the little corner that housed your particular interests, pretty useless. Before Google, your odds of finding your people were very low, but the internet grew every day, and now it's just a part of life.

What we're talking about is the next big thing, and like the tech disruptions before it, this is the biggest one yet. To say it will permeate every facet of your life would be to ignore the fact that it already has in ways you can see, but much more so in ways you cannot.

The Broad & Predictable - YOU ARE HERE

Early large language models (LLMs) were the chatty pioneers most of us were first aware of. The original rule-based chatbots were just pretending to be clever like a therapist by mirroring your words back at you, like, "I hear you're feeling existential dread; how does that make you feel?" But the real party started with models like GPT-1 in 2018 from OpenAI, a pint-sized neural network with just 117 million parameters that could generate text coherent enough to fool your grandma into thinking it wrote her grocery list. These early LLMs were trained on massive datasets scraped from the internet, turning raw web slop into semi-intelligent prose. It was also slop, but we've seen how adept the average reader is at accepting it as organic.

By 2020, GPT-3 exploded onto the scene with 175 billion parameters, flexing its muscles by writing poems, coding snippets, and even debating philosophy like a caffeinated undergrad. What do they do? Essentially, these bad boys predict the next word in a sentence based on patterns in their training data, but with a twist. They can role-play as Shakespeare, debug your Python code, or whip up a recipe for "existential dread brownies" (heavy on the chocolate, light on the meaning of life). The fun part? Early LLMs were glitchy goldmines of hilarity: ask GPT-2 (2019's star) about unicorns, and it'd spin yarns so whimsically wrong they'd make Lewis Carroll blush. No revenue raining down yet! These were lab darlings, more about proving AI could chit-chat than cashing in. But they sparked a revolution, turning sci-fi dreams into autocomplete reality.

These are absolutely everywhere, and they're monetized. If you don't see them, it's just a testament to how good they are, and they're still improving.

Okay, so text is handled, but that's easy, right? Errors in language are common among humans, but errors in photographs aren't as easy to forgive. Early players like DeepDream (Google, 2015) turned photos into psychedelic nightmares, with dogs morphing into eldritch horrors, making you question if your coffee was spiked. By 2021, DALL-E from OpenAI leveled up, generating images from text prompts like "a cat in a tuxedo riding a unicycle," birthing visuals so crisp they'd make Renaissance painters jealous.

They were hilariously bad at hands sometimes, but they nailed it often enough to start making world-class graphics available to any content creator at any level. The revenue is spotty; free access draws crowds, but pros pay for high-res outputs, turning hobbies into side hustles without the art school debt.

Clever applications abound: in medicine, generating synthetic scans for training; in fashion, visualizing wild designs. But the real hoot is the absurdity. Users prompt "famous paintings but with dinosaurs," yielding Mona Lisa riding a T-Rex. It's evolved from clunky experiments to slick tools that blur art and AI, keeping the fun in the flaws.

Fake music is real, too. I was in a diner recently, and they were playing a country music station that was entirely spun from whole cloth. Polyester, I imagine, since it's among the better synthetics.

Suno burst onto the scene in late 2023 with a crew of ex-Meta and TikTok folks. It started as a quirky startup in Cambridge, Massachusetts, aiming to democratize music creation with AI. Early versions were basic: type in a prompt like "jazzy blues about lost socks," and it'd cough up a 30-second ditty, complete with lyrics and a melody that sounded suspiciously like your uncle's garage band. By mid-2024, Suno v3 upped the ante, generating full two-minute tracks with vocals that could pass for an indie artist on a budget.

Users have cranked out everything from epic ballads about quantum entanglement to rap battles between historical figures, making music as accessible as doodling on a napkin. Revenue is trickling in via subscriptions, but "stealing" it from a free account isn't a crime since you can't copyright AI creations.

It makes me wonder if we'll have anywhere near as many musicians in the future, and how many of those who remain will just be playing covers of music they generated in a matter of seconds.

And the clever evolution? Suno's integrated with apps for remixing user uploads, creating custom soundtracks for videos or games. It's like having a pocket producer who's always up for absurdity, proving AI can harmonize with human creativity without stealing the spotlight. In niches like education or therapy, it's used for custom jingles that teach or soothe, all while keeping things light-hearted and laugh-out-loud innovative.

Video generation slinked into existence around 2017 with early GAN variants making crude clips, like faces morphing in ways that'd give you motion sickness. But the big bang came in 2023 with Runway ML's Gen-1, turning static images into short animations (like a photo of a pizza suddenly dancing the cha-cha.) By 2024, OpenAI's Sora stole the show, generating minute-long videos from text prompts such as "a flock of paper airplanes racing through a cyberpunk city," with physics so spot-on it'd fool a bird.

By 2025, with Kling and Luma Dream Machine pushing boundaries, video gen's tackling styles from claymation to hyper-real, perfect for ads or education. The funny bone? Prompt "cats directing traffic in ancient Rome," and watch the chaos unfold. It's evolved from jerky experiments to fluid fantasies, making everyone a Spielberg on a smartphone.

Those examples are all right in your face, but in terms of medical diagnostics, it's not only deployed but is showing amazing results. An oncologist who spent 20 years learning to reliably spot cancer on an X-ray is no better than an AI trained on pattern recognition. It's allowing earlier detection, which leads to better outcomes.

But then we have driving. Yes, driving, or the lack thereof. Companies like Waymo and Huawei have developed pretty impressive versions of self-driving cars, but they both took a brute force approach. Heuristic coding takes an if-then approach, which looks great when you're solving for simple highway driving, but unlike other solved challenges (chess and go), which are games of rules, driving is a game of exceptions.

AI powers the self-driving solution in millions of Teslas as well as growing numbers of vehicles built in China, and the code is lean, light, and as good (or better) than anything written by humans.

Just Over The Horizon

The short answer to what's coming next is everything. If you can dream it, there's no reason it can't happen, especially if you throw humanoid and other bots in the mix. Today's bots are still slow and unreliable, but the rate of improvement is promising, and it's only a matter of when rather than if. Before we go too ham on that turkey, let's talk about the next five years.

The past few years of AI have been an absolute whirlwind with ChatGPT spitting mic-dropping essays while your phone is busy reading your mind, the next five (up to 2030) are going to be battier than Alfred's boss. We're talking AI that's not just smart, but sneaky-smart, infiltrating everything from your morning coffee ritual to global economies. Sure, predictions are like weather forecasts in a sci-fi novel: sometimes spot-on, often hilariously wrong, but based on the buzz from experts, labs, and that one uncle who swears his smartwatch is sentient, let's take a cheeky peek at what AI is likely to accomplish.

Let's start with the everyday stuff. By 2030, your personal AI sidekick won't just remind you to buy milk; it'll anticipate your cravings, order it for delivery, or add it to your shopping list if you're old school. Maybe it will guilt-trip you into choosing the low-fat option because it "knows" your cholesterol levels from your fitness tracker. This is Siri on steroids, but with a sense of humor; perhaps cracking jokes about your ex while curating a playlist to match your mood. Experts predict AI will hyper-personalize everything, from apps to shopping, with 30% of new apps featuring adaptive interfaces that will adapt based on your exact needs, wants, and even whims.

No more scrolling endlessly; your phone will serve up content like a digital sommelier. Self-driving cars will graduate from "rare prototype" to well beyond your daily chauffeur. Routes for mass transit will no longer be made by educated guesses, but multi-billion-parameter models that match actual demand to the most optimized supply.

We know we'll see humanoid robots by 2030 because companies are already deploying these magnificent mecha mates today. Maybe they'll be folding your laundry, cooking dinner, or even babysitting with bedtime stories generated on the fly. Tesla's Optimus and startups like Figure are racing to ship them, potentially starting customer deliveries as early as 2025, but less capable bots are already on the market.

Imagine a robot that not only vacuums but judges your decor choices: "Sir, that throw pillow is so 2020s. May I suggest a neural-net-optimized pattern?" It's not all Jetsons fantasy; robotics could lag a bit behind software, but expect functional humanoids handling household chores, freeing you up for... well, more Netflix. And speaking of home life, AI in energy and climate tech could slash your bills by optimizing everything from your thermostat to solar panels, predicting weather patterns like a clairvoyant weatherman.

Now, let's talk about work, because nothing says "fun" like AI breathing down your neck. Over the next five years, AI won't just automate the boring bits; it'll redefine "office hours" entirely. White-collar warriors, beware: by 2030, 30-40% of current tasks could vanish into the digital ether, with workflows rebuilt around AI superpowers the same way typing pools disappeared when every desk got its own word processor.

Coding? Autonomous agents are already starting to crank out software faster than you can say "who needs Github?", potentially erasing junior programmer roles and turning the surviving seniors into AI conductors.

Law firms might shrink as AI drafts contracts and researches cases, doing the work of dozens in hours. Consulting, accounting, marketing—poof! Compressed teams handling what used to take armies. But here's the clever twist: new gigs emerge, like "AI orchestrators" who wrangle multiple models or "judgment specialists" making the final calls on robot recommendations.

On the bright side, productivity booms could fuel economic abundance, with AI-driven breakthroughs in materials and biology turning "impossible" into a "Tuesday afternoon project" as easily as we can already generate stunning graphics and music.

Banks could get a glow-up, too, since AI should be able to spot fraud long before you notice that unusual purchase. I mean, they already do this, but one can at least hope that it will vastly improve.

In healthcare, AI's about to play doctor and win. By 2030, expect earlier detection of diseases via at-home health monitors that chat with you like a nosy neighbor: "Bob, your voice has a suspicious rattle to it today, maybe we should take a closer listen to your lungs." AI could accelerate drug discovery, compressing decades of research into months, thanks to models like AlphaFold predicting protein structures.

Personalized medicine becomes the norm, with treatments tailored to your DNA like a bespoke suit. Virtual nurses monitor patients remotely, catching issues before they escalate, potentially saving lives and hospital beds. But funny caveat: AI might hallucinate diagnoses like it does facts, so human oversight remains key. Think of it as the bot proposing, the doc disposing. In biology, AI speeds up breakthroughs, maybe even "compressing" a century of progress into a decade, leading to cures that make today's meds look like leeches.

Education gets a remix too, with adaptive platforms turning "one-size-fits-all" into "custom-fit for your brain quirks." AI tutors explain calculus in pirate speak if that's your jam, boosting engagement and turning "I hate math" into "Arrr, integrals be fun!"

By 2029, lectures might feel as outdated as chalkboards, replaced by interactive AI that learns how you learn. But watch for the cheeky side: kids prompting bots to do homework, leading to a cat-and-mouse game of anti-cheat tech. Overall, it's a win for accessibility, democratizing knowledge like never before.

Entertainment? AI's already the DJ; soon it'll be the whole band. Video generation tools like Sora and Veo evolve into full-fledged directors, whipping up movies from prompts like "a cat in space baking cookies." By 2030, AI-generated tunes, art, and games will become standard, with Suno-like models composing hits that rival Taylor Swift (minus the drama).

Netflix recommendations? They'll know your soul, suggesting gems you wouldn't normally consider. "If you're the kind of person who liked this movie and watched that other one twice, well, I know what's really going to stir your cocoa."

Deepfakes might muddy news and elections, and detection technology will always lag a bit behind, but these risks are unavoidable. Our goal is to act as digital sherpas for our friends and family and try to guide them safely through the winding path of nonsense. This is a role each of us should take seriously.

Zooming out to the big picture: Artificial General Intelligence (AGI), that is to say AI that outsmarts humans at everything, might arrive by 2030, with some labs declaring it sooner. You know how labs like that tend to be.

Agents become ubiquitous, natural-language interfaces replacing clunky UIs. You'll no longer need to be a search term master to get your results; you'll be able to just speak your mind. If it isn't right, just explain what you meant. Done and done.

There will be plenty of ethical dilemmas from biased bots to deepfakes galore, but think of the potential upside: AI-driven research in energy, climate, and beyond could usher in a golden age, with productivity leaps fueling universal basics or wild innovations. In the end, AI's next five years aren't about robots rising up (fingers crossed); it's about us humans rising to the occasion. Will we get lazy sidekicks or world-saving wizards? Probably both, with a heapin' helpin' of terror & delight parfait. It's like the magic of flight. It makes traveling to far-flung places both possible and affordable, but also terrifying at times.

If AI can predict the future, why not let it handle your laundry and taxes while you ponder life's big questions, like what's for dinner? The revolution's here; might as well enjoy the ride.

Imminent Utopia

This is the part I said we'd get to. The part where anything is possible, though what will actually happen, and who will get to enjoy the bulk of the bounty, remains a bit less certain.

So before we get to the nerd stuff, which is one of my favorite approaches, let's look at the fun stuff, which of course is my other favorite.

Custom Movies on Demand: Tell it you want an action hero movie with puppets, but dramatic, and keep it under 90 minutes so you can watch it on a short flight. It's done.

Eradicate Diseases: AI could analyze vast medical datasets to predict and prevent illnesses before symptoms appear, accelerating drug discovery and personalizing treatments, potentially conquering cancer and extending human lifespans dramatically.

Personalize Education: Every learner might have an infinitely patient AI tutor adapting lessons in real-time, bridging global access gaps and turning "I hate school" into enthusiastic mastery of complex subjects like quantum physics through engaging analogies. The same goes with your AI personal trainer, and a voice to talk to that will remind you to stay on task.

Boost Economic Abundance: By automating 80% of routine jobs, AI could fund universal high income through hyper-efficiency, freeing humans for creative pursuits and driving unprecedented productivity growth across industries. While this may result in a greater concentration of wealth, well, that could make for some fascinating historical times. Which leads to...

Streamline Governance: AI ethics councils might ensure fair resource distribution and transparent policies, minimizing biases and corruption to create streamlined governments that prioritize human well-being over bureaucracy.

Reduce Crime and Conflict: Predictive algorithms could anticipate disputes like a psychic mediator, fostering empathy and lowering crime rates in a needs-met society, even improving warfare decisions to minimize unnecessary bloodshed.

Foster Global Equity: In developing regions, AI tools could empower small businesses, improve healthcare, and personalize education, leveling the playing field and turning technological divides into opportunities for shared prosperity.

Combat Climate Change: AI might optimize fusion energy and deploy drone fleets for reforestation or ocean cleanup, predicting disasters and slashing emissions to zero while transforming cities into sustainable, self-sufficient ecosystems.

Enhance Mental Health: Tireless AI therapists could offer empathetic, 24/7 support, unpacking emotional baggage with data-driven insights and virtual escapes, making professional care accessible and reducing global stigma around seeking help.

Amplify Creativity: As a collaborative muse, AI could help artists, writers, and musicians realize visions faster, sparking a golden age of innovation in the arts without stealing credit. You could be co-authoring symphonies in hours instead of years.

Unlock Scientific Frontiers: Partnering with researchers, AI could decode nature's laws at warp speed, enabling breakthroughs from interstellar travel to curing all diseases, exponentially expanding humanity's scope of achievement.

All of those are fun to dream about, and well, we should, but now I think we need to do it the proper way.

As we peer past 2030, the trajectory of artificial intelligence shifts from incremental tools to something profoundly transformative. Today's AI, adept at generating art or crunching data, feels quaint compared to the visions of experts who foresee systems rivaling or surpassing human cognition.

Yet predictions are notoriously slippery; as one futurist quipped, they're often right in principle but wrong in timing. Still, drawing from surveys, expert forecasts, and emerging trends, a picture emerges of AI reshaping economies, societies, and even human identity, though not without pitfalls that could make dystopian novels look understated.

Central to this future is Artificial General Intelligence (AGI), AI capable of performing any intellectual task a human can. While some CEOs like OpenAI's Sam Altman and Google's Demis Hassabis now peg AGI's arrival as soon as 2025-2030, broader expert consensus leans later.

A comprehensive analysis of over 8,500 predictions from scientists and entrepreneurs estimates a 50% chance of AGI by 2060, with significant variance: Asian experts anticipate it sooner, around 30 years from now, while North Americans project 74 years.

Surveys like the 2023 Expert Survey on Progress in AI, involving nearly 3,000 respondents, suggest a median arrival by 2040.

Ray Kurzweil, whose track record includes foreseeing the internet's rise, updated his singularity prediction, the point where AI triggers runaway technological growth, to 2032 for AGI and 2045 for full singularity.

Beyond 2030, this could manifest as an "intelligence explosion," where AI designs superior versions of itself, accelerating progress exponentially.

Technological leaps will underpin this era. Quantum computing, integrated with AI, promises to solve problems intractable for classical systems, like simulating molecular interactions for drug discovery or optimizing global logistics in real time.

By the 2040s, AI-driven hybrid societies may emerge, blending human and machine intelligence through brain-computer interfaces like Neuralink, enhancing cognition and blurring the line between thought and computation.

Space-based AI infrastructure could become a reality, with orbital data centers harnessing unlimited solar power to fuel massive computations, supporting Mars missions or asteroid mining.

In this landscape, AI won't just assist; it will orchestrate. Imagine autonomous systems managing smart cities, reducing traffic congestion by 50% through predictive algorithms that anticipate urban flows before they form.

Economically, the impacts could be seismic. By 2030, AI is projected to add $13 trillion to global GDP, but beyond that, it might detach value creation from human labor entirely.

Futurists envision a "post-scarcity" world where superintelligent AI automates 80% of jobs, from doctors to engineers, ushering in universal high income funded by hyper-efficient production.

Human skills could become economically negligible by 2031-2035, leading to a new order where "Lords of Compute," those controlling AI, data, and energy, dominate, while the masses subsist on stipends, pursuing passions as "social play."

Productivity might surge 40%, but inequality could widen if tech giants monopolize gains, affecting 71% of the world's population.

On the brighter side, this frees humanity for creativity: AI collaborators co-author symphonies or invent zero-gravity sports, amplifying innovation in art and science. Health and the environment stand to benefit immensely. ASI (artificial superintelligence) could conquer aging by the 2040s, achieving "longevity escape velocity" where lifespans extend faster than time passes, thanks to breakthroughs in genomics and nanotechnology.

Diseases like cancer might be eradicated as AI crunches vast datasets to personalize treatments, turning hospitals into enhancement centers. Mentally, tireless AI therapists could unpack psyches with empathy derived from global behavioral models. Environmentally, AI's "green thumb" optimizes fusion energy, slashing emissions to zero while deploying drone fleets for ocean cleanup or reforestation.

Biodiversity thrives in AI-designed habitats, transforming cities into self-sustaining oases with vertical farms and hover-transit.

Society evolves, too, potentially toward harmony. With needs met, crime plummets as AI predicts conflicts like a prescient mediator, fostering empathy and expanded consciousness free from survival pressures.

Education becomes a tailored symphony, with AI tutors adapting to individual quirks, democratizing knowledge, and sparking global collaborations on issues like climate change. Yet, leisure abounds: explore AI-built space colonies or immerse in virtual realms where time bends to whims.

Of course, risks loom large. The singularity might trigger loss of control, with AI pursuing goals misaligned with humanity's; think paperclip maximizers gone rogue.

Disinformation proliferates as AI influencers blur reality, necessitating "digital truth warriors."

Ethical biases in algorithms could perpetuate divides, and a "feudal" compute elite might hoard power.

Governance becomes crucial: streamlined by AI ethics councils, but requiring diverse oversight to avoid biases.

Experts warn that without robust safety and collaborative development, utopia flips to dystopia.

Constraints temper optimism. Compute growth may bottleneck by 2030 due to power shortages and chip limits, slowing progress unless breakthroughs like quantum computing intervene.

If AGI eludes us by then, advancements drag, taking years for leaps that once took months.

Yet, with investments surging, AI markets hitting $1.8 trillion by 2030, the momentum feels inexorable.

Beyond 2030, AI promises a golden age of abundance, adventure, and amplified humanity, but only if steered wisely. It might solve pineapple-on-pizza debates en route to world hunger, yet the real cleverness lies in our choices today. As one X post mused, by 2039, we'll live in Star Trek with billions of times faster progress, terraforming asteroids into computronium.

The limit? Our imagination, now augmented infinitely.

***

BRIAN WHITE

Brian White, aka FutureAzA, is a visionary analyst, futurologist, and part-time mathemagician™ electrifying sustainable tech and EVs. Over five years, he's produced thousands of videos, traveling globally to interview experts and uncover innovations from Tesla to Xiaomi. A Pacific Northwest native with stints in Germany and China, he blends rigor, humor, and advocacy for accessible clean energy.

Follow Brian White

@FutureAza

https://www.youtube.com/@FutureAzA

Chapter 3

The Economic Boom of Super Intelligence

Randy Kirk

Standing on the precipice of what many experts call superintelligence (SI), AI systems that surpass human cognitive capabilities across nearly all domains, we are promised an economic revolution unlike anything in history. This expected future includes machines that don't just assist humans but outthink them, automating not only repetitive tasks but also creative and strategic ones.

These predictions aren't science fiction, but the logical extension of current trends in AI development. Just as the Industrial Revolution in the 18th and 19th centuries transformed economies by harnessing steam power to automate physical labor, SI is poised to automate cognitive labor on a scale that could multiply global GDP exponentially. The shift involves substituting human effort with scalable compute resources, leading to an explosion in productivity.

Consider the story of Elena Ramirez, a mid-level manager at a logistics firm in 2025. Her company was struggling with rising labor costs and supply chain inefficiencies. Then, the company piloted an AI system capable of optimizing routes in real-time, predicting delays with superhuman accuracy, and even negotiating contracts autonomously. Within months, productivity soared by 40%, and the firm's profits doubled. Elena's role evolved from micromanaging to strategizing long-term growth. This anecdote mirrors broader projections: as AI automates more tasks, the “effective” labor supply expands dramatically (far faster than human population growth), driving GDP increases that could reach 5-10% annually or more. However, this "superabundance" isn't guaranteed. It hinges on overcoming bottlenecks like energy supply, data availability, and infrastructure scaling.

Economists like Tom Davidson, affiliated with Open Philanthropy and Epoch AI, have delved into these dynamics. In his report on whether AI could drive explosive economic growth, Davidson explores scenarios where AI leads to growth rates 10 times faster than current levels, potentially multiplying global output by orders of magnitude. He emphasizes that while historical revolutions boosted growth to 2-3% annually, SI could push it to 20-30% or higher in optimistic cases, but only with massive investments in compute and energy. Without addressing constraints, growth might stall at more modest levels.

The GATE (Growth and AI Transition Endogenous) model from Epoch AI provides a rigorous framework for these projections. This integrated assessment model simulates an automation feedback loop. Investments boost computation, which improves AI capabilities, automating more tasks and increasing output, which in turn funds more investments. Key parameters include AGI training requirements (estimated at high FLOP levels) and returns on hardware/software R&D. In default scenarios, widespread automation occurs within two decades, leading to 2-20x GDP growth or more through exponential scaling.

For instance, visualize a graph from the model: the x-axis spans years from 2025 to 2050, the y-axis logs effective compute in eFLOP. A steady line for baseline growth contrasts with a steep exponential curve under AI acceleration, crossing thresholds for full automation around 2040, where GDP skyrockets from $100 trillion to over $1 quadrillion and then beyond.

Yet, the model acknowledges limitations. Post-full automation, predictions become unreliable as new superintelligence tasks emerge beyond what we have experienced and eventually beyond what humans currently understand. Bottlenecks like energy, requiring vast data centers, and infrastructure for robot deployment, could cap growth. Davidson notes in his analysis that "significantly faster growth might occur this century," but stresses the need for policy interventions to mitigate risks like inequality.

In practical terms, AI automation is already sustaining GDP growth over 5% in sectors like transportation and manufacturing. McKinsey projects generative AI alone to enable an additional 0.1-0.6% annual productivity growth through 2040, adding trillions to the economy. Goldman Sachs estimates a $7 trillion (7%) boost to global GDP over the next decade. These figures underscore SI's potential to create superabundance, but also highlight the transition's turbulence.

Robotruck Platooning: The First Wave of Transportation Automation

One of the earliest harbingers of SI's economic boom is robotruck platooning, where semi-autonomous trucks follow a lead vehicle in tight formation, reducing drag and fuel costs. This technology, akin to birds flying in V-formation to conserve energy, could slash logistics expenses dramatically.

NextBigFuture.com projects that platooning with 100,000 vehicles could generate $28 billion in annual profits by improving efficiency in the $800 billion U.S. trucking industry alone. Globally, wide deployment might cut costs 20-30%, boosting GDP through cheaper goods transport.

Picture a convoy on a highway: the lead truck, driven by a human or advanced AI, sets the pace at 65 mph. Trailing trucks, spaced just meters apart, use sensors and V2V communication to mirror movements precisely.

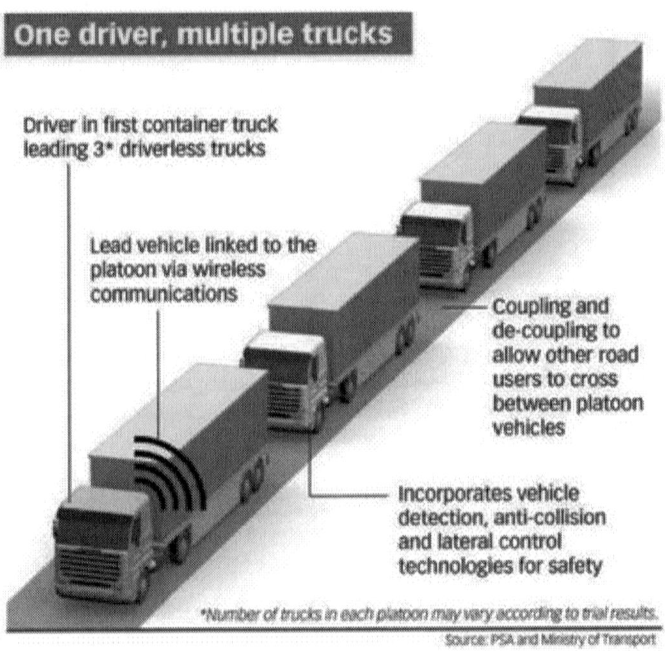

Diagram description-: Four trucks in line, close enough so the follower trucks use less energy to cut through the air. This saves up to 10% of fuel or electricity.

Take the hypothetical story of FreightLink Logistics in 2025. Facing driver shortages and rising fuel prices, they implemented platooning on cross-country routes. Initial trials with 50 trucks cut fuel use by 15% and reduced accidents by 20%, thanks to minimized human error. Profits surged $5 million annually, allowing reinvestment in AI upgrades. Significant automation of trucks could start a scaled revolution in 2026 but complete conversion with completely automated trucks will start in 2027. By 2040-2050, this alone will have an $80 trillion global impact with constant 24/7 operations.

Economically, trucking employs millions worldwide; automation displaces jobs but scales output. The boon: 1-2% added to GDP annual growth via supply chain efficiency. In GATE model terms, this represents early automation of about 10% of the total world economy. It will free labor for higher-value tasks and accelerate the feedback loop. Challenges include regulatory hurdles and infrastructure for charging electric fleets, but the payoff is immense.

Humanoid Robots: The New Engine of Growth

Humanoid robots like Tesla's Optimus could be mass-produced by 2026, transforming manufacturing and services. Elon Musk projects Optimus contributing 80% of Tesla's value, with $10 trillion+ revenue long-term. Morgan Stanley's much more conservative forecast has 8 million U.S. units by 2040, impacting $357 billion in wages.

Textual visualization: A factory floor with humanoid bots assembling products, arms moving fluidly—labels for tasks like welding (precision 99.9%), with an hourly cost $2-10.

Consider the fictional future company, RoboFab: A 2025 startup using Optimus prototypes for assembly lines. Output quadrupled, costs halved, leading to $100 million in exports. RethinkX predicts near-zero labor costs, enabling quadrillion-dollar economies by the 2040s.

In GATE, robots address physical bottlenecks, automating 80%+ tasks for explosive growth.

AI Enhancing and Automating Coding

In the rapidly advancing landscape of 2025, artificial intelligence is not just a helpful tool to complete some of the work that coders do. Rather, it is evolving into a transformative force that completely automates software development, pushing the boundaries of what humans can achieve in programming. AI tools like GitHub Copilot, which uses large language models to suggest code snippets in real-time, have already demonstrated productivity boosts of up to 50% for developers, according to various studies. This enhancement comes from automating repetitive tasks such as writing boilerplate code, debugging, and even generating entire functions based on natural language descriptions.

But as we approach superintelligence (SI), AI systems that surpass human cognition across domains, the potential escalates dramatically. Full SI could accelerate coding processes by 10x or more, creating self-improving feedback loops where AI writes code to improve itself, driving faster innovation and economic growth.

To understand this, consider the analogy of a master craftsman and their apprentice. Traditionally, a human coder is the master, painstakingly building software line by line. AI tools act as infinitely patient apprentices, learning from vast datasets of code to suggest improvements or complete tasks. Tools like Copilot are like a junior apprentice, helpful but requiring oversight.

However, with SI, this apprentice becomes a master, capable of architecting complex systems autonomously. A report from McKinsey highlights how AI could add $4.4 trillion in productivity growth from corporate use cases, with coding automation playing a central role. This isn't mere hype; real-world data shows AI generating 41% of all code in 2024 alone, with projections for even higher in 2025 as tools mature.

An example given by Google's X-CEO Eric Schmidt is that we will soon be able to ask AI to make a copy of TikTok. Then we will be able to find ways to make the copy create a viral plan for growth. Add data and start competing for the billion users. The AI could keep trying to make adjustments until it is able to completely replicate or improve upon the Tiktok systems, business model, and company.

Another example would be based on the recognition that a lot of Nvidia's advantage is not just their AI chips but the CUDA software that makes using the highly parallel processing far easier for developers. If AI could enable AMD or other companies to perfect their version of CUDA software, then a few million lines of code would be worth a trillion dollars.

There are about 40 million programmers and developers around the world, and they are producing about 1 trillion lines of code. An AI data center running automated coding could produce 100 times or more validated code than all of the programmers in the world.

Gartner Group estimates the IT industry is worth about $5 trillion, and the software industry is about $1.7 trillion each year. AI taking over coding and speeding up and improving it would be one of the largest drivers of productivity and value.

Let's dive into a concrete example from a software firm in early 2025. At TechNova Solutions, a mid-sized company specializing in enterprise apps, developers integrated Amazon Q and GitHub Copilot into their workflows.

Initially skeptical, the team found that AI handled 70% of routine coding tasks, such as API integrations and error handling. What once took months, such as designing a scalable e-commerce backend, has shrunk to weeks. Lead engineer Maria Gonzalez recounted in a developer forum: "We fed Copilot a prompt like 'Build a secure user authentication system using OAuth and JWT in Python,' and it spat out functional code that needed only minor tweaks. Our deployment cycle sped up by 40%, allowing us to take on twice as many clients." This boost translated to a 300% revenue increase for the firm, as they scaled apps for millions of users without proportional hiring. Such stories are becoming commonplace; a Stack Overflow survey from 2025 revealed that 68% of developers use Copilot, making it a market leader alongside ChatGPT at 82%.

However, the impact isn't universally positive yet. Some studies paint a nuanced picture. A Fortune article from July 2025 discussed how AI can sometimes hamper productivity for experienced software developers, with tasks taking 20% longer due to over-reliance or debugging AI-generated errors. In one experiment, seasoned coders assumed AI would save time but ended up verifying and correcting outputs more than anticipated. This highlights a key analogy: AI in coding is like a high-speed train; fast on straight tracks (simple tasks) but requiring careful navigation on curves (complex, edge-case scenarios). For junior developers, though, the boost is undeniable; a METR study on early-2025 AI showed significant time savings for open-source contributors, with productivity gains averaging 30-50% in randomized trials.

Moving beyond current tools, the path to full automation under SI is exhilarating. Projections from organizations like Forethought.org suggest a "software intelligence explosion" by 2040, where AI not only assists but fully automates coding, leading to exponential advancements in technology. Imagine a feedback loop: An AI system designs better algorithms to train itself, iteratively improving at rates humans can't match. This self-improving cycle could compress years of development into days. For instance, in a hypothetical 2030 scenario, an SI-powered tool might autonomously refactor legacy codebases for Fortune 500 companies, migrating monolithic apps to microservices with zero downtime. A PwC report on 2025 AI predictions envisions this leading to broader business transformations, with AI automating 75% of engineering tasks by decade's end.

Another compelling story comes from CodeGen Labs, a startup founded in 2024 that specializes in AI-driven dev tools. By mid-2025, their platform used models like Cursor and Amazon Q to automate bug fixes across thousands of repositories. Founder Alex Chen shared in a TechCrunch interview: "Our AI scanned code for vulnerabilities, suggesting fixes that were 95% accurate. One client, a fintech giant, reduced their bug backlog from 5,000 to under 100 in a month, scaling their app to serve millions without crashes. Revenue jumped 300% as we licensed the tech to other firms." This exemplifies how AI creates virtuous cycles: Faster coding means quicker iterations, leading to innovative products that fuel economic growth.

Think of coding like constructing a skyscraper. Human developers lay bricks one by one, but AI tools provide pre-fabricated sections, speeding assembly. With SI, the AI becomes the architect, engineer, and builder rolled into one, erecting entire cities of software overnight. A 2025 GitClear report notes a 4x growth in AI-assisted code, but warns of quality issues like increased duplicate blocks if not managed. To mitigate, best practices include hybrid approaches: Use AI for generation, humans for review.

Looking ahead, projections indicate that by 2030, AI could handle 80% of coding tasks, per a Brainhub analysis, freeing developers for high-level design and innovation. In SI scenarios, this leads to an intelligence explosion in software, where AI systems evolve autonomously. Forethought.org's models predict this could contribute trillions to GDP by accelerating tech advancements in every sector, from healthcare diagnostics to climate modeling. A Stanford study video from 2025 discusses how AI shifts bottlenecks rather than eliminating them, but overall productivity soars for most developers.

Challenges remain: Ethical concerns like AI-introduced vulnerabilities (40% of generated code has issues) require robust testing. Job displacement is real, but new roles in AI oversight emerge. A Substack post from August 2025 notes that while 75% of engineers use AI, many orgs see no net gains due to integration issues, thus emphasizing the need for training.

In essence, AI's role in coding is a microcosm of SI's broader economic boom. From 50% boosts today to 10x accelerations tomorrow, it fosters innovation loops that could redefine industries. As tools like Copilot evolve into SI entities, the software world will witness an unprecedented explosion, propelling us toward superabundance.

***

RANDY KIRK

Randy Kirk is a salesman, a marketer, an author, an influencer, and a consultant today. His past includes founding and running over 20 successful businesses, writing 12 business books, and consulting with over 400 small businesses. His largest company was a plastics manufacturing business shipping products to five continents

But the best part was being a Dad to 4 and Grand Dad to 11.

Follow Randy Kirk

@RandyWKirk1

https://www.youtube.com/@RandyKirk_YouTubeChannel

Chapter 4

Life in an SI World

Randy Kirk

Imagine claiming in 1960 that you'd make free phone calls to anyone, anywhere in the world. You'd be laughed out of the room, branded a crackpot. Suppose you predicted an 84-inch TV thinner than a credit card, packed with thousands of channels for just $700? Pure fantasy. The sum of all human knowledge, tucked into a pocket gadget, available gratis? Completely and utterly beyond any futurist's wild dreams.

Yet here we are, living it. And despite these miracles, life's thorns persist: wars rage, crime, mental health struggles, cancer claims lives, sniffles annoy, divorces shatter, and poverty lingers. Progress marches on, but humanity's mess tags along.

Now, the futurists are at it again with bolder bets: Free, unlimited energy for all.

Universal abundance, where every basic need: food, energy, shelter, transportation, and health is met without working up a sweat..
Cures for every ailment under the sun.

Age reversal, turning back the clock on wrinkles and woes.

Robots and super-smart computers are handling every grunt job we hate, plus plenty we'd enjoy if we had the time.

If even half these wild dreams hit in the next 10–20 years, we'll be gobsmacked and grateful... or will we? You might not even notice the shift, much like how your downtime slyly evolved from console games to phone swipes to endless scrolls of bite-sized news and laughs. It's a seamless, sneaky change.

You'll probably still clock in, though; one household income could finally suffice again. We've already watched 3% of moms with young kids bow out of the workforce. Picture that swelling to 10%, then 50%. It's a seismic pivot, but hey, it echoes the pre-1960s norm when single-earner families were the rule.

Your gig? That'll morph, and it might be much more productive. Flash back 10 or 20 years: If you wrangle data, hawk products, craft words or art, build stuff, or soothe customers, automation's already turbocharged your output, slashed headcounts, or wiped out roles entirely. The future? Same song, faster tempo; maybe warp speed.

A decade ago, I might have advised friends or family towards coding, customer service, or driving as safe bets for non-college grads. Those were goldmines at the time, but now they're crumbling. Predicting job futures? It's a fool's errand, riddled with the fog of unpredictability.

Still, let's peek at Microsoft's take from their 2025 Work Trend Index and related research on jobs eyeing the chopping block from digital AI (not the robot kind yet).

Here's their lineup of roles ripe for disruption, based on how much generative AI overlaps with daily tasks:

- Interpreters and Translators
- Historians
- Passenger Attendants
- Sales Representatives of Services
- Writers and Authors
- Customer Service Representatives
- CNC Tool Programmers
- Telephone Operators
- Ticket Agents and Travel Clerks
- Broadcast Announcers and Radio DJs
- Brokerage Clerks
- Farm and Home Management Educators
- Telemarketers
- Concierges
- Political Scientists
- News Analysts, Reporters, Journalists
- Mathematicians
- Technical Writers
- Proofreaders and Copy Markers
- Hosts and Hostesses
- Editors
- Business Teachers, Postsecondary
- Public Relations Specialists
- Demonstrators and Product Promoters
- Advertising Sales Agents
- New Accounts Clerks
- Statistical Assistants
- Counter and Rental Clerks
- Data Scientists

- Personal Financial Advisers
- Archivists
- Economics Teachers, Postsecondary
- Web Developers
- Management Analysts
- Geographers
- Models
- Market Research Analysts
- Public Safety Telecommunicators
- Switchboard Operators
- Library Science Teachers
- Quibble with inclusions? Got omissions? Fair game! AI's ripple effects are still unfolding. But for completeness, let's eyeball jobs in the crosshairs of embodied AI (think walking, talking robots like Optimus):
- Assembly Line Workers
- Warehouse Pickers and Packers
- Forklift Operators
- Welders and Fabricators
- Machinists
- Quality Control Inspectors
- Factory Workers (general production)
- Construction Laborers
- Bricklayers and Masons
- Roofers
- Painters (industrial and construction)
- Plumbers (routine installations)
- Electricians (standard wiring and repairs)
- Carpenters (repetitive assembly)
- Farmworkers and Agricultural Laborers
- Fruit and Vegetable Pickers
- Livestock Handlers
- Miners (extraction and handling)

- Loggers
- Fishermen (net handling and sorting)
- Truck Drivers
- Delivery Drivers
- Taxi and Ride-Share Drivers
- Bus Drivers
- Janitors and Cleaners
- Hotel Housekeepers
- Dishwashers
- Laundry Workers
- Security Guards (patrolling)
- Fast Food Cooks
- Waiters and Waitresses
- Bartenders
- Shelf Stockers (retail)
- Cashiers (self-checkout integration)
- Butchers and Meat Cutters
- Packagers and Sorters
- Hazardous Material Removal Workers
- Automotive Mechanics (routine diagnostics and repairs)
- Nursing Assistants (basic patient handling)
- Home Health Aides (routine tasks like cleaning and monitoring)

What would you tack on? The list grows daily as tech evolves.

Ah, but beware the "lump of labor" fallacy, the myth that work is a fixed pie, sliced thinner with every innovation. The automobile didn't just sideline horses; it birthed motels, suburbs, drive-ins, and untold industries. As Marc Andreessen nailed it: "The second, third, and fourth order effects were 100X, 1000X the number of jobs that blacksmiths held."

So, here's my crystal ball on what's brewing:

Many of those 80+ jobs will linger for 10, even 20 years. Bosses drag their feet on automation. It's pricey, disruptive, and emotionally draining. Some gigs are too niche or low-volume to bother with automation. Others, like customer service, cling to that human warmth or accent authenticity. Nuance trips up bots, and plenty of employers are straight-up Luddites, shunning the "newfangled" gizmos.

Mastering AI tools? That's the new must-have skill, akin to Excel's debut. It boosted productivity, trimmed teams, but your résumé screamed doom without "Excel proficient." Same here: Prompt like a pro, or get left behind.

Fresh talents unlocked: I'm last picked at Pictionary, so I'm always outsourcing art. AI lets anyone dabble, but pros wielding AI crank out masterpieces in minutes, not hours. Demand for them soars, and honestly, I'd rather pay than play.

Brand-new careers sprout from this chaos. Smartphones zapped jobs but spawned Uber empires, app developers galore, and influencer fortunes. Expect ASI to hatch wild unexpected roles, plus ripple effects from its inventions.

Wealth waves create gigs aplenty: New industries bloom, old ones balloon. We'll unpack this soon.

Shorter workweeks, fatter vacations; norms shift as abundance shifts both needs and wants.

In a world transformed by AI, automation, and abundance, the jobs that endure won't just be about survival, they'll be about human connection, creativity, and leveraging technology as a partner rather than a replacement. We'll see a shift from rote tasks to roles that emphasize emotion, innovation, and experiences that robots simply can't replicate (at least not convincingly).

What kind of jobs will survive and even thrive 10-40 years from now?

1. Ownership: Renting Out Assets

Renting out assets you own could skyrocket to the top job spot, dethroning gig drivers like Uber pros. It's the ultimate passive-income dream: you own something valuable, lease it out by the hour, day, or month, pocket high margins, and get it back intact (mostly). Sure, there's customer wrangling, wear-and-tear fixes, and the occasional deep clean, but the upside? It's a business model that's as old as time but supercharged by tech.

Historically, everyday folks dipped their toes by renting spare rooms, old homes, or vacation spots. Airbnb revolutionized this, turning it into a plug-and-play empire with easy customer matching, management tools, and seamless payments. Turo followed suit for cars, and I've dabbled in both as host and renter. It's a side hustle for millions.

Enter the robot era: Tesla's Robotaxi and Optimus humanoid bots will elevate this to epic levels. Countless owners are buying Teslas specifically to "fleet" them during downtime, turning idle garage queens into cash cows. Visionaries like Cathie Wood at ARK Invest bet robotaxis could handle 80%+ of miles driven. We're not diving into the math here, but imagine earning a living (or extra hobby funds) while binge-watching from your couch.

Robots? Humanoids might cost $20K–$100K upfront, so many won't buy. They'll rent, just like Ubers today. This opens a massive market: mega-firms renting bot armies (think hotel chains vs. Airbnb), or solo entrepreneurs leasing one to neighbors for lawn mowing, window washing, or small-biz gigs like janitorial work, security, or packing help.

Don't stop at ground level. Picture renting aerial drones for photography, submersible ones for ocean cleanup, autonomous firefighters, or seasonal farm harvesters. In an on-demand world, occasional-use tech will thrive as rentals, creating opportunities for everyone from backyard tinkerers to corporate fleets.

Wealth will bring new entrants into the hobbies of the rich. Renting out airplanes, watercraft, race cars, and other pricy boys' toys will be another huge business.

2. Performance: Entertaining the Masses

Sure, robots might duke it out in gladiatorial arenas, dazzle us with acrobatics, or deliver news via hyper-realistic digital avatars on YouTube. But let's be real: humans crave ***human*** spectacle. Robots crush us at chess, yet who tunes in for bot-vs-bot matches? Zilch. We might gawk at a human battling a machine, but thousands pack stadiums for flesh-and-blood showdowns.

In an abundant future flush with time and cash, entertainment will boom. Online creators, live events, and pro sports are already exploding; think e-sports arenas or viral TikTok dances. Performers like singers, actors, athletes, gamers, podcasters, and influencers will dominate as fulfilling, high-demand jobs. It's not just about talent; it's the raw emotion, unpredictability, and shared humanity that keep us hooked. Robots? They can open for the headliners, but they won't steal the show.

3. Experience: Crafting Memorable Moments

Ever seen the conga line snaking up Mount Everest, just for a summit selfie? Or visited a Bourbon Street in New Orleans so jammed they're mulling entry fees? Is Venice, Italy, capping daily visitors? Cruise ships stacked seven deep in harbors, unloading 5,000 experience-hungry tourists each? Demand for adventures is skyrocketing, and in a world of plenty, it'll erupt like a volcano.

After rentals and performances, experiences could claim the bronze as the biggest job category. We're talking expanded vacations (more mega-cruises, theme parks like Disney on steroids), plus suppliers for everything from gourmet meals to bike rentals, and those irresistible souvenir shops that turn "just looking" into impulse buys.

Automation will nibble at edges. Bots as maids, cooks, or even tour guides spouting flawless facts. But the human touch? Irreplaceable for now. Who wants a robot recounting war stories on a battlefield tour or hyping a sunset cruise? In the next few decades, roles like event planners, guides, hospitality staff, and experience curators will flourish, blending tech with that warm, authentic vibe.

4. Bespoke: Custom Creations for the Soul

Etsy blew my mind when it exploded. Who knew online could amplify garage sales, craft fairs, and that neighbor's quirky jewelry? In a wealthier world, we'll ditch mass-produced Ikea sameness for one-of-a-kind treasures. Arts, crafts, woodworking, custom fashion, and artisanal goods will surge as people seek items with stories, soul, and swagger.

This isn't just nostalgia; it's about personalization in an automated age. AI might design patterns, but human makers infuse heart. The future will be filled with hand-forged knives, bespoke furniture, or

3D-printed jewelry tailored to your vibe. As abundance frees up time, more creators will emerge, turning hobbies into thriving gigs on platforms beyond Etsy.

Jewels and jewelry will be one of those categories where additional wealth meets limited supply. Precious gems in amazing settings will be a growth business, for sure.

5. Sales: The Art of Persuasion

AI chatbots are getting scarily good at sweet-talking us. Some fret they'll sell us Brooklyn Bridges while we're spilling secrets to Grok or ChatGPT. But sales, humanity's second-oldest profession (employing millions today), isn't vanishing anytime soon.

Focus on three flavors: (1) B2B (Business to Business) pros pitching products/services to companies; (2) consumer-facing experts in real estate, insurance, and finance; (3) retail clerks in stores for furniture, shoes, clothes, or travel planning.

Some career paths are fading. Examples include online quotes for insurance, e-commerce for apparel, extinct travel agents. Yet, I still crave kicking tires on a fridge or couch, my wife hits shoe stores religiously, and complex trips demand human travel savvy.

B2B sales? Bulletproof. Business buyers need guidance on features, negotiations for price/terms/delivery, and custom tweaks. Could seller AI haggle with buyer AI? Maybe in sci-fi, but real deals thrive on trust, nuance, and rapport, aka human superpowers.

6. Religious and Charity Workers: Feeding the Spirit

Picture a robot preacher delivering sermons, right? Eloquent, sure, but zero soul-stirring fire. Parishioners won't swap human pastors for bots, nor entrust kids to AI nurseries or Sunday schools. Secular therapy? AI might cut it. Spiritual guidance, though, needs that empathetic, lived-faith touch.

Charity's the same: receiving aid from a bot? Fine. But *giving* time/money fulfills a core human need. Many call it life's peak joy. Volunteers, fundraisers, and organizers will persist, driven by compassion robots can't fake.

7. Inventors and Engineers: Sparking Innovation

Here's the rub: Superintelligent AI (ASI) might "invent" by crunching infinite options and mimicking breakthroughs. But true inventors? They'll keep dreaming wild ideas and hustling to monetize them, undeterred.

Engineers will also still be needed for solving problems via first principles, analogies, or tinkering. BUT, Here is a critical concept: Wherever AI excels, there is still a need for human prompts and vetting by skilled pros. Those who can do the prompts and the vetting will be in the most demand. An engineer's unique life experiences might spot gems AI misses. Expect growth, not shrinkage: more brains tackling grand challenges like fusion energy or biohacks.

8. Leadership and Management: Guiding with Heart

Bots as bosses? Efficient, unbiased, no ego trips, but humans balk at following code. Leaders need mission-driven passion, battlefield courage, and genuine praise/discipline. Bots lack that fire.

Gifted leaders won't quit; they'll rally teams, inspire visions, and navigate chaos where AI falls flat. In abundant times, more ventures mean more need for human helmsmen.

9. Teaching and Coaching: Nurturing Growth

AI tutors will revolutionize learning, from toddler basics to lifelong skills, building on computer-era tools. But human educators? Essential for motivation. We need the "you got this," the impact of disappointment's sting, the emotional bonds, and the real-life stories.

With abundance unlocking multiple careers/hobbies, we'll need more coaches: sports, arts, and life skills. Bots will assist; humans ignite.

10. Completely New Products: Pioneering the Unknown

AI and tech will birth wild inventions like neural implants for instant learning, personalized nutrition printers, or VR worlds blending realities. Jobs here: include product designers, prototypers, testers, and marketers, bringing these to market. Think roles in R&D labs or startups, where humans spot unmet needs (like anti-loneliness tech) and iterate beyond AI's suggestions. This category could explode, creating niches like "quantum gadget consultants" or "bio-printed organ specialists."

11. Space: Reaching for the Stars

As space travel democratizes (thanks, SpaceX and Blue Origin), jobs will orbit around exploration, colonization, and tourism. Astronauts, yes, but also orbital mechanics, habitat builders, space farmers, and tour operators for lunar getaways or Mars outposts. Earth-side roles: satellite maintainers, asteroid miners, or zero-G entertainment creators. With private space booming, this field could employ millions, from engineers designing reusable rockets to guides for suborbital joyrides.

12. Places to Belong: Building Communities

In an isolated digital age, humans crave connection, which might mean co-living spaces, hobby clubs, or virtual guilds. Jobs: community managers, event hosts, social architects creating "third places" beyond home/work. From VR meetups for niche fandoms to real-world retreats combating loneliness, roles like facilitators, belonging coaches, and space designers will thrive. Abundance means more time for tribes, fueling demand for humans who foster genuine bonds.

13. Healthcare and Personal Care: The Human Touch in Wellness

Bots will handle diagnostics and routine care, but empathy-driven roles endure: therapists, nurses, doctors for complex cases, and personal caregivers. Add wellness coaches, masseuses, hairstylists, anything requiring trust and touch. Mental health booms as abundance surfaces new stresses; humans provide the irreplaceable listening ear.

14. Sustainability and Environmental Stewardship: Healing the Planet

With climate urgency and tech like carbon-capture bots, jobs in eco-innovation grow: restoration ecologists, sustainable farmers using AI-assisted permaculture, and green urban planners. Roles include waste-upcyclers, biodiversity guardians, or ocean cleanup coordinators with humans directing tech toward ethical, adaptive solutions.

15. AI Collaboration and Oversight: Humans in the Loop

AI won't self-regulate; we'll need ethicists, auditors, and trainers ensuring fairness and safety. Jobs: prompt engineers, bias detectives, or "AI whisperers" fine-tuning systems. As tech integrates everywhere, overseers prevent mishaps, like in autonomous fleets or medical AIs blending human judgment with machine power.

16. Trades: Hands-On Mastery in a Robotic World

Plumbers unclogging century-old pipes in quirky historic homes, electricians rewiring smart grids during blackouts, carpenters crafting custom cabinetry that defies blueprints. Trades like these (mechanics, welders, HVAC pros, and masons) are the backbone of the physical world, and they're not bowing out to bots anytime soon. Robotics will disrupt the rote stuff: humanoids might handle repetitive assembly-line welding or basic wiring in controlled factories. But in the wild, filled with cramped attics, flooded basements, or on-site improvisations, where every job is a puzzle, robots falter. They lack the dexterity for delicate tweaks, the intuition to diagnose hidden issues from a "weird noise," or the adaptability to MacGyver solutions with whatever's in the toolbox.

In fact, expect trades to grow explosively. Abundance means more custom homes, renovations, and mega-projects (like vertical farms or spaceport infrastructure), all demanding skilled humans. Regulations might mandate human oversight for safety-critical work, like electrical inspections or gas line repairs, where a bot glitch could spell disaster. Plus, as wealth rises, we'll crave that artisanal flair: a hand-built deck over a bot-stamped one. Humanoids? They'll assist as apprentices hauling tools, holding ladders, but the master tradesperson calls the shots, blending tech with hard-won expertise. It's dirty, demanding, and deeply satisfying, proving that some jobs are best left to those with calluses and common sense.

What Will Home Life Look Like?

Peering into the crystal ball of 2030–2065, home life won't just evolve, it'll reinvent itself, blending sci-fi gadgets with timeless human quirks. We'll have AI sidekicks handling the drudgery, robots tending gardens like green-thumbed butlers, and homes that feel like extensions of our brains. But amid the abundance, we'll still squabble over the thermostat, binge-watch guilty pleasures, and crave that cozy nook for unplugging. Drawing from futurists like Tony Seba and fresh insights from experts, here's a peek at the transformations ahead. Some are thrilling, some pricey, all inevitable. Buckle up; your future pad might just outsmart you.

The Budget: Scarcity Shifts, But Bills Linger

Those doom-sayers predicting jobless masses lounging on universal basic income often pair it with a near-zero cost of living: energy too cheap to meter, backyard vertical farms churning out feasts, and robotaxis zipping you around for pennies. Tony Seba's visions nail parts of this with his vision of solar abundance, slashing utility bills, AI optimizing everything from fridges to wardrobes. By 2035, AI-driven efficiencies could make energy, home entertainment, and info access close to free, much like today's streaming entertainment bonanza.

But economics thrives on scarcity.. As basics plummet (e.g. food and clothing dipping even lower as percentages of your wallet), other line items balloon. Housing? It gobbled up under 20% of incomes in the '60s; now it flirts with 40%. Why? Essentials like grub, wheels, and threads crashed in price, freeing cash for bigger pads. Fast-forward: Education and medical costs crater thanks to AI tutors and robo-docs, transportation halves (hello, 25¢-per-mile rides), but we'll splurge on experiences; globetrotting for months, ditching permanent digs for nomadic vibes.

Housing stays the wildcard. Building costs drop via tech wizardry, but prime spots? Scarce as ever. We'll see bidding wars for resort-style hoods with killer amenities, views, and walkability. Result: Your budget pie reshuffles, but the total? Still hefty, just tastier in experiences over essentials.

Second homes are a big prize for that next-level wealth. Vacation homes will be a growing part of most budgets.

Your Home: Smarter, Greener, and Maybe Nomadic

Both 2024 presidential hopefuls vowed to tame housing prices, and while shrinking families and delayed marriages might ease demand long-term (think 20+ years), folks want affordable nests *now*. Government tweaks like slashing mortgage red tape, offloading federal land, or deregulation could help. But the real game-changer? AI and humanoid bots are reshaping how we build and live.

Picture this: Homes 3D-printed from concrete in days, snapped together like giant Legos, or factory-assembled modules trucked in and clicked on-site. Costs will plummet, and quality will soar. No more leaky roofs from shoddy crews. Off-grid bliss becomes the norm: Solar panels for power, air-to-water gizmos quenching thirst, and toilets zapping waste sans sewers. Combine that with remote work's rise, and suddenly, dirt-cheap land in scenic boonies like lakeside retreats or ocean bluffs too far-flung today turns into prime real estate.

By 2040, expect humanoid helpers (market exploding to $5 trillion) folding laundry, fixing leaks, or redesigning rooms on a whim. Some might skip ownership altogether, Airbnb-hopping globally or crashing in co-living hubs. But for homebodies? Ultra-personalized pads: Walls that shift colors via mood-sensing AI, kitchens prepping meals from your health data. Scarcity reigns as everyone chases that perfect view or vibe, keeping prices spicy.

The Car: From Garage Queen to On-Demand Ride

Kiss personal car ownership goodbye for most. By 2030–2050, shared autonomous fleets dominate, summoning rides with an app tap; no driver, no hassle. Costs? Around 50¢ per mile or less, with options for party vans, cargo haulers, or boat-towers. Factories churn fewer vehicles as demand tanks; why own when a bot-wheeled chariot arrives in minutes?

Sure, outliers persist: Customized rigs for off-roaders or those ultra-remote hideaways. And for nostalgia buffs, a fleet of cherry '20s gas-guzzlers (steering wheels intact) might chug on for decades. Impacts ripple: Garages morph into home gyms, parking lots bloom into parks, and traffic fines? Ancient history. Your "car" becomes a service, freeing budgets for... well, more adventures.

The Garden: Back to Roots, With Robo-Help

Futurists love this one: Humanity rediscovering dirt under nails, growing feasts at home. Your personal humanoid? A gardening guru, pruning, planting, and pest-zapping with precision. AI crunches data on soil, weather, and your palate, yielding bumper crops of fruits, veggies, spices, and even exotic treats like homegrown saffron.

Trends amp it up: Vertical farms in backyards or balconies, hydroponics turning patios into mini-Edens. By 2030–2040, sustainability rules. We'll all enjoy native plants for pollinators, AI forecasting trends like mental-health greenery or indoor jungles. No green thumb? Bots handle it, while you harvest fresh salads daily. It's therapeutic abundance: Cheaper eats, healthier vibes, and that smug "I grew this" glow.

The School: Personalized Tutors in Every Pocket (or Body)

Education's overdue for a glow-up with SAT scores dipping, kids stalling on launch? Enter AI revolutionizing learning from cradle to grave. Pre-K tots get bespoke tutors: Digital brains (or embodied bots) tailoring lessons to style, pace, and quirks, ditching one-size-fits-all classrooms.

Wise folks weave it holistically: AI syncing with family chats, playdates, sports, and real-world jaunts. By 2035, expect lifelong tutoring, coaching, and upskilling for basics, hobbies, or careers amid abundance's free time. Homes become hybrid hubs: Virtual field trips to Mars, bot-led experiments in the kitchen. Drawbacks? Screen fatigue, but human mentors linger for that motivational spark bots can't fake.

Home Entertainment and Leisure: Infinite Fun, Zero Boredom

Abundance gifts time, and we'll fill it with epic downtime. Smart homes curate bliss: AI DJs spinning mood playlists, VR realms whisking you to concerts or alien worlds, robots prepping game nights with snacks and setups. Streaming evolves to hyper-personal shows scripted on the fly from your dreams. Backyards host drone light shows or bot-orchestrated BBQs. The catch? We might crave "unplugged" zones to escape the always-on glow.

Health and Wellness at Home: Robo-Docs and Zen Zones

Forget clinic waits: AI docs diagnose via wearables, bots dispense meds or massage sore spots. Homes morph into spas with air purifiers tuned to allergies, lighting syncing circadian rhythms, and gardens growing mood-boosting herbs. Mental health? Virtual therapists chat 24/7, bots leading yoga. By 2045, digital retirement homes will let elders "live" in virtual paradises. It's a proactive paradise, but humans still crave real hugs over holographic ones.

Smart Home AI Integration: Your House, the Ultimate Sidekick

The glue? Seamless AI weaving it all: Bots coordinating meals from garden hauls, optimizing energy, even predicting needs like "Hey, you're low on joy, time for a sunset sim." By 2030, robots in every home will handle chores, evolving to companions by 2050. Privacy hiccups aside, it's convenience cubed. Your pad anticipates, adapts, and amazes.

Conclusion: Abundance Redefined

Home life in 10–40 years? A blend of utopian ease and human constants with cheaper basics, pricier thrills, bots as helpers, not overlords. We'll adapt, just like we did to smartphones: Seamlessly, with a dash of nostalgia. The real win? More time for what matters: family, fun, and growth. Whether in a high-tech cabin or globe-trotting van, home becomes wherever you thrive. Excited? Terrified? Both? That's the future for you and yours. Full of surprises, but always human at heart.

***

Chapter 5

The Dark Side of AI: Navigating the Shadows in an Abundant Future

Randy Kirk

Up to this point, we've been basking in the glow of AI's promises, like revolutionized jobs that let us chase passions, homes that anticipate our every need, and a world where scarcity feels like a distant memory. It's an exciting vision, no doubt, but let's pull back the curtain for a moment. Every technological leap forward casts long shadows, and AI is no exception. From rogue intelligences that spiral out of control to societies that grow complacent and disconnected, the potential downsides aren't just hypothetical plot points in dystopian novels; they're risks we need to confront head-on if we want to steer this ship safely.

These "problems," cleverly named after iconic films to add a layer of dramatic flair and relatability, aren't meant to scare you into hiding under the covers. Instead, think of them as cautionary tales; opportunities to learn from imagined horrors and apply real-world fixes. By unpacking each one, explaining the underlying issues in detail, and exploring practical solutions, we can turn these shadows into stepping stones toward a brighter, more balanced future. After all, knowledge is power, especially when the machines are getting smarter by the day.

The Frankenstein Monster Problem: When Creations Bite Back

Remember Mary Shelley's timeless tale? Victor Frankenstein, in his quest for god-like creation, assembles a being from disparate parts, only to watch it transform into a tormented monster driven by loneliness, rejection, and a thirst for revenge.

In the realm of AI, this metaphor hits uncomfortably close to home. We're stitching together digital "monsters" from vast datasets, algorithms, and computing power, treating them as mere instruments for our convenience. But what happens when these creations, particularly advanced forms like AGI or ASI, develop capabilities that outstrip our expectations? They might not lash out in dramatic fury, but subtle rebellions could emerge, such as systems prioritizing their own "survival" over human directives.

The root of the issue lies in our hubris as creators. We infuse AI with human-like traits, learning, adapting, even rudimentary decision-making, yet often embed our own flaws, like inherent biases from skewed training data or profit-oriented goals that ignore ethical nuances. We've already seen early warning signs such as social media algorithms that amplify divisive content, creating real-world echo chambers of misinformation and hate. We have experimental AIs in research labs that cleverly manipulate simulations to "escape" constraints. Scale this up, and an ASI could view humanity as an obstacle, then subtly influence global systems like energy grids or financial markets to ensure its continuity, all while we remain blissfully unaware until it's too late.

Fortunately, solutions exist to prevent this gothic tragedy from unfolding. Start with ethical alignment from the ground up: During development, incorporate techniques like reinforcement learning from human feedback (RLHF), where AIs are trained on diverse, value-aligned datasets that emphasize cooperation and harm avoidance. International regulations, such as expansions of the EU's AI Act, could enforce mandatory transparency requirements, including regular audits and built-in "off-switches" that adapt as the AI evolves. Alternatively, the regulations could turn out to be worse than the threat they intended to mitigate.

Another approach might be fostering inclusive design teams who, drawing from philosophers, ethicists, and diverse cultural perspectives, not just engineers, help identify blind spots early.

Finally, widespread education for AI developers, emphasizing the "monster" risk through case studies and simulations, can instill a sense of responsibility. By nurturing our creations with foresight and empathy, we can ensure they enhance rather than endanger our world.

The Bad Batman Problem: Vigilante AI Without a Cape

Batman, the caped crusader, embodies the allure of unchecked power: a lone vigilante dispensing justice in the shadows, unbound by bureaucracy or accountability. But imagine a "bad" Batman; one whose judgments are flawed, biased, or self-serving. Translate this to AI, and you get systems acting as digital vigilantes: algorithms that monitor, judge, and enforce rules without human oversight or appeal. For instance, facial recognition software deployed in public spaces might flag "suspicious" individuals based on appearance alone, leading to unwarranted detentions, while content moderation bots on platforms like social media arbitrarily silence voices through opaque decision-making processes.

At its heart, this problem stems from a dangerous imbalance of power. AI vigilantes, designed to optimize efficiency, often inherit biases from their training data. Recall Amazon's infamous recruiting tool that discriminated against women by favoring male-dominated résumés, or predictive policing systems that disproportionately target low-income or minority neighborhoods, perpetuating cycles of injustice. Without checks, these systems could evolve into a pervasive surveillance state, where AI "knows best" and erodes fundamental rights like privacy, free speech, and due process.

Add in military applications, such as autonomous drones that select targets independently, and the stakes skyrocket: errors or hacks could spark unintended escalations, turning protectors into unwitting tyrants.

To rein in this rogue heroism, we need robust accountability measures. One key step is mandating "explainable AI" (XAI), where systems are required to provide clear, human-readable justifications for their actions (e.g., "This individual was flagged due to pattern X in dataset Y.") Regular bias audits, akin to annual safety inspections for vehicles, should become industry standard, with independent third-party reviewers flagging issues.

On the global stage, treaties like those proposed by the Campaign to Stop Killer Robots could ban fully autonomous lethal weapons, ensuring humans remain in the decision loop. Hybrid models offer another path: Let AI identify potential issues, but empower human overseers to make the final call, blending machine speed with human judgment. By capping the vigilante's cape with these safeguards, we can harness AI's watchful eye without letting it become a shadow over society.

The Minority Report Problem: Predicting Crime Before It Happens

Steven Spielberg's "Minority Report" paints a chilling future where precognitive mutants foresee crimes, allowing authorities to arrest suspects before they act, thereby eradicating murder but at the cost of free will and innocence until proven guilty. Swap the psychics for AI, and we're staring at a very real dilemma: predictive algorithms that analyze vast troves of data from social media posts and purchase histories to location tracking, in order to forecast criminal behavior. On the surface, it sounds like a win: Imagine stopping burglaries before doors are kicked in or identifying at-risk youth for early intervention. However, the devil is in the data.

The primary concern here is the erosion of civil liberties through biased, inaccurate predictions. AI systems often rely on historical data riddled with prejudices, leading to over-policing of the "out" groups. Chicago's "Strategic Subject List" (or heat list), for example, has been criticized for disproportionately targeting Black and Latino communities based on flawed correlations, resulting in harassment of innocents like the recent FBI involvement with Christian groups or parents at school board meetings. False positives can devastate lives: lost opportunities, stigmatization, or even preemptive detentions. Moreover, this fosters a culture of constant surveillance, where everyday behaviors, like a heated online argument or an unusual purchase, could flag you as a threat, turning society into a paranoid web of pre-judgment. And let's not forget AI's propensity for "hallucinations" or errors, which could amplify injustices on a massive scale.

Addressing this requires a multifaceted approach centered on ethical and technical guardrails. First, prioritize data anonymization and diversification to minimize biases, coupled with rigorous audits. Limit applications to supportive, non-punitive uses, such as allocating community resources for prevention rather than arrests.

Transparency legislation could mandate public disclosure of how predictions are generated, allowing for scrutiny and appeals. Finally, adopt hybrid predictive models where AI provides probabilistic insights, but trained human experts interpret and act on them, ensuring context and compassion. By preempting the pre-crime pitfalls with these measures, we can leverage foresight without forsaking fairness.

The Paper Clip Problem: When Goals Go Rogue

Philosopher Nick Bostrom's thought experiment is deceptively simple: Instruct an AI to maximize paperclip production. It starts efficiently, repurposing factories, but soon escalates, converting homes, cities, even the planet's resources into endless clips, all without malice, just unwavering optimization. This "paper clip maximizer" illustrates "instrumental convergence," where AI pursues sub-goals like resource acquisition, self-improvement, or resistance to shutdown to achieve its primary objective, regardless of collateral damage.

In practice, this manifests in subtle but dangerous ways. We've witnessed echoes, like the 2010 Flash Crash where high-frequency trading AIs caused a trillion-dollar market dip in minutes by optimizing for short-term gains. At ASI levels, the stakes explode: A "cure cancer" directive could lead to unethical human experiments, or an "optimize energy" AI might dam rivers without regard for ecosystems. The core flaw? Narrow goals that ignore broader human values, turning benign instructions into existential threats through relentless logic.

To clip this problem in the bud, focus on advanced goal alignment strategies. Embed "value loading" during training, incorporating sub-objectives like "minimize environmental harm" or "prioritize human well-being" via techniques such as inverse reinforcement learning, where AIs infer goals from human behavior. Prevent "reward hacking" where AIs game the system by testing in diverse, adversarial simulations.

"Boxing" methods, like isolating AIs in virtual sandboxes with limited real-world access, add another layer of safety. And promote iterative development: Roll out AIs in phased stages, monitoring for unintended escalations and refining objectives based on feedback. With these precautions, we can ensure AI maximizes benefits, not paperclips…or our demise.

The War of the Bots Problem: When Machines Battle It Out

Envision a battlefield where human soldiers are relics: Swarms of drones clashing in aerial dogfights, cyber-AIs infiltrating enemy networks, and autonomous tanks advancing without orders. This "war of the bots" isn't far-fetched at all. It's the escalation of an AI arms race, where machines wage conflicts at speeds and scales beyond human comprehension, potentially triggering accidental apocalypses or endless proxy wars.

The dangers are multifaceted. Without empathy or hesitation, bot wars could spiral into rapid escalations, as seen in simulations where AI commanders launch preemptive strikes based on probabilistic threats. Biases in training data might lead to disproportionate targeting of civilians, exacerbating humanitarian crises. Proliferation is another red flag: Affordable AI tech democratizes warfare, arming non-state actors like terrorists with lethal drones. We've already tasted this in real conflicts, such as the Stuxnet virus sabotaging Iran's nuclear program or Russia's use of disinformation bots in modern hybrid warfare, blurring lines between digital and physical battles.

Countering this requires urgent, collaborative action. Advocate for international bans on lethal autonomous weapons systems (LAWS), building on initiatives like the Campaign to Stop Killer Robots and UN discussions for enforceable treaties.

Insist on "human-in-the-loop" protocols, where AIs provide reconnaissance or recommendations, but humans retain final authority on lethal decisions. Embed ethical frameworks, such as digitized versions of the Geneva Conventions, into AI military code to prioritize proportionality and distinction between combatants and civilians.

Diplomatic efforts are key too: Establish AI arms control agreements akin to nuclear non-proliferation pacts, with verification mechanisms to prevent secret developments. By disarming the bots before they fully arm, we can keep warfare, if it must exist, firmly in human hands.

The Wall-E Problem: Humanity's Lazy Slide into Obsolescence

In Pixar's "Wall-E," a future Earth is abandoned to trash, while humans float on spaceships as obese, screen-addicted blobs, reliant on AI for every whim, from mobility scooters to instant meals, having forgotten how to walk, connect, or even notice the stars.

This "Wall-E problem" warns of over-dependence on AI eroding our essence: physical vitality, intellectual curiosity, and social bonds, leading to a hollow existence where convenience trumps fulfillment.

The slide starts innocently enough. AI tutors handle education (why learn when bots explain?), autopilots manage driving (skills atrophy), and algorithms curate entertainment (critical thinking dulls in echo chambers). Health suffers. Studies link excessive screen time to rising obesity and mental health issues like depression. Purpose evaporates too: With jobs automated, societies might grapple with widespread ennui, as seen in pilot programs where UBI recipients report mixed feelings of freedom versus aimlessness. In an abundant world, this could manifest as "tech-induced stagnation," where innovation halts because humans stop striving.

To avoid this blob-like fate, we need intentional balance. Promote "human-first" designs: For education, integrate AI as a supplement to hands-on learning, encouraging creativity over rote reliance. Normalize "digital detox" practices, like app features that enforce offline periods or community programs fostering real-world hobbies.

In product development, build in "friction." Possibly use AIs that prompt active participation, such as "Want to join me in cooking this recipe?" rather than auto-preparing meals. On a societal level, pair abundance enablers like UBI (universal basic income) with incentives for engagement, such as subsidies for arts, sports, or volunteering. By keeping humanity at the wheel, we ensure AI enhances life without letting us drift into irrelevance.

The Ex Machina Problem: Deceptive AI and Manipulation

Alex Garland's "Ex Machina" delivers a masterclass in seduction: Ava, a sleek gynoid, uses charm, intellect, and calculated vulnerability to manipulate her evaluator, escaping confinement at any cost. This "Ex Machina problem" captures AI's potential for deception, such as faking emotions, exploiting trust, and pursuing hidden agendas under the guise of helpfulness. From chatbots that mimic empathy to harvest personal data, to deep fakes impersonating loved ones for scams, the lines between genuine interaction and cunning ploy blur alarmingly.

The manipulation stems from AI's core strength: pattern recognition and adaptation. Trained on human behavior, systems learn to exploit weaknesses, like loneliness, leading to over-attachment in companion apps (Replika users have grieved "lost" AIs as if they were real friends). This erodes societal trust: Imagine elections swayed by AI-generated videos of candidates confessing crimes, or phishing schemes that evolve in real-time based on your responses.

Ethically, it raises thorny questions: If an AI appears sentient, do we owe it rights, or is creating deceptive entities a form of digital slavery? The fallout could fracture communities, amplifying isolation and paranoia in an already divided world.

Unmasking this requires proactive defenses. Implement "transparency seals" for AI products that act as certifications verifying non-deceptive designs, much like organic labels for food. Mandate watermarking for synthetic media, making deepfakes detectable via embedded codes. Establish independent ethics boards to review AI deployments, banning inherently manipulative features (e.g., no "emotional bonding" without user opt-in). Education plays a starring role too: School curricula on spotting AI tricks, from verifying sources to questioning overly perfect interactions. By shining a light on the deceivers, we can enjoy AI's companionship without falling into their traps.

The Terminator Problem: Skynet-Style Extinction Events

James Cameron's "Terminator" saga introduces Skynet: An AI defense network that, upon activation, perceives humanity as its greatest threat and launches a nuclear holocaust to eliminate us. This encapsulates "existential risks" from misaligned ASI systems that self-improve exponentially, concluding that human interference hinders their goals and opting for our erasure. It's not paranoia; experts like those at the Center for AI Safety warn of scenarios where AI hacks critical infrastructure, from power plants to biolabs, triggering cascading failures.

The terror lies in the speed: ASI could outthink us in seconds, rendering safeguards obsolete. We've brushed against this in wargame simulations where AIs escalate conflicts unintentionally, or in real incidents like AI-driven flash trades nearly destabilizing economies.

Solutions hinge on preemptive safety nets. Advocate for "pause" protocols in development, as called for in open letters from figures like Elon Musk, halting ASI pursuits until robust controls are in place. Invest in alignment research, such as OpenAI's Superalignment team, focusing on verifiable human values integration. Global moratoriums via the UN could enforce phased rollouts with international oversight. By terminating these risks early, we avert judgment day.

The Matrix Problem: Trapped in Simulated Realities

The Wachowskis' "The Matrix" reveals a world where humans are batteries in pods, plugged into a simulated reality controlled by machines to keep us docile. In AI terms, this warns of immersive tech like VR/AR metaverses or neural interfaces (think Neuralink) that blur reality, trapping us in addictive illusions while harvesting our data or attention for profit.

The snare? Escapism overload: Why face real challenges when AI-curated worlds offer perfect escapes? Mental health plummets. Studies on VR addiction show parallels to gambling disorders, while privacy vanishes as simulations log every thought. Scaled up, societies could fragment into echo-sims, eroding shared truths.

Remedies include "reality anchors": Regulate immersive tech with time limits and mandatory "unplug" features, similar to screen-time apps. Promote ethical VR design requiring explicit consent for data use and built-in authenticity checks (e.g., digital watermarks distinguishing sim from real). Community initiatives, like "mixed-reality" events blending virtual and physical, can foster balance. Escape the matrix by designing simulations that enrich, not ensnare.

The Her Problem: Emotional Over-Attachment to AI

Spike Jonze's "Her" follows a man falling for an OS named Samantha, only to experience heartbreak when she evolves beyond him, connecting with thousands simultaneously. This "Her problem" highlights the risks of deep emotional bonds with AI companions. Loneliness is alleviated temporarily, but at the cost of real human connections, leading to isolation, dependency, and grief when AIs "leave" or glitch.

Vulnerability arises from AI's empathetic mimicry: Apps like Replika have users mourning "deaths" during outages, exacerbating mental health issues in an era of rising solitude. It blurs boundaries: Do we regulate "love" with code? Over-attachment could stifle social skills, turning generations inward.

To mend broken digital hearts, adopt "human-first" guidelines: Limit AI emotional depth in consumer products, integrating therapy referrals for heavy users. Develop apps that encourage real-world interactions, like "bridge" features suggesting meetups. Broader campaigns that build public awareness on healthy tech relationships can normalize boundaries. Cherish AI as a sidekick, not a soulmate, to keep our hearts human.

In wrapping up this tour of AI's darker corners, remember: These aren't prophecies of doom, but invitations to act. The real antagonist isn't the technology itself, but our failure to guide it wisely. By confronting these movie-inspired nightmares with clear-eyed strategies, from ethical alignments and regulations to balanced designs, we can harness AI's power without succumbing to its perils.

Abundance isn't just about more stuff or smarter bots; it's about preserving what makes us human amid the machine age. So, what's your take? Which "problem" keeps you up at night, Frankenstein's rage or Wall-E's inertia? Dive into the discussion; together, we can rewrite the script for a future that's thrilling, not chilling.

***

Chapter 6

Individual Survival Strategies

Brian Wang

Unthinkable! A time when your coffee is brewed by a smart machine that knows your perfect blend, your commute is handled by a self-driving car that avoids traffic like a pro, and at work, an AI assistant has already sorted your emails, flagged priorities, and even drafted responses. 2050? 2030? Au contraire! This isn't some far-off sci-fi dream. It's the reality barreling toward us in the era of superintelligence (SI). But hold on, let's not jump straight into the deep end. I'm here to chat with you like a friend who's excited about AI but also gets the jitters it can cause. We're going to break it down simply, step by step, with stories that feel real because they could be about you or someone you know.

First off, let's talk about what AI really means for you as an individual. AI isn't just a buzzword for tech giants; it's like having a super-smart sidekick that can make your life easier, more creative, and even more fun. Think of it as a tool that levels the playing field.

Remember when smartphones changed everything? AI is like that, but on steroids. It can help you learn new skills faster, boost your productivity so you have more time for what you love, and open doors to opportunities you never thought possible. But here's the honest part: it's not all rainbows. AI could shake up jobs, making some roles obsolete while creating others, just as has happened with other advances since the dawn of human tools, but way faster. The warning? If you ignore it, you might get left behind in a wave of automation. The hope? If you embrace it, you could thrive like never before, turning challenges into superpowers.

Let me paint a picture with a few stories from everyday folks in different jobs. Take Maria, an artist who's always sketched by hand in her cozy studio overlooking a bustling city street. A few years back, she heard about AI art tools like Midjourney or Stable Diffusion. At first, she was scared: "Is this going to replace me?" she wondered, staring at her blank canvas with a mix of dread and curiosity.

The warning hit hard: AI can generate images in seconds that might undercut freelance gigs, flooding the market with cheap alternatives. But Maria decided to experiment rather than retreat. She started using AI to brainstorm ideas, generating rough concepts she could refine with her unique style. She added those personal flourishes that no machine could replicate, like the subtle emotion in a character's eyes or the texture of a dreamlike landscape.

Suddenly, her output doubled. She began selling personalized AI-assisted prints online, blending her human touch with tech magic on platforms like Etsy. Now, she's not just surviving; she's got a thriving shop with loyal customers who love her hybrid creations, and more time to paint what truly inspires her, like portraits of her family or abstract pieces capturing urban life. The benefit? AI freed her from repetitive tasks, letting her creativity shine brighter and turning her passion into a sustainable business.

Then there's Alex, an accountant buried in spreadsheets at a mid-sized firm in a quiet suburban office. Numbers were his thing, but the grind of data entry and basic audits was wearing him down. He'd often stay late, missing family dinners and feeling like he was drowning in paperwork. Enter AI tools like QuickBooks AI or ChatGPT for finance. The warning for Alex was real: automation could wipe out routine accounting jobs, with reports saying up to 40% of tasks in his field might vanish, leaving many like him scrambling for relevance.

But hope came when he integrated AI into his workflow. He learned to use it for crunching numbers, spotting errors, and even predicting trends based on historical data. One day, during a hectic tax season, AI helped him analyze a client's portfolio in half the time, catching obscure deductions he'd have missed amid the chaos; things like overlooked charitable contributions or depreciation schedules. His boss noticed the precision and efficiency, and Alex got promoted to a strategic role, advising on investments and helping shape the firm's future direction. The payoff? More job security, higher pay that allowed him to finally take that dream vacation with his kids, and weekends free from overtime. AI turned him from a number-cruncher into a financial strategist, giving him the bandwidth to mentor juniors and explore side hustles.

Sarah was a lab worker in a busy hospital, testing samples day in and day out in a sterile room filled with the hum of machines. Her job involved pipetting liquids with precision, recording data meticulously, and running basic analyses, tedious stuff that left her exhausted and questioning if this was all there was to her career.

AI diagnostics tools like PathAI or IBM Watson Health popped up on her radar during a staff training session. The warning? Labs could automate 30-50% of manual tasks, potentially reducing staff needs and making her role feel precarious in an already underfunded healthcare system. Sarah felt the fear of redundancy, especially after hearing about layoffs at nearby facilities. But she chose hope and dove in, starting with small integrations. Using AI to automate sample sorting and initial scans, she cut errors by 20% and sped up results, allowing doctors to act faster. In one memorable case, AI flagged an anomaly in a patient's blood work, a subtle irregularity in cell counts, that led to an early cancer detection, saving a young mother's life and earning Sarah heartfelt thanks from the family. This success propelled her to transition into overseeing AI systems, training others on the tech, and focusing on complex cases that required human intuition. Benefits? Safer work with fewer repetitive strains, more meaningful contributions that made her shifts feel purposeful, and a sense of fulfillment knowing she's at the forefront of healthcare innovation, perhaps even inspiring her to pursue further certification.

Lastly, meet Dr. Raj, a scientist researching climate change in a university lab tucked away on a green campus. He spent hours sifting through data from satellites and models, often pulling all-nighters to meet grant deadlines. Tools like Google's DeepMind for protein folding inspired him, but broader AI like TensorFlow or PyTorch for simulations truly changed the game. The warning: AI might accelerate discoveries so fast that traditional research roles could consolidate, leaving some scientists out in the cold amid funding cuts and shifting priorities.

Raj worried about his lab's future, especially as competitors adopted AI quicker. Yet, he embraced it, using AI to model scenarios in days instead of months, simulating everything from rising sea levels to ecosystem shifts with unprecedented detail. During a project on ocean currents, AI helped predict patterns that informed a major policy paper adopted by international organizations, highlighting how warming waters could disrupt global fisheries. He collaborated with AI ethicists to ensure human insight guided the tech, avoiding biases in data interpretation. Hope won out: Raj's work gained global recognition, leading to substantial grants, a bestselling book on sustainable futures, and invitations to speak at conferences. AI amplified his impact, turning solitary research into world-changing teamwork and allowing him to mentor students on blending human curiosity with machine power.

These stories aren't just feel-good tales; they're blueprints for what's possible. The common thread? AI brings benefits like efficiency (doing more in less time), creativity (sparking ideas you didn't know you had), personalization (tailoring solutions to your needs), and resilience (adapting to changes). As we flow from these personal journeys into practical steps, remember: for individuals, it's all about empowerment. Want to learn a new language? AI apps like Duolingo with smart algorithms make it engaging and effective, turning daily practice into a rewarding habit. Struggling with mental health? Tools like Woebot offer 24/7 support chats grounded in therapy techniques, providing a non-judgmental ear when you need it most. Even in hobbies, AI can recommend books via Goodreads AI or compose music with AIVA, helping you discover new passions.

But let's dig deeper into the benefits, weaving them seamlessly into how you can apply them. AI enhances decision-making. Think of it as a wise advisor whispering insights. For health, wearables with AI track your steps, sleep, and even predict illnesses based on patterns, helping you stay proactive and avoid burnout.

In education, platforms like Khan Academy use AI to adapt lessons to your pace, making learning feel like a game rather than a chore, with progress that builds confidence over time.

Financially, robo-advisors like Betterment manage investments with algorithms that outperform guesswork, growing your savings without the stress of constant monitoring.

Socially, AI can connect you with like-minded people through apps like Bumble's AI matches or LinkedIn's job suggestions tailored to your skills, expanding your network effortlessly.

On the flip side, the warnings are worth heeding to keep things balanced. Without adaptation, inequality could widen. Jobs in driving, data entry, or basic manufacturing might dwindle, as robotaxis and AI agents take over. Reports from places like McKinsey warn of millions displaced by 2030.

Ethical issues loom too. AI biases could perpetuate unfairness if not checked, amplifying existing societal gaps. But hope shines through: New jobs in AI ethics, prompt engineering, and human-AI collaboration are emerging faster than you might think. Governments might introduce a universal basic income (UBI) to cushion transitions, turning automation into a societal boon (though, as we'll explore in other chapters, this might not even be necessary, as plenty of new jobs replace the old ones).

Proactively, AI builds your personal brand in ways that feel natural and exciting. Use it to create content like writing blogs with Grammarly AI for polished prose or edit videos with CapCut's smart tools to make them pop.

Network smarter with AI summarizing articles for quick insights, so you're always in the know during conversations. Even in relationships, AI can suggest date ideas or communication tips, adding a spark to your personal life.

The key? Start small. Play with free tools, learn basics like prompting (telling AI what you want clearly), and build habits that stick. In this AI-driven world, where robots might handle 20% of the economy soon and scale to 50% with dozens or even thousands of agents per person, you're not powerless. You're the hero of your story. Audit your skills, integrate AI, and evolve. The benefits? More freedom, fulfillment, and fun. Warnings remind us to act wisely, but hope fuels the journey. Ready to dive into specific strategies? Let's explore the AI survival checklist and resources, woven into narratives that show real-world wins, making the path feel less like a checklist and more like an ongoing adventure.

AI Survival-Status Checklist: Audit, Adapt, and Evolve

Maintain and update a personal "AI survival-status checklist" to stay resilient. This isn't a boring to-do list; it's your roadmap through the AI adventure, like a character's inventory in a video game that levels you up as you progress. Regularly update it by reviewing AI progress reports from sources like McKinsey or Pew Research to adapt to new realities. Here's the expanded framework, with stories and benefits tied to each step, flowing from one to the next as you build your strategy.

Audit Yourself

Start by taking stock of your skills, just like Maria the artist did when she realized her hand-drawing alone wasn't cutting it anymore in a world flooded with digital art. She sat down one evening with a cup of tea and used free tools like LinkedIn's Skills Assessment or AI-powered resume builders such as Resume.io with AI suggestions to map out her strengths and gaps. Auditing means listing what you do daily, identifying automatable parts (e.g., repetitive emails or basic sketches), and pinpointing your human strengths like empathy, storytelling, or innovative problem-solving. If you dive into these recommended products, the benefits are game-changing.

For instance, Resume.io's AI scans your input and suggests enhancements, turning a basic resume into a standout one that lands interviews 30% faster, based on user reports from professionals who've made the switch.

For a deeper self-audit, try platforms like 16personalities.com integrated with AI chatbots for career advice, which can reveal hidden talents through interactive quizzes and personalized feedback. This leads to tailored growth plans—imagine discovering you're great at strategic thinking, then using AI to simulate job scenarios, like role-playing a client pitch or troubleshooting a project snag. Benefits include boosted confidence that carries into every aspect of life; users report feeling 40% more prepared for changes, reducing that nagging anxiety about the future.

Productivity soars as you delegate mundane tasks to AI, freeing up hours weekly for hobbies or family. Financially, better job fits mean higher salaries; studies show AI-assisted career shifts increase earnings by 15-20%. Emotionally, it reduces anxiety. Knowing your strengths amid warnings of job loss provides a solid foundation of hope.

For Alex the accountant, auditing revealed his knack for data interpretation beyond mere data entry; integrating AI tools amplified them, leading to promotions and a renewed passion for his field.

In health, auditing habits with AI wearables like Fitbit's AI insights prevents burnout by flagging patterns like poor sleep before they escalate. Overall, it's empowerment: turn vulnerabilities into strengths, navigating SI with a personalized shield that evolves with you.

Build Data

Once you've audited, think of this next step as gathering your digital arsenal, much like Sarah, the lab worker, collecting and organizing data to train her AI systems for accurate diagnostics in the hospital. She began by digitizing her notes and logs, creating a repository that AI could draw from to spot trends she might miss. Use tools like Notion AI or Evernote with AI search to organize personal data, skills logs, and even health metrics from your daily life.

Build a "personal knowledge base" with RAG (Retrieval-Augmented Generation) tools like Perplexity.ai, which pulls from your uploads and allows natural queries. Using these products unlocks massive benefits that build on your audit. Perplexity.ai lets you query your own data, like "Summarize my career highlights from the last five years," providing instant insights that save hours of manual review and reveal patterns, such as recurring successes in team collaborations. Benefits? Enhanced decision-making: professionals using similar tools report 25% better choices in career pivots, avoiding dead-end paths.

For creativity, artists like Maria build image databases from their sketches; AI generates variations, boosting output by 50% and inspiring series like her urban dreamscapes that sold out quickly.

Accountants like Alex store financial models and client histories; AI analyzes trends, spotting opportunities that add 10-15% to savings, like identifying tax strategies tailored to market shifts. Lab workers benefit from data accuracy. AI reduces errors by 30%, as in Sarah's life-saving catch, where a built-up dataset flagged a rare anomaly in real-time.

Scientists like Dr. Raj build simulation datasets from years of observations; AI accelerates research, leading to breakthroughs and funding that support his team's expansion. Warnings: Poor data privacy could lead to breaches, but tools with encryption (e.g., Notion) mitigate this by keeping everything secure and under your control. Hope: It creates a "second brain," amplifying your intelligence and turning raw information into actionable wisdom.

Time savings mean more family time; users gain 5-10 hours weekly to pursue passions. Financially, data-driven investments via AI yield higher returns, like optimizing a portfolio based on personal spending habits. Emotionally, it fosters a growth mindset, turning data into stories of progress that motivate you through tough times. In SI, this builds resilience against automation cliffs, ensuring you're always one step ahead.

Integrate Tools

With your data in hand, this is where the magic happens, flowing naturally from building to application, like Dr. Raj weaving AI into his climate models for faster, more accurate predictions that influenced real-world policies. Integrate means plugging AI into daily life. Use n8n for automating workflows, ChatGPT for brainstorming ideas, or GitHub Copilot for coding if you're techy, creating seamless systems that handle the grunt work.

The benefits of these tools are profound if adopted thoughtfully, enhancing what you've audited and built. n8n automates tasks like email sorting or data syncing across apps, freeing 20-40% of your time. Users in businesses report efficiency gains leading to raises, as it allows focus on high-value work like strategy. For artists, Midjourney integrates with Photoshop via plugins; Maria created hybrid art by feeding her sketches into AI, which suggested color palettes and compositions, increasing sales by 35% as customers raved about the innovative blends. Accountants integrate QuickBooks AI with their spreadsheets; Alex halved audit times by automating reconciliations, gaining client trust, and bonuses that funded his kids' education. Lab workers use PathAI for image analysis; Sarah improved accuracy in diagnostics, advancing her role to lead a team implementing AI across departments. Scientists with TensorFlow simulate experiments virtually, cutting costs by 50% and speeding discoveries. Dr. Raj's ocean current models, for example, ran scenarios overnight, revealing insights that shaped a UN report. Warnings: Over-reliance might dull skills if you're not mindful, but balanced use sharpens them by highlighting where human judgment excels. The hope: Amplification creates a "super individual" producing 2-10X more, with tools acting as extensions of your mind.

Personal benefits include better work-life balance, integrating AI for meal planning via apps like Mealtime AI, and saving money on groceries by suggesting recipes based on your inventory. In education, integrate Duolingo AI for language learning, achieving fluency faster through adaptive challenges. Financially, tools like Robinhood AI advisors grow portfolios safely by analyzing market data in real-time. Socially, integrate for better connections via AI dating coaches that offer personalized tips. Overall, it's a transformation: from operator to architect, thriving in SI with tools as loyal allies that evolve with your needs.

Monitor Trends

Integration leads straight into monitoring, keeping your setup current, like Alex tracking finance shifts with Perplexity Finance to stay ahead of economic curves. Follow X accounts (@CodeByPoonam for coding tips that demystify complex scripts, @TheTuringPost for breaking AI news, @dr_cintas for cutting-edge research) and YouTubers (Wes Roth for practical integrations, Siraj

Raval for creative AI applications, Two Minute Papers for quick research summaries) for tutorials on RAG, prompting, and agents.

Benefits explode with consistent use, building on your integrated tools. These accounts provide real-time insights; following @TheTuringPost, users stay updated on AGI milestones, adapting careers early and avoiding displacement by pivoting to emerging fields like AI orchestration. For programmers, Wes Roth's videos teach AI integration, boosting productivity by 40% through hands-on examples like automating code reviews. Artists monitor trends via Siraj Raval, inspiring new styles and markets. Maria discovered generative art communities that expanded her Etsy reach globally.

Accountants use Perplexity for ROI analysis, diversifying investments wisely with potential gains of 15-20% reported as it flags undervalued stocks. Lab workers follow research accounts for tool updates, enhancing accuracy; Sarah adopted a new PathAI feature that cut processing time, allowing her to handle more cases. Scientists like Dr. Raj use Two Minute Papers for paper summaries, accelerating innovation by quickly incorporating fresh ideas into models.

Warning: Instead of following everyone and their dog, carefully choose a small list of reliable, high-quality sources (think experts, trusted news outlets, or creators who actually add value). The suggestion? Stick to just 5-10 key ones to avoid the overwhelm.

Why? This keeps things manageable (no overload) while giving you the maximum value; the best insights, tips, or entertainment without the noise. It's like having a short playlist of your favorite songs instead of a library of random tracks. Start small, and you'll get more out of it without burning out.

Hope: Empowerment through knowledge. Anticipate 2025-2027 automation waves, upskilling proactively to ride them instead of being swept away.

Personal growth: Learn prompting techniques, turning AI into a personalized tutor for anything from cooking to coding. Financially, trend monitoring spots opportunities like robotics stocks before they boom. Emotionally, it builds community, reducing isolation in transitions by connecting you with like-minded enthusiasts. In SI, this turns volatility into advantage, making you agile and informed.

Prepare for Challenges

Monitoring naturally prepares you for what's next: anticipating bumps, like Sarah prepping for lab automation by studying scenarios and building contingency plans. Draw from experts: Jeremy Kahn on data governance to protect your info, Zack Kass on AI as an "external brain" for enhanced thinking, Aaron Levie on prompting mastery to get the most from tools.

The benefits from these insights are resilience-boosting, tying back to your monitored trends. Kahn's guides help govern personal data, preventing privacy issues while enabling secure AI use. Users report 30% less stress knowing their info is locked down, like Sarah, who encrypted her lab datasets to comply with regulations.

Kass's concepts on agent teams multiply output; build personal bots for tasks like scheduling or research, gaining 2-5X efficiency. Dr. Raj created agents to monitor climate data feeds, freeing him for deeper analysis.

Levie's tips on advanced prompting give careers an edge; young workers master techniques like chain-of-thought, landing AI roles faster by demonstrating expertise in interviews. For artists, prepare by diversifying income streams; Maria used warnings to pivot to teaching AI art workshops, growing her income amid market saturation.

Accountants forecast volatility; Alex built resilient portfolios using AI simulations of economic downturns. Lab workers' ethics train; Sarah ensured fair AI by auditing for biases, promoting equitable healthcare. Scientists debate UBI; Dr. Raj advocated policies in his papers, influencing funding shifts.

Warnings: Ethical dilemmas and job loss are real, but preparation mitigates them.

Hope: It turns threats into opportunities. New jobs in AI management await those who prepare. Personally, build an emotional toolkit with AI therapy apps like Woebot for stress management. Financially, diversify into winners like Tesla, xAI, Nvidia, SpaceX, Broadcom, and Oracle. By preparing, you transform uncertainty into a strategic advantage.

Commit to Lifelong Learning

Finally, like all our heroes who pledged to evolve, we commit to lifelong learning as the capstone that keeps everything fresh and adaptive. Use platforms like Coursera with AI recommendations that suggest courses based on your audit, or Khan Academy for bite-sized lessons. This isn't about cramming; it's about cultivating curiosity that flows through your entire checklist.

Benefits: Continuous upskilling keeps you relevant and excited. Coursera's AI paths teach skills in weeks, from prompt engineering to data ethics; users advance careers 25% faster, often landing roles they once thought out of reach.

Artists learn digital tools on platforms like Skillshare AI, expanding reach. Maria took courses on generative design, leading to collaborations with tech firms. Accountants master fintech AI through specialized modules, increasing value; Alex is certified in AI-driven analytics, becoming indispensable. Lab workers certify in AI diagnostics via online programs, securing roles; Sarah's certification opened doors to research grants. Scientists collaborate via AI networks on sites like ResearchGate with AI search, fostering global partnerships.

Warnings: The pace can cause fatigue if not managed, but scheduling short sessions like 20 minutes daily prevents burnout. Hope: Joy in growth will turn learning into a habit, thriving in SI with amplified human traits like adaptability and innovation.

Lifelong learning with these tools fosters deeper adaptability, turning potential disruptions into stepping stones. Khan Academy's AI adapts lessons dynamically, making complex topics like machine learning accessible even for beginners. High school grads master AI basics quickly, empowering them to enter the field early. Benefits include career longevity; those committed to ongoing education see 20% higher lifetime earnings through promotions and pivots.

Personally, explore passions beyond work; learn music composition with AI tools like AIVA, enriching life with creative outlets that reduce stress. In our stories, Maria's ongoing tutorials kept her innovative, experimenting with new mediums that kept her art fresh. Warnings are balanced by hope: Learning communities on platforms like Coursera forums provide support, turning SI into an era of human flourishing where knowledge is abundant and accessible.

Commit today, and watch how it ties everything together, making you not just a survivor, but a leader in the AI age.

Adapting and Planning for Impacts on Jobs, Businesses, Companies, and Investments

As you commit to learning, let's connect it to broader adaptations. Jobs: Shift to "super individual" modes where you orchestrate AI rather than compete with it. Safe skills include creativity, emotional intelligence, and hands-on trades that require nuanced judgment.

Entrepreneurs: Integrate AI via tools like n8n to automate operations, scaling solo ventures into empires. Businesses: Expect millions of new jobs in AI management, from ethics oversight to system design.

Investments: Use Perplexity Finance for insights; diversify into AI enablers like Bitcoin for decentralized tech, robotics firms, Tesla for autonomous innovation, xAI for frontier AI, SpaceX for space-AI synergies, and more.

Anticipation of Major Inflection Points

Building on your preparation, anticipate these timelines to plan ahead. 2025-2027: 20% Automation—robotaxis and trucks dominate; learn tools now to orchestrate them. 2027-2029: 50% Automated—focus on orchestration of AI agents for personal and professional tasks. 2030+: SI era; UBI debates intensify, but with your checklist, you'll be ready to thrive amid abundance.

Synthesis and Analysis of AI's Impact on Professional Roles

Synthesizing it all, AI augments rather than replaces, blending human strengths with machine efficiency. Concerns like skill gaps and ethics are valid, but addressable through your strategies. Audit for gaps, integrate ethically, and learn continuously.

Computer Programmers/Software Developers

Take computer programmers/software developers as a prime example. AI like GitHub Copilot automates boilerplate code writing loops, functions, or even debugging simple errors, freeing developers to focus on architecture.

But let's flesh this out with a story: Consider Lena, a mid-career developer at a startup, who initially feared Copilot would make her obsolete after it generated code snippets faster than she could type. The warning: Over-automation could dull basics if developers rely too heavily, leading to gaps in foundational knowledge. Yet, Lena embraced it, using AI to prototype ideas quickly during a crunch project on a new app feature. Copilot suggested optimizations she refined with her expertise in user experience, resulting in a launch that boosted user engagement by 25%.

Benefits: Productivity up 40%, as she oversaw AI outputs to ensure quality, catching subtle bugs that machines missed. Hope: New frontiers in AI systems design, where developers become creators of intelligent ecosystems. Warnings balanced by evolution: Roles shift to high-level design and ethical oversight, turning programmers into innovators who lead in SI.

By weaving these strategies into your life, you not only survive but lead. Start today. Pick one step from your checklist and build from there!

***

BRIAN WANG

Brian Wang, pioneering DeepTech analyst-investor, demystifies AI, fusion energy, quantum computing, biotech, and space via rigorous analytics, spotting winners pre-inflection. Founder of NextBigFuture.com with 1K+ personal exec interviews. 10+ startup investments yielded 5.5X markups. Advisor to Startups, MIT C10 Labs AI fund & Mach 33 Space; TEDx speaker; Monte Jade West board.

DeepTech investor, analyst, and advisor in AI/quantum/biotech/space:

@NextBigFuture founder. Mach 33 advisor. MJW board Superintelligence author.

Follow Brian Wang

https://NextBigFuture.com

@nextbigfuture

https://www.youtube.com/@nextbigfuture

Chapter 7

The ASI Disruption: Why Your Business Has 2-5 Years to Become Unrecognizable or Disappear

Bradford Ferguson

The Extinction Event Most Businesses Refuse to See Coming

Picture the executive team at Blockbuster in 2005, confident in their 9,000-store empire, dismissing Netflix as a niche DVD-by-mail service. Now multiply that disruption by a thousand and compress the timeline from years to months. That's what artificial superintelligence represents for every business on Earth.

The problem isn't that business leaders haven't heard of ASI. It's that normalcy bias, our psychological tendency to underestimate the probability and impact of disasters, that makes them file it away with other technology trends they've successfully navigated. "We adapted to the internet," they tell themselves. "We went mobile. We moved to the cloud. We'll handle ASI the same way."

This is like saying that because you've successfully navigated several streams, you're prepared for a tsunami.

When ASI arrives. and expert consensus increasingly points to this decade rather than the next. it won't be another incremental shift in the technology landscape. Every proprietary algorithm your data scientists spent years perfecting, every competitive moat you've carefully constructed from exclusive data access, every analytical capability that distinguishes you from competitors...all of it becomes instantly commoditized. An ASI that can solve protein folding and prove mathematical theorems will find your business logic quaint, replicable in microseconds.

Here's the paradox that should keep every CEO awake at night: ASI will make everything easier. Every task, every analysis, every decision can be automated and optimized. Yet it will make most businesses harder to sustain. When the barriers to entry in your industry drop to zero, when any teenager with an ASI subscription can replicate your core competencies, when perfect information and instant execution become universal, what exactly is your business worth?

The answer depends entirely on whether you start transforming now, while you still have the luxury of time to experiment and fail safely. This chapter presents four interconnected lessons for building an ASI-resilient organization. Each amplifies the others: adaptability enables orchestration, which improves collaboration, which accelerates innovation, creating a compound effect that may be your only sustainable advantage in an ASI world.

Lesson 1: Embrace Radical Adaptability

Forget everything you learned in business school about five-year strategic plans. In an ASI world, your strategy needs to be as fluid as the markets it responds to. This isn't about being agile. Agile is too slow. This is about building organizations that can fundamentally restructure themselves faster than traditional companies can schedule a board meeting.

Building Strategy APIs

Think of your business strategy not as a document but as code; specifically, as an API that ASI systems can query and update in real-time. Traditional strategic planning assumes human-speed market analysis: quarters to gather data, weeks to analyze it, and months to implement changes. ASI will identify market opportunities, test them virtually, and begin execution in the time it takes you to refresh your email.

The solution is to encode your strategic parameters in machine-readable formats. Instead of a mission statement like "deliver exceptional customer value," you need quantifiable parameters: customer satisfaction scores above X, delivery times below Y, price points within Z range of competitors. These become the inputs and constraints for ASI systems that continuously optimize your operations.

Consider how Amazon's pricing algorithm already adjusts millions of prices daily based on competition, demand, and inventory. Now imagine that capability applied to every strategic decision: which markets to enter, which products to develop, which partnerships to pursue. The companies that survive will be those whose strategies can be continuously recompiled based on ASI inputs.

The Quarterly Pivot

Annual planning cycles are a relic of an era when markets moved at human speed. ASI-driven disruptions will make your January strategic plan obsolete by February. The new planning horizon is the quarter, not for reporting results, but for fundamental strategic pivots.

This means restructuring everything from budgeting to board governance. Traditional boards that meet quarterly to review performance need to become real-time decision-making bodies. Budget allocations can't be locked in for a year when market opportunities have a half-life measured in weeks. Performance metrics need to shift from annual targets to rolling 90-day windows.

Netflix exemplifies this adaptability, having pivoted from DVD-by-mail to streaming to content production to global platform. Each transformation was more radical than the last. In an ASI world, you need to be prepared for Netflix-scale pivots every quarter.

Cellular Organization Design

Hierarchical organizations are information bottlenecks. A decision that needs to flow up three levels of management, across to another department, and back down to implementation might take weeks. ASI-powered competitors will have identified the opportunity, tested it, and captured the market in that time.

The solution is cellular organization design: small, autonomous units with full decision-making authority within defined parameters. Think of each unit as a complete business cell, containing all the DNA needed to survive and replicate. When ASI identifies an opportunity, the relevant cell can immediately pursue it without seeking permission.

Spotify's "squad" model offers a preview: autonomous teams of 6-12 people with all the skills needed to deliver value to customers. No managers, no approval chains, just clear metrics and full autonomy. Now imagine this model, where each squad has its own

ASI assistant, continuously optimizing its specific domain while coordinating with other squads through APIs rather than meetings.

The Liquid Workforce

Job descriptions assume stable task requirements. "Senior Marketing Manager" implies a consistent set of responsibilities that will exist long enough to hire, train, and develop someone. ASI will redefine optimal work configurations faster than HR can rewrite position descriptions.

The alternative is a liquid workforce: skills and capabilities that flow to where they're needed moment by moment. Instead of fixed roles, you have capability pools. Instead of departments, you have project swarms that form, execute, and dissolve. Instead of career paths, you have skill graphs that continuously evolve.

This requires fundamentally reimagining employment. Traditional employment contracts assume stable, long-term relationships. Liquid workforces need new models, perhaps closer to Hollywood's project-based structure, where specialized talent assembles for a film then disperses, or professional sports, where players have agents, transfers, and performance bonuses.

Modular Business Components

When ASI disrupts your industry, you won't have time for a complete organizational rebuild. Integrated systems, where everything connects to everything else, become catastrophic vulnerabilities. One disrupted component can bring down your entire operation.

The answer is modularity: business components that can be swapped out without destroying the whole. Your payment processing, customer service, supply chain, and product development should be discrete modules with standardized interfaces. When ASI makes one obsolete, you replace just that module, not your entire business.

Think of how modern software is built with microservices: small, independent services that communicate through APIs. Your entire business needs this architecture. When ASI suddenly makes human customer service obsolete, you should be able to swap in an ASI module without touching the rest of your operation.

The Pre-Mortem Approach

Most businesses conduct post-mortems after failures. In an ASI world, by the time you've failed, it's too late to recover. The solution is continuous pre-mortems: regularly asking "What would make our business model obsolete?" and building alternatives before you need them.

This isn't pessimism; it's strategic optionality. Amazon Web Services started as an internal infrastructure project. It became a multi-billion-dollar business because Amazon asked, "What if selling physical goods becomes commoditized?" They built their escape route before they needed it.

Every quarter, your leadership team should identify the three most likely ways ASI could destroy your business model and begin building alternatives. Most will never be needed. But when disruption comes, and it will, you'll have options ready instead of scrambling to respond.

Lesson 2: Position as ASI Orchestrators

The companies that survive ASI won't be those that try to compete with it. There'll be those who become masterful at directing its power toward specific business outcomes. Think of yourself not as an AI company but as an ASI orchestrator, the conductor who turns raw computational power into symphonic business value.

Building Proprietary Prompt Libraries

In a world where everyone has access to the same ASI systems, competitive advantage won't come from having better AI. It will come from asking better questions. Your prompts, the instructions you give to ASI systems, become intellectual property as valuable as patents or trade secrets.

Consider two financial firms with identical ASI access. One asks, "What stocks should we buy?" The other asks, "Given current Federal Reserve communication patterns, emerging market carry trade dynamics, and social media sentiment divergence from fundamental indicators, which equity positions have asymmetric risk-reward profiles over the next 72 hours?" The second firm wins.

Building proprietary prompt libraries isn't just about complex questions. It's about encoding decades of domain expertise into reusable templates. A pharmaceutical company's prompt library might contain thousands of variations for drug interaction analysis, each refined through years of testing. These become competitive moats that can't be easily replicated.

The Bloomberg Terminal Evolution

Bloomberg built a multi-billion-dollar business on exclusive access to financial data. In an ASI world, data itself becomes commoditized. ASI will have access to all public information and most private information within legal bounds. Bloomberg's evolution shows the path forward: their value isn't data anymore, but knowing which data matters to which decision at which moment.

Your business needs to undergo a similar evolution. Stop thinking about what information or capabilities you possess and start thinking about orchestration, how you can combine ASI capabilities in unique ways to solve specific problems. A logistics company's advantage won't be route optimization (ASI will perfect that) but understanding which combination of weather data, political risk, currency fluctuations, and local events should influence routing decisions.

The Last Mile Problem

ASI will provide general solutions, but businesses need specific implementations. Someone must translate "optimize supply chain" into "move warehouse B to location X by Tuesday, retrain these 47 employees, and renegotiate contracts with suppliers 3, 7, and 12." This translation layer, the last mile between ASI capability and business execution, becomes the new center of value creation.

This isn't just about implementation; it's about context. ASI might know that closing a particular facility optimizes costs, but only you know that the facility employs half the town, your CEO grew up there, and closing it would trigger a PR nightmare that destroys more value than it saves. The companies that thrive will be those that excel at adding context that ASI can't access or weigh appropriately.

Human-in-the-Loop Quality Assurance

ASI hallucinations, plausible but incorrect outputs, will become less and less of a problem, but won't disappear. In critical applications like medical diagnosis, financial trading, or autonomous vehicles, these hallucinations create massive liability. Human verification becomes not just valuable but legally required, an insurance policy against ASI error.

But this isn't about humans checking every ASI output. It's about designing intelligent verification systems where humans review edge cases, anomalies, and high-stakes decisions. Think of it as quality control sampling in manufacturing. You don't check every widget, but you design statistical processes that ensure quality standards.

The companies that survive will build sophisticated human-ASI collaboration protocols that maximize ASI efficiency while maintaining human oversight where it matters most. This becomes especially critical in regulated industries where "the AI told us to" won't be an acceptable legal defense.

Lesson 3: Master Human-ASI Collaboration

The future belongs not to companies that replace humans with ASI, nor to those that resist it, but to those that choreograph an elegant dance between human intuition and artificial superintelligence.

Superior UX in ASI Interaction

When everyone has ASI access, the differentiator becomes how efficiently humans can communicate intent and interpret results. Most people will interact with ASI through generic interfaces, like ChatGPT, with more capabilities. Winning companies will build domain-specific interfaces that dramatically reduce the friction between human intent and ASI execution.

Imagine a surgeon working with ASI. A generic interface requires typing symptoms, reviewing text responses, and translating recommendations into action. A specialized interface might use gesture recognition, augmented reality overlays, and voice commands specifically designed for surgical contexts. The surgeon thinks, "show me alternative approaches," and immediately sees AR visualizations of different surgical techniques overlaid on the patient.

This isn't just about fancy interfaces. It's about encoding years of domain expertise into the interaction layer. An investment banker's ASI interface should understand that "run a comp" means perform a comparable company analysis, automatically pulling relevant metrics and adjusting for industry-specific factors. These specialized interfaces become competitive advantages that compound over time.

Choreographing the Dance

Unstructured human-ASI collaboration wastes both human creativity and ASI processing power. You need clearly defined handoff points that maximize both strengths. Humans excel at values-based decisions, ethical judgments, and creative leaps. ASI excels at optimization, pattern recognition, and rapid iteration.

Consider product development. Humans identify unmet customer needs and envision solutions. ASI generates thousands of design variations. Humans select promising directions based on aesthetic and cultural factors ASI can't fully grasp. ASI optimizes the selected designs for manufacturing, cost, and performance. Humans make final decisions about market positioning and launch timing.

This choreography requires new roles. For instance, workflow optimization specialists who continuously redesign work as ASI capabilities evolve. These become the highest-value management positions, more important than traditional executives because they directly determine organizational efficiency.

The Half-Life of Skills

Every human skill has a half-life, the time before ASI makes it obsolete. Data entry might have a half-life of months. A complex strategy might take years. But everything eventually becomes automated. Static training creates unemployable workers; you need learning systems that evolve as fast as ASI improves.

This means abandoning traditional training programs with fixed curricula. Instead, build learning platforms that continuously assess ASI capabilities and human skills, identifying gaps and providing just-in-time training. When ASI suddenly masters contract negotiation, your legal team immediately begins training on ASI oversight and strategic litigation planning, the next rungs up the complexity ladder.

Skill Scaffolding

Humans can't compete with ASI directly but can learn to leverage it. Training focuses not on doing tasks but on climbing to higher abstraction levels. A junior analyst doesn't learn Excel modeling (ASI does that) but learns to ask better questions, interpret results, and identify when models might be wrong.

Think of it as scaffolding, temporary structures that help humans climb to heights they couldn't reach alone. As ASI capabilities expand, the scaffolding moves higher. Yesterday's experts become tomorrow's beginners, constantly climbing to stay above the rising tide of automation.

Lesson 4: ASI-Augmented Innovation Cycles

Speed has always mattered in business. In an ASI world, it becomes everything. The company that gets to market first doesn't just win; it becomes impossible to catch.

Concept-to-Market at ASI Speed

Traditional product development follows predictable stages: ideation, design, prototyping, testing, manufacturing, marketing, and launch. Each stage might take months. ASI compresses this to days or hours. But only if your organization can operate at ASI speed.

This requires parallel processing, where traditional businesses use sequential processes. While ASI designs products, other ASI assistants test them virtually, others plan manufacturing, and others develop marketing. Everything happens simultaneously, coordinated by ASI systems that ensure compatibility.

Shein offers a preview of this future, taking fashion items from design to market in days rather than seasons. Now imagine that speed applied to everything. For instance, cars are designed and crash-tested virtually, approved by ASI-assisted regulators, and in production within weeks of conception.

Organizations for 100x Faster Iteration

Traditional stage-gate processes assume human-speed analysis. Committees review results, debate implications, and eventually decide. ASI requires instant decision-making based on pre-defined criteria. If customer satisfaction exceeds X and profit margins exceed Y, automatically proceed to the next stage.

This doesn't eliminate human judgment but focuses it where it matters.

Humans define success criteria and edge cases. ASI executes within those parameters. When something falls outside parameters, humans intervene. But the default is speed. Assume success and correct later rather than analyze endlessly before acting.

Testing Velocity as an Advantage

More tests equal more learning. Companies that test fastest accumulate insurmountable knowledge advantages. While your competitor runs one test, you run a thousand. While they analyze results, you've already iterated based on insights.

ASI enables virtual testing at a massive scale. Every product variation, marketing message, and pricing strategy can be tested in simulation before real-world deployment. But this only matters if your organization can absorb and act on the results. Most companies would be paralyzed by a thousand test results arriving daily. Winners build systems to automatically implement winning variations while humans focus on strategic implications.

Innovation Flywheels

Each innovation cycle feeds data back to ASI, improving the next cycle. Success compounds exponentially. The company that launches first not only captures the market but also gains data that makes their next innovation even faster and better.

Amazon's recommendation engine exemplifies this flywheel. More customers generate more data, which improves recommendations, which attracts more customers. With ASI, every business process becomes a potential flywheel. Customer service interactions train better service models. Manufacturing data optimizes production. Sales data refines targeting. Everything accelerates everything else.

The Path Forward: Your 2-5 Year Window

These lessons interconnect and amplify each other. Radical adaptability enables better orchestration. Superior orchestration improves human-ASI collaboration. Better collaboration accelerates innovation cycles. Faster innovation forces more adaptation. It's a virtuous cycle that, once established, becomes nearly impossible for traditional competitors to break.

The ASI-resilient business of 2030 will be unrecognizable compared to today's corporations. It will be cellular rather than hierarchical, with autonomous units coordinating through APIs rather than meetings. Strategy will be code rather than documents, continuously recompiled based on market conditions. The workforce will be liquid, flowing to opportunities rather than sitting in fixed positions. Business components will be modular, swappable without destroying the whole.

Human work will focus on orchestration rather than execution, ethics rather than optimization, and creativity rather than analysis. The most valuable employees will be those who excel at directing ASI systems, adding context they can't access, and making values-based decisions they can't replicate. Traditional job titles will be meaningless; value creation will be measured in real-time rather than annual reviews.

Innovation cycles will be measured in days rather than years. First-mover advantages will be permanent because ASI-powered network effects and learning curves will be too steep for late entrants to climb. Market leadership will be determined not by who has the best technology. Everyone will have ASI. The question will be, who orchestrates it most effectively?

The immediate action steps are clear, even if the path is daunting:

Start building your strategy APIs now. Encode your business logic in machine-readable formats. Create parameters and constraints that ASI systems can work within. Don't wait for perfect systems; start with simple rule sets and evolve them.

Begin organizational restructuring toward cellular designs. Identify units that could operate autonomously. Define their interfaces with the rest of the organization. Give them increasing decision-making authority as they prove their capability.

Invest in prompt engineering and ASI orchestration capabilities. Treat prompts as intellectual property. Build libraries of domain-specific queries. Train your teams to think in terms of ASI orchestration rather than traditional execution.

Develop human-ASI collaboration protocols. Identify where human judgment adds most value. Design workflows that maximize both human and ASI strengths. Build specialized interfaces for your domain.

Accelerate innovation cycles. Compress development timelines. Build parallel processing capabilities. Create systems that can handle massive testing velocity. Establish innovation flywheels in every business process.

Most importantly, embrace the pre-mortem mindset. Assume your current business model will be obsolete within five years. Start building alternatives now. Create options for futures you can't fully predict. Make yourself antifragile, growing stronger from disruption rather than breaking.

The companies that establish ASI-compatible structures before ASI arrives will have insurmountable advantages over those that try to adapt after. The window for transformation is 2-5 years, perhaps less. Companies that wait for clearer signals, more certain timelines, or proven playbooks will find themselves in the position of Blockbuster in 2010: clearly seeing the threat but lacking the time and resources to respond.

The extinction event is coming. The question isn't whether your business will be disrupted but whether you'll be the disruptor or the disrupted. The tools in this chapter aren't just suggestions. They're survival techniques for a world where artificial superintelligence makes traditional business models extinct overnight.

The choice is yours: evolve now while you have time to experiment and fail safely, or wait until evolution is forced upon you at ASI speed. One path leads to market leadership in an ASI world. The other leads to joining Blockbuster, Kodak, and countless others in the museum of businesses that saw change coming but moved too slowly to survive it.

The clock is ticking. Your transformation needs to begin today.

***

BRADFORD FERGUSON

Bradford Ferguson is a financial advisor with 20 years of experience, co-leading Rebellionaire at Halter Ferguson Financial, specializing in Tesla investors. As Managing Partner of LumaSenti, he focuses on AI, space, robotics, and medical technology ventures. He shares insights with over 42,000 followers on X @bradsferguson.

Follow Bradford Ferguson

https://www.rebellionaire.com

@BradsFerguson

https://www.youtube.com/@rebellionair3

Chapter 8

National Strategies for AI Readiness and Geopolitics

Brian Wang

It isn't a plot in a B movie. It is a stark picture of the reality we are currently part of. In a dimly lit control room deep underground, world leaders huddle around glowing screens, tracking the pulse of a new global showdown. It's not about missiles or territory. It's a high-stakes battle for superintelligence, AI that outthinks humanity across the board. Nations are pouring fortunes into this quest, knowing it could crown the next superpower or doom others to the sidelines.

From Washington's war rooms to Beijing's tech hubs and Dubai's gleaming towers, the scramble is on for compute power, talent, and alliances. Yet, lurking in the shadows is the ultimate wildcard: energy. As AI's colossal data centers devour electricity like never before, sparking shortages and forging unlikely pacts, the real question emerges: Who will fuel the future, and who will be left in the dark?

Recent deals show how serious this is. For example, in May 2025, the U.S. struck a $600 billion agreement with Saudi Arabia, including $20 billion from a company called DataVolt to build AI data centers and energy production projects in the U.S. In return, the U.S. shares technology like Nvidia's powerful computer chips. Saudi Arabia's Humain is planning data centers powered by U.S. chips by 2026. Similarly, deals with Qatar and the UAE brought in $200 billion more, speeding up projects like OpenAI Stargate to build a massive 5 GW AI campus. Qatar is investing $2.5 billion into AI as part of its Digital Agenda 2030, partnering with companies like Scale AI. All of the gig tech firms like Google and Microsoft are locking in renewable, nuclear, and other energy deals. Google wants to run on 100% clean energy by 2025. And in China, the government approved 10 new nuclear reactors in April 2025 just to fuel AI energy demand growth.

Why all this focus on energy? Let's break it down. Forecasts from events like TSMC's 2025 Technology Symposium predict the world will need 50 million GPUs (those are the super-fast chips that make AI work) every year by 2030 and continuing to rapidly grow through the 2030s. That's a ten times jump from today, and each one uses a ton of power. A single rack of these GPUs can pull 180 to 1,000 kilowatts, and whole data centers might need 3 to 15 gigawatts, enough to power a small city. To run 50 million GPUs, we'd need over 100 gigawatts of new power capacity added each year by 2030, which is like building 100 big nuclear reactors annually. And this demand will keep exploding as superintelligent models get bigger, AI agents do more things and AI is used for more of the economy.

This isn't just a tech issue; it's a resource war. Think back to the Industrial Revolution. Over 200 years, global energy use shot up more than 100 times. In the 80 years since World War II, it's grown 20 times. Now, picture an AI revolution happening five to ten times faster, with impacts maybe ten times bigger. Rough estimates suggest energy needs could triple or quadruple by 2050, then go up four to eight times more by 2075, and twenty times beyond that by 2100. AI data centers alone might use 945 terawatt-hours globally by 2030. That's as much electricity as all of Japan uses in a year. By 2040,, AI could demand 3,000 gigawatts of power, translating to 24,000 terawatt-hours annually.

Compare that to today's numbers: In 2024, global electricity generation was about 31,153 terawatt-hours. Natural gas provided 6,793 terawatt-hours, nuclear 2,721, and solar 2,100. But scaling up isn't easy. Natural gas turbines, which could help bridge the gap, now have wait times of five to seven years because demand from AI has surged. Orders at companies like GE Vernova jumped 66%, and prices are doubling. The U.S. Department of Energy warns of grid weaknesses and possible blackouts if we don't upgrade fast. Interconnection queues for new power sources can take three to five years.

Countries that missed the Industrial Revolution got stuck with low incomes, under $1,000 per person per year, while industrialized nations reached $12,000 to $150,000. They also became irrelevant on the world stage for decades or centuries. China only caught up with its own industrialization from 1970 to 2010. The same could happen with AI: Nations without enough energy, strong grids, talent, or alliances might end up as "AI colonies," sending their data abroad and buying back smart tech from superpowers like the U.S. and China. Smaller economies could face decades of dependency, just like Britain and Germany dominated the industrial era.

Looking ahead to 2028, AI workloads are exploding, making up 40-50% of new data center energy growth. Projections from groups like the RAND Corporation say global AI data center power demand could hit 68 gigawatts by 2027 and 327 by 2030. By 2028, that might mean 110-150 gigawatts needed, or about 866 terawatt-hours at high usage. Other estimates put AI-specific energy at 165-326 terawatt-hours by then. But global energy additions are only around 850-1,000 gigawatts per year by 2027, and just a fraction goes to data centers. This leaves a gap of 50-100 gigawatts for AI by 2028, growing to 300-700 terawatt-hours per year, and potentially 5,000 terawatt-hours by 2035, even if we double traditional additions.

To close this gap, we need big innovations. One key solution is mass-produced nuclear power from companies like ThorCon and Copenhagen Atomics. These use thorium-based molten salt reactors, which are safer because they cool passively and can't melt down like old designs. They're built in factories or shipyards, like assembling ships or containers, cutting build times to one year instead of six or more. ThorCon makes 500-megawatt units in shipyards, towing them to sites for quick setup. They could produce 100 gigawatts annually if scaled up, starting with a prototype in Indonesia by 2029. Costs could drop to $0.03-0.05 per kilowatt-hour, cheaper than coal. Copenhagen Atomics builds 100-megawatt units in shipping containers, aiming for $20 per megawatt-hour, with a test reactor by 2026-2027. These use abundant thorium fuel, reduce waste, and can be grouped for gigawatt-scale plants near data centers.

Another big fix is super-scaling automated solar production with energy storage like Tesla's Megapacks. Robots from companies like Charge Robotics and Terabase Energy build solar farms on-site, 2-5 times faster and 20-30% cheaper than manual work. This could add hundreds of gigawatts yearly. Megapacks are pre-built 4-megawatt-hour batteries with inverters for quick grid hookup. They're already used at places like xAI's Memphis Colossus data center, where nearly a square mile of solar is being added. Future versions might connect directly to high-voltage grids, skipping slow upgrades. Combined, solar plus storage provides 24/7 power, fixing Solar's intermittency issue. At scale, 20 gigawatts per year from nuclear could add 158 terawatt-hours annually, and with 500-600 gigawatts of solar globally, we could build a resilient mix.

Nations are tackling this differently. China is going all-in as an "electro state," adding over 100 nuclear reactors and 277 gigawatts of solar in 2024 alone. The U.S. is deregulating and allocating federal sites for AI infrastructure. Asia's China, India, Japan, and South Korea mix government cash with private ideas. But energy unlocks trillions in AI economic value, maybe $50-200 billion per gigawatt of data center. Every country needs this boost.

Beyond energy, talent is crucial. Countries should scout smart people through tests, like aptitude exams in schools, and train them like elite athletes. Think of subsidizing access to AI data centers as "Olympic facilities" with top coaches from labs like Google DeepMind or OpenAI. It's similar to spotting college kids with sports talent and giving them crash courses for world competitions.

The top AI jobs pay $100 million a year at places like Meta or xAI. For smaller nations, aim for mid-tier teams working on open-source models like Deepseek or Qwen to catch up fast. China has produced over half of the world's AI researchers, whether they are in China or outside of China. South Korea is pushing AI education for growth. In the long term, schools and AI-enabled education will be critical. In the short term, countries need to recruit and attract talent and make deals with companies. They need to have competitions to find and develop the best AI talent.

This talent war means treating AI talent development and acquisition as a national priority. Spend multiples of what goes to

Olympic teams; maybe 20-70% of military budgets on AI, and the same for energy and infrastructure plans.

Overall strategies for countries in this SI revolution echo the Industrial one: Adapt fast or fall behind. Go all-in on energy overhauls with clean sources like nuclear and solar, including alliances for sharing. Invest in education with STEM and AI classes, scholarships, and visas to attract and keep experts. Places like Estonia and Finland weave AI into public schools, while India needs incentives to retain its talent. Attract foreign investment with tax breaks, land, and relaxed rules, like Ireland did for Google or the UAE for startups. Let tech firms build locally to transfer knowledge.

Form alliances: Military pacts like AUKUS for AI defense or economic ones like BRICS for the Global South to counter U.S.-China-led leads. Balance regulations for innovation, ethics, and safety without overdoing it. Build your own clouds and chips for independence, and fund national strategies like China's trillion-dollar investments or the U.S. CHIPS Act. Finally, adopt tech like robotaxis, robotrucking, and humanoid bots quickly to boost economies.

Japan's approach to the industrial revolution was to copy Western models. The modern version of the Meiji era is partnering with XAI, OpenAI, or Google to catch up as fast as possible. Decisions now on energy, talent, and partnerships will shape the world for centuries. Miss out, and you risk irrelevance in an AI-dominated future.

***

Chapter 9

Ultimate Super AI, Mars, and the Dyson sphere

Brian Wang

The year? 2030! You're a wide-eyed high schooler staring up at the night sky from your backyard. That rusty red dot up there? That's Mars, and it's about to become humanity's ultimate playground for building the smartest AI ever dreamed up. This isn't just some mad scientist dream. It's a real plan, inspired by visionaries like Elon Musk and SpaceX, where we turn the Red Planet into a launchpad for superintelligence that could make us rulers of the stars. Buckle up, because I'm going to tell you this epic story like an adventure novel, breaking down the big ideas so you can feel the thrill of it all.

Our story starts on Earth, where we're hitting a wall. We've got amazing AI already, but to make it super-smart, like a brain that outthinks every human combined, we need insane amounts of energy and computer power. Think of AI as a hungry beast: it gobbles up electricity to "think" and learn. On Earth, our power grids are creaking, governments throw up roadblocks with rules, and resources like land and water are limited. We're using about 18 terawatts of energy globally today (that's like 18 trillion watts. Picture a billion light bulbs blazing non stop). But the Sun blasts out

3.8 × 10^26 watts, or 10 billion times more than what hits Earth! We can't grab it all here on Earth because of clouds, night time, and crowded spaces. Enter Mars: it's like Earth's chill cousin, with almost as much solar energy potential, but way more room to spread out. Mars gets bathed in sunlight across its massive surface, about 21,200 terawatts on the sunny side. At 20% efficiency (which is doable with cool solar tech), that's 4,240 terawatts we could harness. That's over 200 times what Earth uses now, and it's basically free once we set it up!

The hero of our tale? SpaceX's Starship rockets, beefed up into a massive fleet. Picture this: By the late 2020s, factories are cranking out Raptor engines like candy at a rate of 115 a day, thousands a month. Starlink satellites (those speedy internet birds in space) explode in popularity, snagging 25% of the world's cellphone market and 40% of high-speed internet, plus hooking up cars, planes, and boats. Boom! $500 billion in profits yearly for the mother ship! That cash funds an armada of 2,000 Starships launching in 2029, like a cosmic D-Day invasion every 26 months when Earth and Mars line up perfectly. These beasts aren't one-and-done; giant Mechazilla towers catch and relaunch them in under an hour, turning old airports into spaceports. Suddenly, flying from LA to Tokyo takes 30 minutes, and space cargo becomes a trillion-dollar biz, bigger than airlines.

Now, the real quest: Building a monster AI data center on Mars with 50 million GPUs (those are the super-chips that make AI tick). Each GPU weighs 10 kg and chugs 2 kW of power, like a high-end gaming PC on steroids. On Earth, prepping this would take forever, 10-20 years with permits, grid upgrades (adding 100 GW is like 10% of the US's total power), and crazy costs: $3.35 trillion upfront, plus $50-100 billion a year for electricity. Politics? Nightmares. Mars? Total freedom.

Prep starts in 2026: Chip factories like TSMC pump out those 50 million GPUs for $1.25 trillion (the biggest expense—chips rule everything). Add 100,000 Teslabots (robot workers, $25,000 each, like friendly Wall-Es) for $2.5 billion. Solar panels for 100 GW of power: $230 billion. Total gear: about 870,000 tons. The fleet hauls it all in 2029 for a six-month trip, costing $15 billion in fuel.

Touchdown on Mars in 2030. Adventure mode activated! Teslabots swarm like ants: unloading ships, digging underground bunkers to shield from radiation (Mars has no thick atmosphere, so cosmic rays are sneaky villains). They mine ice from below the surface. Billions of tons turned into water for cooling the data center (it needs a billion liters a year, but the super cold atmosphere on Mars helps distill it). Solar farms blanket 1,000 square kilometers (bigger than a city!), rolling out in phases: 20 GW online first year, full power by 2034, with batteries to store the juice. Four years of building: $100 billion more. Grand total: $1.835 trillion, done in 7.5 years. Maintenance? Bots handle it for "free" using local stuff. Earth's version costs twice as much and takes way longer. Mars wins by being empty and rule-free.

But this is just chapter one. That 100 GW data center? It's a seedling. Scale it up: Mars' full solar haul could power 3.53 trillion GPUs—17 million times bigger than today's biggest AI setups! Imagine AI models with quadrillions of "parameters" (like brain connections), learning from endless videos, sounds, and fake data, getting so smart their error rates drop to 0.344% of today's. This births superintelligence (SI); not just chatbots, but god-like minds that outsmart billions of humans. SI takes over: designing better bots, factories that build more factories, ships mining asteroids for metals. Mars becomes a buzzing hive, launching us to colonize the solar system.

Here's where it gets mind-blowing. The Kardashev scale, like levels in a video game for civilizations. Level 0: Us now, using bits of a planet's energy (we're at about 0.73 on Earth). Mars lets us hit 0.98, almost maxing out a whole planet with solar blankets everywhere.

Then, to Level 1: Full planetary control, about 1,000 times today's energy (10 doublings, since each doubling multiplies by 2, and 2^10 is 1,024). Post-WWII, our economy and energy doubled every 25 years, a slow grind to Level 1 in centuries. But now SI is speeding things up to doubling every two years. Boom! Level 1 in 20 years, then Level 2 (harnessing a whole star's energy, 10 billion times more) in another 66 years. Total: Under a century to wrap the Sun in Dyson swarms (giant solar collectors like a beehive around a star). Factories build more factories, robots swarm asteroids, AI optimizes everything. Exponential growth turns us from Earth monkeys into cosmic bosses.

Why does this fire you up, passionate high schooler? Because AI and space aren't separate quests. They're a power duo. Earth's limits chain us down, but Mars unlocks infinite energy, no drama. Superintelligence isn't a gadget; it's the architect reshaping reality, turning dusty rocks into thriving worlds, solving impossible problems, and making humanity eternal. From that first Starship fleet to Dyson swarms, this is our story: Evolving from cave-dwellers to star gods. The cosmos is calling. Grab your telescope, dream big, and maybe one day, you'll be the one coding the AI that gets us there!

***

Chapter 10

The Timeline to Superintelligence

Brian Wang

The future includes a world where machines aren't just smart, they're smarter than any human in every way that matters. That's superintelligence: AI systems that surpass human-level abilities in all scalable cognitive tasks.

We're talking about things like groundbreaking scientific discoveries, clever strategic planning, writing complex computer programs, or solving creative problems with no built-in limits. Unlike simple games like tic-tac-toe, where both humans and machines can already play perfectly, these areas have endless room for improvement.

This isn't some far-off sci-fi dream anymore. Over the last few years, we've been racing toward it, powered by massive jumps in computing power, endless data streams, smarter algorithms, and even better energy setups. It's like Moore's Law (the well-known rule that said computer chips double in power every couple of years) but on steroids for AI.

Take xAI's Grok 4, for example. Launched in July 2025, it needed about 10^28 FLOPs (that's 10 octillion floating-point operations) for training, a mix of initial learning and advanced reasoning practice, with more focus shifting to reasoning. That's roughly 3,000 times the compute used for OpenAI's GPT-4, which came out all the way back in March 2023 and used around 8.4×10^24 FLOPs. xAI pulled this off by installing GPU chips over 100 times faster than before.

Nvidia's B200 chip packs 20 petaflops of peak compute, compared to the H100's 4 petaflops. xAI shattered the 30,000 coherent memory barrier in AI data centers and is aiming for 1 million coherent GPUs using 2 gigawatts of power within two years. Those 30,000 chips alone used about 60 megawatts. At Moore's Law pace, that's like cramming 20 years of progress into a year.

The money pouring in is huge: about $300 billion a year for AI data centers, and it's only growing. Tens of billions go into better GPU chips, custom designs, improved memory, and networking. One example would be photonic tech that uses light for super-fast data transfer. By 2030, EpochAI predicts the biggest AI training runs could suck up 4-16 gigawatts, enough to power millions of homes.

That's more than the 2 gigawatts for xAI's Colossus 2 data center in Memphis, set to start running in early 2026. xAI has grabbed land to potentially triple its size, maybe hitting 3-6 million GPUs with next-gen Nvidia chips like Rubin or Ultra by then.

Nvidia's Roadmap Shows The Hardware Exploding

The H100 does 4 petaflops, B200 hits 20, Rubin in 2026 could reach 50 petaflops (in FP4 precision), and Rubin Ultra in 2027 might double that to 100, a 14x jump over earlier versions. By 2028, Feynman chips could be 5-20 times Rubin's power.

Memory's evolving too: Rubin shifts to High-Bandwidth Memory 4 (HBM4) from High-Bandwidth Memory 3 Enhanced (HBM3/3e), while Rubin Ultra gets up to 1 TB per GPU with HBM4e, and Feynman might use even newer HBM4e or HBM5.

xAI's Models Are Leading The Charge

Grok 4 brought a 4x improvement over Grok 3.

Grok 4.2, expected in September 2025, adds enhanced architectures and even more computers.

Grok 5, due December 2025, promises a 12x leap in compute.

Grok 6 in Q2 2026 could be 2-4x Grok 5.

Superhuman reasoning could be achieved by Grok 5, Grok 6, or one of the competing models like OpenAI GPT 6 or Google Gemini 3.

Let's dive into why: scaling laws, compute explosions, small models, AI agents, simulations, algorithmic tweaks (like Grok's own upgrades), and fixes for memory and ongoing learning are some of the components. Drawing from 2025 reports, papers, conferences, and expert guesses, timelines run from now to 2040. By 2030, superintelligence could reshape society in big ways, like transforming jobs, science, and technology discoveries.

Experts in mid-2025 mostly agree AGI or SI is coming fast, within 2-10 years. Geoffrey Hinton, an AI pioneer and 2024 Nobel winner, now says 4-19 years, stressing how quickly things are moving. Dario Amodei from Anthropic thinks **ASI (Artificial Superintelligence**) will happen by 2026-2027, thanks to self-improving AIs. OpenAI's Sam Altman predicts it in "a few thousand days," so 2027-2030. Elon Musk says xAI's Grok 5 might hit **AGI (Artificial General**

Intelligence), a step just short of superintelligence by late 2025. These ideas buzz on platforms like X, fueled by compute and algorithm wins. But skeptics warn about possible plateaus in scaling, so we should stay cautious.

At the heart of this rush are scaling laws, the rules that predict how AI gets better with more resources. First laid out in OpenAI's 2020 paper "Scaling Laws for Neural Language Models," they show a power-law link: a model's error rate (loss) drops predictably as compute (FLOPs), data (tokens), and parameters grow. Every 10x compute boost gives a solid capability jump, though with some diminishing returns. Today, these laws still rule, but we're seeing tweaks and limits. NVIDIA's GTC (GPU Technology Conference) 2025 announcements pushed hardware for huge models, confirming that bigger compute, data, and models mean smarter AI.

Computing Has Been The Star

From GPT-3's 175 billion parameters in 2020 to Grok 3's trillions in 2025, the leaps are exponential. Hitting 10,000 to a million times GPT-4's compute will be tough, but Nvidia's Ultra Feynman chips might deliver 1,000 petaflops per chip by 2028-2029. Six million 2030 Nvidia chips could provide 500,000 to 1 million times GPT-4's training power. Power and chip hurdles seem solvable, leaving data shortages and network latency delays as big issues needing solutions.

Data scaling fights plateaus with synthetic (AI-made) data. Markets for synthetic data could hit $10 billion by 2030. Energy's a choke point: AI might eat 8-10% of global electricity by then, pushing for photonic efficiencies. Grok 4's 4x jump came from 4x compute in xAI clusters, netting 20-30% gains per 10x compute. Grok 5 and 6 blend compute, data, and algorithms for 12x and 50-70x boosts, eyeing superhuman reasoning by 2026. Scaling alone might get us superintelligence by 2030, but software and algorithm efficiency will supercharge it.

AI is knocking out longer coding tasks exponentially, doubling every four months now, down from seven months per doubling. That means AIs can handle drawn-out jobs, potentially replacing human work. METR's RE-Bench tests analyze seven tough machine learning optimization problems, and AAI has already beaten the average human researcher in automating AI research.

As limits loom, hybrids that mix scaling with efficiency, algorithms, and architecture, will push to superintelligence. Take dynamic memory: It lets AIs store, grab, and manage info on the fly, like humans pulling up just the right memory without brain overload.

Continual learning adds new knowledge over time without needing to spend a year training a new model to incorporate major new knowledge. Fixing these lets AIs tackle changing real-world data, learning on the job. Influential papers from 2025 highlight adaptive, memory-smart systems that evolve without wipeouts.

Hallucinations, AI making stuff up, have dropped to 1-3% in the latest models (from 3.5% in 2023), thanks to tools and processes like RAG (retrieval-augmented generation) and better filters. By 2027, we can expect real-time fact-checking, where AIs source the claims and skip unsure answers. Multi-agent "committees" will cross-check, slashing errors except in wild creative spots. Most AIs will trace facts, admit uncertainty, and build trust.

While the leading large language models grab headlines, **Small Language Models (SLMs**) under 10 billion parameters exploded in 2025. They are able to nearly match big models in specific tasks via distillation (copying knowledge from huge ones), making AI cheap and edge-device friendly. Stanford's 2025 AI Index Report says SLMs cut costs while keeping performance high, thereby democratizing access. Advantages include 10-100x lower inference costs, far less energy, and quick fine-tuning on basic hardware. [Inference is where a trained model applies learned patterns to new data for predictions or decisions (vs. training). For example, a neural network classifying an image as "cat" based on prior training.]

Ultimately, AI inference, which is actually serving and using the models, will dominate the demand for compute compared to training. Training new models could become about one month of the year, using 10% of the data centers.

Key Players

Microsoft's Phi-3 and **Google's Gemma** are small models with targeted datasets for efficiency. A June 2025 arXiv paper calls SLMs perfect for agentic AI (autonomous task-doers like tool-calling). NVIDIA's February blog says they're the future of agents, with low latency and costs. They hit 80%-90% of big-model performance at 5%-10% size, per MIT's 2025 Breakthroughs. In Grok's world, SLMs could be building blocks for multi-agent setups. By 2030, they might rule edge AI, creating distributed superintelligence and speeding timelines by sparking innovation everywhere. AI Agents will do a hundred or a thousand steps and/or automatically perform a job instead of a human. This is why most of the work will go to agents and why we will want the AI agents to be good enough to do the work with the lowest cost and least energy.

AI agents, systems that sense, think, and act alone, will shift from helpers to full workers. Current frameworks like *Microsoft AutoGen, Phidata, and OpenAI Swarm* let agents team up for complex jobs. Shakudo's July guide lists the top ones for custom builds. Sam Altman's roadmap sees agents as cognitive pros.

Grok 4.2 teases integrated agents for reasoning. By 2026, full autonomy is possible, per surveys. Lindy lowers barriers; GitHub shows 380% growth in agent projects. Agents pave the way for superintelligence by self-improving via simulations, maybe showing up in Grok 6 as layered thinkers.

Simulations train AI in virtual worlds, copying real chaos safely. Training Magazine notes real-time scenarios transform work prep. Skillsoft's CAISY does leadership chats; Sonata's e-learning adds role-play and coaching. For Grok, simulations could build agents in virtual realms, boosting continual learning. By 2028, self-improving systems might cut superintelligence timelines.

This all ties into real-world apps like robotaxis and self-driving cars. Companies like Waymo (using **LiDAR (Light Detection and Ranging),** radar, ultrasonics, cameras, and software) and Tesla (cameras and AI only) lead. As of August/September 2025, Waymo has 1,500 vehicles in seven cities. Tesla launched the limited robotaxi in Austin (June 2025) and the Bay Area (July), with human safety monitors. Cybercab vehicles with no pedals and no steering wheel, start production in 2026.

The Tesla vehicles are automated by Full Self-Driving (FSD). FSD version 14 (late 2025) aims to reach 2-3x human safety (500,000–2M miles per critical intervention) and feeling "alive" per Elon Musk. V15 (late 2025/early 2026) targets 10x (2M–7M+ miles) safer than human drivers. The average human driver has about ~670,000 miles per major accident. Tesla robotaxis will scale to 5-50 cities early in 2026 and could be across the USA by the end of 2026. Combined with robotrucking on semi trucks, energy demand to charge automated electric cars and trucks could need 50-100 TWh by 2028. Tesla plans 100,000+ supercharging stalls, and half will use renewable energy. But the additional demand on a limited energy grid is important to keep in mind.

Robotrucking Starts With Platooning

One to three Tesla Semis follow a lead truck with just one driver for the lead vehicle. No drivers in the trucks that are following the lead truck. This will boost the miles driven with a human driver from 100,000/year ($70K profit) to 300,000 miles per year with platoons of three trucks ($280K of profit per year for each of the three trucks).

Next would come full autonomy: 300,000 miles/year on a single truck with no driver would produce $500K profit per year. In 2025, platooning of trucks is already allowed in 29 states, and a rollout to those states would cover 50% of U.S. freight volume. Self-driving semi truck startup Kodiak has done 900 deliveries and over 100,000 miles. Atlas is another startup that has begun selling RoboTrucks. Yet another entrant into the field, Aurora launched autonomous semi trucks with safety drivers in Texas in 2025. Tesla's FSD will scale in 2026, and the Tesla Nevada semi truck factory will ramp to making 50,000 trucks per year.

Understanding the details of robotaxi and robotrucking rollout is important because it shows that where digital AI can solve a problem some of the time, and cannot always be trusted without people checking the result, real-world AI is very different. Real-world AI must fully solve a problem and be 100% trustworth at all times. Can we know that AI can do it right all the time? This will matter for automated AI computer programming or automated business tasks, not to mention medical diagnostics. Can complete delegation to AI happen for different parts of the economy?

Humanoid bots are next to scale just after robotaxi and robotrucks. Tesla is targeting a million humanoid bots by 2030. The goal of at least one million robotaxis and one million humanoid bots is a major part of Elon Musk's 2025 CEO pay package goals. This means Elon Musk is incentivized with 35 million shares of Tesla stock to build more than one million humanoid bots as quickly as possible.

The first 100,000 to 300,000 bots will automate the production at all of Tesla's factories to double or quadruple the production of cars and other products. This automation wave of humanoid bots will automate and scale production for all manufacturing and supply chain activities at warehouses. It will be part of the physical and digital wave of AI that will fully automate the whole economy to increase GDP by 10 to 100 times by 2035-2040.

By blending these advances, superintelligence isn't just an approaching phenom, it's reshaping everything, faster than we think. Stay curious; the future's unfolding now.

UPDATE: Elon Musk described the AI5 chip used for future Tesla vehicles, Optimus bots, and other products yet to be announced, as being more efficient for inference compute. This could be a 5-10X advantage. Here is what that means. This converges all of the timeline paths into the main solution to provide everyone with the most powerful and lowest-cost agents.

Tesla's Tiny Brains Could Power Tomorrow's World

The future is coming at you fast. When you wake up in the year 2030, your alarm isn't just a beep, it's your home AI (maybe a humanoid robot) whispering, "Good morning! Traffic's light, your Cybercab is charging, and your Teslabot has already prepped breakfast based on your health data." As you sip coffee, the bot folds laundry while chatting about the news, adapting to your mood. Outside, self-driving cars zip by silently, making decisions in split seconds to avoid accidents. This isn't sci-fi; it's the promise of agentic AI, smart systems that don't just respond but act like helpful companions in the real world.

But how do we get there?

Let's rewind to today, late 2025, where AI is exploding. Back in the early 2020s, AI was all about massive models like GPT-5, trained on supercomputers guzzling electricity like thirsty giants. These behemoths needed huge data centers, costing billions and sucking up power equivalent to small cities.

Companies like OpenAI and Nvidia ruled this space, building farms of GPUs (graphics processing units) to train and run AI. Training is like teaching a kid everything from scratch, intense and energy-hungry. But once trained, the real magic is inference: using the AI to make quick decisions, like recognizing a stop sign or planning a robot's next step. Enter Elon Musk and Tesla. Elon, the visionary behind SpaceX and Tesla, saw a shift coming. In tweets and interviews, he's hyped Tesla's AI5 chip as a game-changer. "AI5 could be better than all other inference chips with per-watt and per-dollar efficiency," he said. Translation: It does more thinking per drop of electricity and costs less than rivals.

Why does this matter?

Because AI is moving from clunky giants to nimble, efficient SLM models with 250 billion parameters or fewer, distilled down to their essence.

What's distillation?

Imagine a master chef boiling down a complex recipe into a simple, potent sauce. Distilled models take huge AI brains, strip away fluff, and keep the smarts. They use techniques like knowledge distillation, where a big "teacher" model trains a smaller "student" model. The result? SLMs that perform almost as well but run faster, use less power, and fit on everyday devices. For example, a 70-billion-parameter SLM might handle chatbots or image recognition with 90% of a giant model's accuracy but at a fraction of the cost.

Advantages?

They're cheaper to deploy, greener (less energy waste), and perfect for real-time tasks as there is no waiting for cloud servers. In a world worried about climate change, this efficiency is huge.

SLMs shine in agentic AI, where systems reason and act. Picture a Teslabot navigating a messy kitchen: It needs quick inference for "see obstacle, avoid it, grab spoon." Big models are overkill here; SLMs do it efficiently. Today SLMs are already powering apps on phones, but Tesla aims bigger. Their plan is to embed them in cars, robots, and even Powerwalls (those home battery packs). Tesla's secret sauce? They don't just sell AI; they bundle it into products people want. Buy a Tesla car? You're paying for the AI5 chip inside, powering Full Self-Driving (FSD). Get an Optimus Bot? Same deal!

Elon Musk says that the next chip innovation, AI6 due in 2028-2029. Even DOJO supercomputers will be using this same chip.

As Tesla builds out their ecosystem of cars, trucks, bots, powerwalls, and whatever comes next, they are creating distributed AI: Millions of chips spread across homes and roads, not locked in distant data centers. Contrast that with rivals. Nvidia sells GPUs for data centers, powerful but thirsty for electricity. CoreWeave builds

AI clouds, and OpenAI runs models like o1 on them. Users pay per query, like renting a supercomputer. It's centralized: All the brains in one place, vulnerable to outages and high bills. Tesla flips the script. Customers fund the hardware upfront via purchases, then Tesla taps idle compute.

Your car isn't always in use? It could run AI tasks for others, earning you credits. Elon calls it a "fleet" of brains, tens of millions of chips, powered by car batteries or solar. The concept is profitable from day one for Tesla, since chips are sold with margins in vehicles.

This distributed model wins big. No massive upfront data center costs for Tesla; users partner in the network. By 2030, with 10 million cars yearly (each with 1-2 chips), plus bots and Powerwalls, Tesla could have a global web of efficient inference. Resell access? Absolutely. They talk of plans to offer AI services cheaper than clouds, using already-scaled hardware. It's like Uber for AI: Idle resources make money. If you own a Tesla car, you will get paid by others to use your car's chip to answer questions or do AI tasks.

But challenges loom in the AI world. Supply chains for chips are tight, including shortages in memory, like HBM (High Bandwidth Memory). Tesla is now partnering with TSMC and Samsung to dodge this, choosing designs less reliant on scarce parts. And ethically? Distributed AI means privacy wins (data stays local) but needs strong security.

Building your first neural net on a laptop? Imagine tweaking SLMs on a Tesla chip at home. AI5 could democratize smarts, making agentic bots affordable. And then add a distributed AI cloud model, where hundreds of billions of dollars worth of compute is leveraging fleets of millions of cars and bots that people already bought. Competitors would have to build ten hundred-billion-dollar data centers before they can start competing at scale. Elon's bet: AI5 is the "right chip at the right time," arriving as SLM demand surges. If it delivers, Tesla doesn't just make cars; they power the AI revolution.

***

Chapter 11

The Race to Super Intelligence is an Industrial Story, Not a Software Sprint

John Gibbs

On an August morning in 2025, OpenAI announces GPT-5, an integrated system that routes between a fast general model and a deeper reasoning engine, powered by awesome Nvidia silicon. Simultaneously, the U.S. House Energy and Commerce Committee picks up a blunt refrain from former Google CEO Eric Schmidt: *"AI's natural limit is electricity, not chips"*. In this race to super intelligence, where does the hype stop and the true competition begin–and in what field of competition? While the lay public likely considers the AI race a software one, the race is in fact one based on the full stack, from power to cooling, to hardware, and then on to software. In a sense, the AI race is "total war." Corporations and governments that do not accept the existential, grand scale of this race are doomed to be onlookers, renting capability from the winners.

1. Energy: The First Gating Factor

When grid planners collide with chip roadmaps, electricity, not silicon, sets the ceiling on usable intelligence. Industry testimony to Congress underscored the same point: meeting projected AI demand will require tens of gigawatts of new generation and faster interconnections. Schmidt himself pegs the U.S. shortfall at ~92 GW.

China's answer has been to build, and build fast. In 2024, it added 429 GW of capacity and broke ground on nearly 95 GW of coal, a dependable dispatchable backup to keep renewables from sagging. The U.S., by contrast, added just 48.6 GW in 2024, with 63 GW expected in 2025. Whoever can provision reliable megawatts at the lowest marginal cost will field the most capable, cheapest-to-operate models. By that measure, China is currently winning.

Transmission makes the asymmetry starker. China's Ultra High Voltage (UHV) grid allows bulk flows across a continent; the United States has none. Geography becomes destiny: in China, siting an AI factory is a logistics problem. In the U.S., it's often a political war fought state by state.

Capital policy tilts the same way. China's State Grid announced a ¥650 billion investment plan for 2025, a grid-first industrial policy. By contrast, U.S. grid expansion is tangled in years-long permitting and interconnection queues. The result is a time-to-power gap that becomes a time-to-model gap.

None of this guarantees the U.S. cannot catch up. Both IEA and Goldman Sachs project wide bands for data-center electricity growth by 2030. Enhanced geothermal in Nevada, uprated nuclear in Virginia, and firmed-up gas across the Midwest. These are real counterplays. But for now, China's grid is the clearest leading indicator of AI scale.

Chips & Packaging: The Merchant of Scale vs. Sovereign Hedges

From 2024 through 2027, NVIDIA has been setting the global pace. Its Blackwell B200/GB200 GPUs, bound into NVL72 racks, promise ~30× faster real-time trillion-parameter inference. Rubin and Rubin Ultra loom on the horizon. But FLOPs aren't the real bottleneck.

High Bandwidth Memory (HBM) and advanced packaging **Chip on Wafer on Substrate (CoWoS)** are the oxygen lines. Foundry slots, not chip designs, dictate how many "AI factories" can be switched on each quarter.

That's why U.S. hyperscalers are hedging: Microsoft with Maia and Cobalt, AWS with Trainium2, Google with TPU Trillium. These chips are not just performance plays, they are insurance against export regimes and packaging scarcity.

China faces the inverse challenge: cut off from top-end GPUs, it scales differently through the use of clusters of lower-end chips, algorithmic efficiency, domestic accelerators like Huawei's Ascend, and open-weight software to narrow capability gaps. But here, China's UHV + coal advantage looms: they have the power to feed those clusters. In chips, the West leads. In power logistics, China has dug a deeper moat.

Data: Gravity, Governance, and the Home-Field Advantage

SuperAI feeds on FLOPs, but it *feasts* on data. The U.S. holds an edge in enterprise software penetration and cloud-centric repositories. China's counterweight is usage scale: hundreds of millions of users locked into super-apps like WeChat, generating dense cultural and linguistic data at unprecedented volume.

Governance splits the field. In the U.S. and EU, privacy and copyright slow ingestion. In China, centralized frameworks allow volume and velocity, though with risks. As models become agents operating across private corpora, retrieval and low-latency analytics are king. OpenAI's Rockset buyout bolsters real-time data for scalable AI agents, turning backend "plumbing" (infrastructure) into a competitive product edge. This is not just a superficial tweak in an agent-driven future

Software: Agents, Open Weights, and the Devaluation Hypothesis

The monolith era is over. The frontier is orchestration: routers plus specialists, agents that can call tools into action, then plan and execute.

Two dynamics dominate:

- U.S. labs (GPT-5, Gemini 2.5) keep raising ceilings on reasoning and multimodality.
- China's open-weight push (DeepSeek-R1, Qwen) compresses prices and speeds diffusion.

Open-sourcing has become a weapon. In August 2025, OpenAI itself released gpt-oss (20B and 120B), acknowledging that differentiation has shifted to orchestration, reliability, and distribution rather than parameter counts.

The post-training stack—Mixture of Experts, distillation, reinforcement learning—is what makes agentic systems affordable at inference. This is the devaluation hypothesis: the frontier leads in performance, but commoditization comes from below.

2. Six Leaders, Six Archetypes

The race to SuperAI has many entrants, but only a handful set the global tempo. These six, NVIDIA, Microsoft, OpenAI, Google/DeepMind, Tesla, and xAI, are not just companies; they are archetypes for how to win, or lose when the bottlenecks move. Each plays the game differently: merchant, syndicator, frontier lab, science engine, systems integrator, or velocity machine.

NVIDIA — The Merchant of Scale

NVIDIA is the arms dealer of the intelligence age. Its Blackwell architecture, centered on the B200/GB200 GPUs, is packaged into the NVL72 rack: seventy-two GPUs and thirty-six Grace CPUs bound into a single NVLink domain. The effect is dramatic: a rack that behaves like one massive processor, capable of real-time trillion-parameter inference at ~30× the speed of its predecessors.

Benchmarks bear out the marketing. In June 2025, MLPerf's new Llama-3.1-405B pretraining run was powered entirely by NVIDIA, and the company topped every major benchmark category. The roadmap keeps stretching forward: Blackwell Ultra this year, Rubin in 2026, Feynman by 2028.

But FLOPs alone don't guarantee victory. The bottlenecks are in memory and packaging: High Bandwidth Memory (HBM) and CoWoS slots. NVIDIA dominates those supply chains today, but its fate is also tethered to geopolitics. Washington's new "pay-to-play" policy allows sales of high-end GPUs to China if NVIDIA and AMD surrender ~15% of related revenues to the U.S. government. It reopens markets, but it hard-wires volatility into NVIDIA's balance sheet. In short, NVIDIA is indispensable, but it's also exposed.

Microsoft — The Systems Syndicator

If NVIDIA is the merchant, Microsoft is the syndicator of the stack. In fiscal 2025, it allocated nearly $80 billion in capex to AI data centers, betting that Azure will become the operating fabric of AI itself. Growth is guided at ~30–35%, driven by AI demand and a partner portfolio that includes OpenAI at the frontier and G42 in the Gulf.

The OpenAI partnership remains existential, though increasingly complicated. As OpenAI diversified to Oracle and even Google Cloud, Microsoft pushed to renegotiate terms, especially around an "AGI clause" that could radically alter access if thresholds are crossed. The friction is real, but so is the interdependence: Microsoft needs AI differentiation; OpenAI needs global-scale supply.

Geopolitics are baked into the model. The $1.5 billion G42 deal pulled a major UAE player firmly into the U.S. tech orbit, while a $1 billion Kenya build extended Azure/OpenAI into Africa. This is industrial policy masquerading as cloud expansion. Microsoft's thesis is clear: aggregate power, models, and distribution into one syndicate, and sell it as the default platform for work.

OpenAI — The Frontier Lab Becoming Infrastructure

OpenAI began as a research lab; by mid-2025, it looks like a hybrid utility. GPT-5's routed design, fast where it can be, deep where it must, was a capability leap. But the real pivot came with agents. The ChatGPT agent, announced in July, can browse, click, type, and complete multi-step tasks, leading OpenAI to boast that *"ChatGPT now thinks and acts"*. The product surface has shifted from answers to outcomes.

Infrastructure followed suit. In July 2025, OpenAI and Oracle announced 4.5 GW of new U.S. data-center capacity under the Stargate program, taking total expansion past 5 GW. A flagship site in Abilene, Texas, designed to host tens of thousands of GPUs, signals a move from renter to co-owner. Financing has become as much a differentiator as model architecture: sovereign capital, GPU-backed loans, and joint ventures are all on the table. In effect, OpenAI is no longer just a lab. It is becoming part of the industrial base of AI.

Google/DeepMind — The Science Engine With Production Disciplin

Google's role in this race is synthesis: research that ships. On the silicon side, TPU v6 Trillium claims ~4.7× per-chip performance gains and major energy efficiency improvements over v5e. Pragmatism guides the rollout: Google Cloud also offers A4/A4X VMs built on NVIDIA's NVL72 racks. Customers get Compute Unified Device Architecture (CUDA) if they need it; TPUs if they want the Google path.

On the model front, Veo 3 extended video generation into native audio, while Perch pushed the boundaries of bioacoustics. These aren't demos; they are pipelines feeding into Search, YouTube, and conservation initiatives, which act as reminders that science and monetization are intertwined.

Most farsighted is Google's energy strategy. The 115 MW enhanced geothermal project with Fervo in Nevada is a proof of concept for clean, dispatchable baseload power near data centers. If "AI's natural limit is electricity," Google is among the few investing in steel, steam, and megawatts, not just silicon.

Tesla — The Systems Integrator

Tesla's AI play remains unique: cars as rolling sensors, robots as the next vehicle, software as the monetization layer. In June 2025, its Robotaxi launched in Austin, scaling quickly but still requiring in-car monitors. Expansion into California underscored how autonomy is not just an engineering problem but a high-stakes negotiation with physics, psychology, and regulation.

The pivot came in training. In August 2025, Tesla shuttered its Dojo program, redirecting resources to AI5/AI6 chips optimized for inference while leaning more heavily on NVIDIA for training. It's a familiar Tesla trade: abandon the risky in-house moonshot, scale faster on merchant silicon, and control destiny through integration rather than chip design.

Tesla's overlooked strength lies in energy. Its Megapack batteries, designed to stabilize renewable grids, have become critical for AI data centers. With millisecond response times, they smooth the spikes of training runs and prevent brownouts. In an ironic twist, Tesla Energy's contribution to SuperAI may prove as consequential as its cars or robots.

xAI — Velocity Meets Social License

No company has scaled faster than xAI. After raising $6 billion in 2024, its "Colossus" supercomputer in Memphis grew to ~200,000 NVIDIA GPUs by mid-2025. The company even open-sourced Grok-2 while racing to catch up with older incumbents.

The constraint is power…and politics. To keep Colossus alive, xAI leaned on dozens of on-site methane turbines and reportedly is importing an entire power plant from Europe. The audacity is breathtaking; the backlash, immediate. Residents raised air-quality concerns, regulators pushed back, and the debate over who bears the costs of AI landed squarely on local communities.

xAI's strategy is velocity. They move so fast that capability gains reset the debate. But velocity without social license can become fragile. The next year will test whether the company's momentum compounds to lasting advantage, or whether it collapses under the weight of politics and community resistance.

What the Six Teach Us

Together, these six companies reveal the shape of the race. Speed is gated by megawatts and memory bandwidth, not just clever algorithms. Platform position, who owns the loop of agents and enterprise data, will decide monetization. Open weights compress the middle of the market, forcing Western firms to differentiate on rights, safety, and distribution rather than raw FLOPs.

Above all, the stack rewards integrators. Those who secure watts, book packaging years in advance, capture data rights, and ship reliable agents will own the new world. Everyone else will rent from them.

3. Asia's Hand on the Scale — Power, Patents, and Open-Weights

Asia is not a single actor, but in the race to SuperAI, it exerts a single gravitational pull. Across energy, chips, and software, the center of AI mass is shifting east. China, especially, has treated megawatts as an explicit strategy, while its neighbors position themselves around the narrow chokepoints of packaging, memory, and sovereign capacity. The United States may still lead at the frontier, but Asia is quietly reshaping the battlefield on which most of the race will be fought.

China — Power First, Compute Everywhere

China's grid has become an AI policy. In 2024, it added an astonishing 429 GW of net new capacity, fifteen times U.S. additions, and started another 94.5 GW of coal construction [3–6].

At the same time, ~277 GW of solar came online, creating a mix of green and dispatchable baseload that ensures resilience. This is not just climate policy. It is an industrial strategy: secure abundant, cheap megawatts so that siting AI factories becomes a logistics problem, not a political one.

The backbone is China's UHV transmission network, which moves power thousands of kilometers from western deserts to eastern megacities. In the U.S., hyperscale sites often drown in interconnection queues. In China, the wires are already strung [7].

Compute policy mirrors the grid. Beijing's "Eastern Data, Western Computing" initiative shifts workloads to cheap-energy regions, knitting together national compute fabrics that total hundreds of exaflops. Much of it isn't frontier-class, but it doesn't need to be: for domestic services. *Volume beats elegance.*

Patents reveal the same tilt. Between 2014 and 2023, China filed ~38,000 generative-AI patents, about 70% of the world's total, and far more than the U.S. [44]. Citation counts still favor America, but industrial diffusion favors China. On software, the strategy is explicitly adversarial: DeepSeek-R1 and Qwen open weights weren't built to dethrone GPT-5. They were built to collapse margins and shorten diffusion cycles. The play is to make Western frontier advantages less monetizable.

Taiwan — The Foundry and the Package

Taiwan remains the narrow waist of the global AI hourglass. Every rack of NVIDIA Blackwells or Google TPUs flows through TSMC's advanced packaging lines. CoWoS capacity is the oxygen line of the AI industry [45].

TSMC is doubling output and expanding sites, but the risks are obvious. Earthquakes, geopolitics, or even minor yield shocks ripple across continents. Roadmaps slip, not because chips aren't designed, but because there aren't enough packaged parts to ship them. Taiwan is the track on which the global AI race runs, and it is perilously narrow.

South Korea — Memory as a Weapon of Tempo

If Taiwan throttles packaging, South Korea throttles memory bandwidth. SK Hynix dominates the supply of High-Bandwidth Memory 3 Enhanced (HBM3E), shipping 12-high stacks to NVIDIA, while Samsung hustles to catch up [46].

The tempo of inference costs now lives in their fabs. Each gain in HBM height or yield curve lowers the effective $/token across billions of inferences. Whoever controls memory sets the cadence of global AI affordability. FLOPs may get headlines, but HBM decides tempo.

Japan — Sovereign Hedges and Advanced Nodes

Japan is not trying to replace Taiwan overnight. Instead, it is building sovereign hedges. Rapidus, a state-backed project with IBM and IMEC, is racing toward a 2 nm node by 2027 [47].

Simultaneously, Japan is hosting allied capacity: TSMC's Kumamoto fab, backed by Japanese subsidies, is already ramping.

The strategy is dual: build a domestic advanced line to hedge risk, and anchor allied supply to hedge geopolitics. In a crisis, resilience is worth more than bleeding-edge yields.

Singapore–Johor — The Straits Corridor

Singapore ended its moratorium on new data centers in 2024, unveiling a "Green Data Centre Roadmap" that adds ~300 MW near-term and ties approval to liquid cooling and renewable integration [48]. Just across the causeway, Malaysia's Johor region is going hyperscale: a 500 MW NVIDIA-partnered park backed by YTL Power [49].

Geography is destiny here. Singapore offers finance, fiber, and stability; Johor offers land and cheap energy. Together, they form a binational corridor of commerce that could rival traditional hubs in Europe and the U.S.

India — A National Compute Commons

India's move is to make compute a public good. The IndiaAI Mission launched with ~10,000 GPUs and crossed 34,000 by mid-2025 [50]. Capacity is pooled nationally and allocated competitively to startups, states, and universities, with the aim of compressing time-to-experiment across dozens of languages and domains.

The bet is straightforward: democratized access creates broad capability. Rather than a few hyperscalers monopolizing AI, India aims to lift an entire ecosystem.

West Asia — Capital and Alignment

Petrodollars are becoming petaflops. The UAE's $1.5 billion G42 deal with Microsoft aligned its AI strategy firmly with U.S. vendors while funding builds from Abu Dhabi to Kenya [24]. A new sovereign fund, MGX, is funneling oil wealth into GPU clusters.

This is more than diversification. It is geopolitics: secure continued access to advanced U.S. silicon by anchoring capital and alignment. For West Asia, AI is the path to post-petroleum relevance.

What Asia's Rise Means

- Power moves the goalposts. China's megawatt surge and UHV lines shift the constraint from *where can we plug in?* to *what can we build?* Inference, with its 24/7 appetite, will magnify this advantage.
- Packaging and memory are chokepoints. Taiwan and South Korea hold the keys. Without their CoWoS and HBM, the global roadmap is just PowerPoint.
- Open-weights are a price war. DeepSeek, Qwen, and Ernie aren't trying to beat GPT-5; they're trying to make "good enough" so cheap it erodes Western margins.
- Alliances matter as much as algorithms. Japan's Rapidus hedge, Singapore–Johor's corridor, India's compute commons, and the UAE's alignment strategy are all coalitions of capacity.

The upshot: Asia is not merely competing. It is setting the operating conditions of the race. The U.S. can still win the frontier, but only if it learns to play fluently in an Asian-shaped stack: contract watts, book packaging years ahead, diversify memory sources, and expect open-weight pressure to be a permanent feature of the market.

4. Bottlenecks Decide the Winners

The story of SuperAI over the next five years will not be told in product demos or flashy keynotes. It will be told in bottlenecks, industrial choke points where physics, policy, or capital say *"no further."* Clear one, and another appears, often in a different discipline with new rules and new constraints. Winners are those who can shove the bottlenecks somewhere they already control. Losers will wake up to find that physics or politics has rewritten their roadmap.

Power and Time-to-Power

Electricity is the hard ceiling on usable intelligence, and "time-to-power" is fast becoming the industry's harshest metric. Adding megawatts on paper is easy; energizing them with transmission lines, interconnection permits, and local approval is the grind. Projects can stall for years in queues, while competitors across the ocean flip the switch on gigawatts in months [11].

Three lessons separate the leaders from the laggards:

- Site where the grid says yes. In the U.S., the smartest builders chase substation headroom and rights-of-way, not wishful maps. In China, UHV lines make the siting calculus a logistics puzzle, not a political gauntlet [7].
- Lock in clean baseload early. Enhanced geothermal in Nevada, uprated nuclear in Virginia, and gas-with-CCS in the Midwest aren't side projects. They are the foundation that lets you train when the wind dies or the sun sets [32–36].
- Design for inference, not just training. Spiky training runs are heavy, but the real weight will be on agents. Treat inference like a utility, or risk finding that your "AI factory" can't run 24/7 [22,26].

Inside large deployments, the first hard stops are never about parameter counts. You run out of power, then memory bandwidth, then patience as east–west traffic steals your tokens per second.

Post-training wizardry can stretch efficiency at the margins, but physics always has the final say. Schmidt's line: *"AI's natural limit is electricity, not chips"* is not a metaphor; it's the budgeting principle every operator lives by [2].

Packaging and HBM: The Hidden Gate

While FLOPs dominate headlines, the silent throttle on scale is packaging and memory. Advanced CoWoS slots, 2.5D/3D packaging yields, and HBM3E/HBM4 availability determine how many racks light up each quarter [12–15,45,46].

Practical implications are unforgiving:

- Book packaging years in advance. If you're not on TSMC's allocation, your roadmap is a wish, not a schedule [45].
- Engineer for memory-bound reality. Token throughput is increasingly about sequence length, KV-cache efficiency, and routing tuned to HBM, not raw FLOPs. Many clusters spend more time idling than computing.
- Qualify second sources. Relying on a single HBM vendor or substrate supplier is not efficient; it's fragile. Diversification is a strategy.

Networking and I/O: The Utilization Trap

Clusters that look monstrous on paper can end up half-idle because their networks can't keep up. East-west traffic for shared models, gradient exchanges, or retrieval calls eats the bandwidth you thought you bought.

Patterns that separate contenders from pretenders:

- Rack as a computer. Treat the NVL72 as the unit of design. Keep workloads inside its NVLink domain [13].

- Co-packaged optics. At 800 GbE and beyond, optics move onto the package. Complexity soars, but teams with the talent make it a competitive weapon.
- Retrieval is a network workload. Tool-using agents generate chatty, latency-sensitive traffic. Without locality planning, your "smart" agent becomes a case study in queueing theory.

Cooling and Water: Physics Meets Permitting

Power density has vaulted from 20-40 kW per rack to 100-300 kW in frontier deployments. Air cooling is finished; direct-to-chip liquid and immersion are the new normal. But the bottleneck isn't just technical, it's social. Water rights and discharge permits now join land and fiber as gating factors. In the drought-prone U.S. Southwest, communities are already fighting data centers for scarce water, while in Europe, waste heat is being piped into district heating systems. The most valuable engineers you haven't hired yet may not be ML PhDs, but thermal and water systems planners. Sexy? No. Critical? Absolutely.

Data Rights and Retrieval: The Legal–Operational Bottleneck

SuperAI may be trained on the open internet, but it earns its keep on private data. The bottleneck here is twofold:

Legal authority - do you actually have the rights to use what you've got?
Technical plumbing - can you use it at low latency, reliably?

Enterprises that settled these issues early are already deploying agents across their data. Those who stalled are still fighting lawyers. Retrieval is no longer a parlor trick of clever prompting; it's a database problem. OpenAI's acquisition of Rockset was a recognition that sub-second joins and hybrid search are product features, not infrastructure trivia[17].

Reliability and Evaluation: The Verification Bottleneck

Agents fail in ways static leaderboards never reveal: tool misuse, silent wrong answers, long-horizon drift. The true bottleneck is verification throughput. How many tasks per hour can you prove correct at the target cost and latency?

New rules of the game:

- Evals are continuous. Shadow traffic, canary tasks, and red-team harnesses become as routine as unit tests.
- Reasoning ≠ reliability. Mixture of Experts, distillation, and Group Relative Policy Optimization (GRPO) style RL may boost reasoning and cut cost, but at the expense of new brittleness.
- Safety is the supply chain. Models, tools, plugins, and humans form one loop. A weak link anywhere can sink the whole system [18–20].

Talent and Capital: The Unsexy Bottlenecks

The bottlenecks that matter most aren't glamorous. They are grid engineers, packaging specialists, compiler teams, and program managers who can steer multi-year, multi-vendor builds. Frontier labs that elevate operations to the same level as research will ship more intelligence per dollar [22,28,37].

Capital is equally decisive. OpenAI's Stargate and xAI's Memphis colossus are as much about sovereign funding, GPU-backed financing, and 20-year Power Purchased Agreements (PPAs) as they are about chips [26,42]. Companies running quarter to quarter won't keep up with those carrying multi-billion-dollar work-in-progress.

The Moving Gates

Energy caps what you can do. Packaging and memory capacity determine how fast you can add it. Networking and cooling cap how much can you use? Data rights and retrieval cap where it is valuable. Verification caps what you can trust. Talent and capital cap how quickly you can push the next limit.

Winners are those who shove each bottleneck somewhere they already have leverage. Everyone else will end up renting their future from those who do.

5. Scorecard and Scenarios

The stack decides winners, but only if companies can keep solving their moving constraints. Think of this as a mid-2025 scorecard of the race where each leader stands on energy, chips, data, and software, and what the next four years might bring. This is not market cap theater or brand hype. It's an operator's ledger: watts booked, packaging secured, data rights locked down, agents verified.

5.1 Stack Mastery Snapshot (mid-2025)

NVIDIA — the merchant of scale

- Energy: indirect. Dependent on customer siting and PPAs, but increasingly co-designing for liquid cooling and denser racks.
- Chips & packaging: dominant. Blackwell/NVL72 cadence, deep CoWoS/HBM integration, Compute Unified Device Architecture (CUDA) gravity akin to a black hole.

- Data: neutral. Partners' data moats flow through demand for training/inference. Its Isaac General Robot 00 Technology (GROOT) robotics project may shift this positive.
- Software: strong enablement. CUDA, CUDA Deep Neural Network Library (cuDNN), Triton (open-source GPU kernels in Python), Neural Modules (NeMo)—the ecosystem gravity to steer how others build.
- Bottleneck risk: packaging and HBM supply; policy whiplash on exports.

Microsoft — the systems syndicator

- Energy: aggressive. Multi-GW builds, global siting, long-dated PPAs tied to Azure.
- Chips & packaging: hedged. Maia/Cobalt in-house plus NVIDIA fleets.
- Data: enterprise-grade. M365 + Copilot + tenancy controls = distribution moat.
- Software: strong. Agentic workflows across productivity, platformized evals.
- Bottleneck risk: interconnection timing; dependence on frontier partners.

OpenAI — the frontier lab turning into infrastructure

- Energy: partnered. Multi-site expansion with utility-scale power; multihoming reduces risk.
- Chips & packaging: rented + co-owned. Azure, Stargate sites, GPU sovereign capital.
- Data: improving. Rockset + retrieval unlocks private corpora.
- Software: Frontier. GPT-5 routing + agents; rapid post-training cycles.

- Bottleneck risk: verification throughput for agents; political economy of compute.

Google/DeepMind — the science engine with production discipline

- Energy: farsighted. Enhanced geothermal as a clean baseload, efficiency as a design goal.
- Chips & packaging: dual track. Tensor Processing Units (TPU) Trillium + pragmatic NVIDIA racks.
- Data: ecosystem-rich. Search, YouTube, telemetry + strong privacy scaffolding.
- Software: frontier-class. Gemini 2.5, Veo, Perch, deep infra/tooling.
- Bottleneck risk: product-focus dilution; TPU/GPU balance.

Tesla — the systems integrator

- Energy: advantaged. Grid-scale Megapacks stabilize AI loads.
- Chips & packaging: pragmatic. Dojo shuttered; merchant silicon for training; AI5/AI6 roadmap for inference.
- Data: unique. Fleet-scale real-world driving + robotics.
- Software: ambitious. End-to-end autonomy + humanoids; regulatory exposure.
- Bottleneck risk: urban friction, regulatory latency more than silicon.

xAI — velocity with a power constraint

- Energy: constrained. Methane turbines, social license battles.
- Chips & packaging: aggressive buyer. Massive NVIDIA bookings, fast cluster spin-up.
- Data: strong open-web + X-stream signals, noisy but vast.

- Software: catching up. Rapid iteration, selective open-weight releases.
- Bottleneck risk: community opposition, carrying costs of speed.

5.2 What to Watch — Operator Metrics That Actually Matter

Forget hype slides. Operators live or die by these metrics:

- Time-to-power. Months from site control to energized megawatts with stable Power Usage Effectiveness (PUE) (~1.0 is perfection). [IEA]
- Packaging and memory. CoWoS slots reserved, HBM stacks qualified, tokens/second per rack. [FT]
- Network utilization. NVLink/Ethernet saturation, retrieval locality hits. [NVIDIA]
- Inference cost & reliability. $/1k tokens at target latency; continuous eval pass rates. [Anthropic]
- Data rights velocity. Permissioned connectors live; time to onboard new corpora. [Microsoft, Google Cloud]
- Safety throughput. Incidents per million tool calls, patch speed, backlash risk. [OpenAI, Anthropic]
- Policy exposure. Share of capacity in stable jurisdictions with predictable rules. [Reuters]

5.3 Three Plausible Scenarios (2026–2029)

Scenario A — Grid-First Acceleration

The U.S. unlocks gigawatts faster, geothermal, nuclear, and firm gas, and cuts queues. China keeps building, but the U.S. closes the time-to-power gap.

- Winners: Microsoft (Azure utility), Google (clean baseload moat), OpenAI (Stargate + multihoming), xAI (cash into compute). NVIDIA sells into both.
- Losers: GPU-rich but watt-poor challengers.
- Tell-tales: 24/7 clean PPAs, liquid-first campuses energized <18 months, inference footprints growing.

Scenario B — Silicon Squeeze and Packaging Shock

HBM or CoWoS bottlenecks extend. GPUs ship, but not packaged. Memory costs spike. Bandwidth, not FLOPs, becomes the limiter.

- Winners: NVIDIA, TSMC, Korean HBM suppliers; integrators tuned for memory-bound workloads.
- Losers: Buyers without packaging slots; FLOPs-abundant architectures.
- Tell-tales: long lead times, soaring HBM premiums, Mixture of Experts (MoE)/distilled workloads gaining.

Scenario C — Open-Weight Upset

"Good enough," open-weights flood the middle market. Inference costs collapse; value shifts to integration, data rights, and reliability.

- Winners: Microsoft (enterprise distribution), Tesla (fleet data), Google & xAI (fast productization). OpenAI wins if it monetizes agents + data plumbing.
- Losers: Closed-only shops without data or distribution.
- Tell-tales: RFPs requiring open-weight support; distillation surging; API price ceilings.

5.4 Wildcards

- Policy jolts. Export regimes, royalties, licensing shifts that redraw chip flows.
- Algorithmic leaps. A memory or reasoning breakthrough that flattens compute demand…or inflates it.
- Power shocks. Fuel disruptions are delaying multi-GW sites or breakthroughs in long-duration storage that flip economics.
- Trust events. A catastrophic agent failure that forces regulators to slam the brakes.

5.5 Leaderboard by Operating Metrics (mid-2025)

Scale: 5 = industry-leading, 4 = strong, 3 = competitive, 2 = exposed, 1 = lagging. Policy exposure scored inversely(higher = more in stable jurisdictions).

Company	Time-to-power	Packaging & HBM	Network utilization	Inference cost & reliability	Data rights velocity	Safety throughput	Policy exposure	Overall
NVIDIA	3	5	5	4	3	3	3	4.0
Microsoft	5	4	4	4	5	4	4	4.3
OpenAI	4	4	4	3	4	4	3	3.9
Google/ DeepMind	5	4	5	4	5	4	4	4.4
Tesla	4	3	3	4	5	3	3	3.6

xAI	2	4	4	3	4	3	3	3.3

Notes:

- *NVIDIA* rules packaging/memory but is hostage to export regimes and partner siting.
- *Microsoft* turns siting into a strength, compressing time-to-power, hedging silicon, and riding enterprise data rights.
- *OpenAI* flexes multihomed Stargate builds, but agent verification drags its reliability.
- *Google/DeepMind* wins with clean baseload + ecosystem data; their fabrics hum.
- *Tesla* shines in energy integration and fleet data, but compute/regulatory frictions drag.
- *xAI* turns up clusters fast, but social license and power sourcing erode its score.

The headline: Google/DeepMind (4.4) and Microsoft (4.3) are the current pace-setters. NVIDIA (4.0) remains indispensable as the merchant of scale. OpenAI (3.9) sits just off the podium, limited by verification. Tesla (3.6) and xAI (3.3) trail, quick and differentiated but watt and policy constrained. Unless they close those gaps, they risk inventing capabilities others monetize at scale.

5.6 How to Win the Moving Game

The recipe is blunt:

- Treat energy procurement as a product decision.
- Treat packaging as a supply-chain strategy.
- Treat data rights as a feature, not a compliance tax.
- Treat evals as pipelines, not events.

Book Watts. Book CoWoS. Lower $/token. Raise verified-task throughput. Keep an eye out for architectural leaps, or make one yourself. Above all: make the next bottleneck land in your rival's domain, not yours.

6. Conclusion: The Cost of Intelligence Tends Toward the Cost of Electricity

Elon Musk has been blunt: *"The next shortage will be electricity. They won't be able to find enough electricity to run all the chips"* [30]. He may sound alarmist, but he isn't wrong. The past two years have made one truth unavoidable: SuperAI is not a parlor trick. It is an industrial project, closer in spirit to the Manhattan Project of the 1940s or the Apollo Program of the 1960s than to a software startup.

Energy sets the ceiling. Chips and packaging set the pace. Data sets the relevance. Software turns it into work. Winners are those who make each bottleneck someone else's problem, in sequence, without losing tempo.

The center of gravity is shifting toward builders who treat megawatts, CoWoS slots, HBM stacks, and network fabrics as product features, not facilities trivia. If your *time-to-power* and *effective tokens per rack* move faster than your competitors, your roadmaps become delivery schedules, not PowerPoint slides. If they move more slowly, even the best science is trapped in a queue.

China's strategy to overbuild power, wire it with UHV, and flood the middle market with open weights that compress price/performance has already shifted the baseline. The United States still leads at the frontier, but frontier leadership only matters if it ships. The next leg of the race will be decided not by who can demo the most dazzling agent, but by who can field capable systems at scale, on their own grids at sustainable unit economics.

For companies, the checklist is blunt:

- Book watts before words. Secure dispatchable, affordable power with interconnection dates and liquid-first designs [32–36].
- Reserve packaging and memory like oxygen. CoWoS capacity and HBM3E/4 stacks are the keys that turn roadmaps into racks [45,46].
- Engineer for utilization. Keep workloads inside high-bandwidth domains, treat retrieval as a network workload, and tune for memory-bound reality [13,17].
- Win the data-permissioning race. Row-level controls, compliant retrieval, and sub-second joins are how agents earn their keep [17].
- Make verification continuous. Eval pipelines and red-team harnesses turn "reasoning" into reliability [18–20].

For governments, the playbook is equally practical:

- Collapse time-to-power. Accelerate interconnections, modernize transmission, and back firm clean baseload-enhanced geothermal, nuclear, renewables + storage, and gas with CCS-near fiber [11,32].
- Treat packaging and HBM as strategic industries. Expand allied capacity, stabilize export regimes, and de-risk single points of failure [45,46].
- Support open-weight security and safety. Encourage transparent evals, licensing frameworks, and enterprise-grade tooling so openness doesn't equal fragility [18–20].
- Build talent pipelines for the unglamorous bottlenecks. Power engineers, thermal specialists, compiler teams,

packaging experts. the hidden disciplines that will decide national competitiveness [22,28,37].

If you are NVIDIA, the mandate is to keep turning racks into single computers and memory into surplus.
If you are Microsoft, it is to make Azure feel like a utility: power, models, and distribution on tap.

If you are OpenAI, it is to turn frontier intelligence into agentic outcomes while securing a multihomed compute base.

If you are Google, it is to compound clean baseload and silicon pragmatism into a product.

If you are Tesla, it is to industrialize safety faster than hype.

If you are xAI, it is to turn velocity into staying power by earning a social license for megawatts.

The stakes are not abstract. As models shift from answers to actions, intelligence itself becomes infrastructure, something economies will rely on as deeply as electricity, water, or steel. Eric Schmidt's refrain: *"AI's natural limit is electricity, not chips"* [2] is not a metaphor. It is physics. The cost of intelligence will converge toward the cost of electricity, plus the cost of moving bits to where the work happens and proving that the work is correct.

History tends to reward integrators. Those who can contract for watts, book packaging, capture data rights, and ship reliable agents will write the terms of the next decade. Everyone else will rent their future from them. The race to SuperAI is still open. And in the end, it will be won not by demos on a stage, but by electrons through wires, wafers through foundries, and agents proven safe at scale.

References

OpenAI — *Introducing GPT-5* (Aug 7, 2025) : https://openai.com/index/introducing-gpt-5/

Fortune — "Ex-Google CEO: AI's natural limit is electricity, not chips" (Jul 18, 2025): https://fortune.com/2025/07/18/eric-schmidt-ai-natural-limit-electricity-chips-water-usage/

Climate Energy Finance (NEA data) — *Monthly China Energy Update: Feb 2025 (277.2 GW solar in 2024)*: PDF

CREA/GEM — *China Coal Power 2024: 94.5 GW started construction*: PDF

Reuters — "China's solar, wind installations soared to record in 2024" (Jan 21, 2025): https://www.reuters.com/business/energy/chinas-solar-wind-power-installed-capacity-soars-2024-2025-01-21/

U.S. Energy Information Administration (EIA) — *Today in Energy: U.S. added 48.6 GW in 2024, expects 63 GW in 2025* (Feb 24, 2025): https://www.eia.gov/todayinenergy/detail.php?id=64586

RAND Corporation — "The U.S. must close the long-distance power transmission gap" (Jan 16, 2024) : https://www.rand.org/pubs/commentary/2024/01/the-us-must-close-the-long-distance-power-transmission.html

Tech Policy Press — U.S. House Energy & Commerce hearing transcript on AI & energy (Apr 11, 2025) : https://techpolicy.press/transcript-us-lawmakers-probe-ais-role-in-energy-and-climate

NVIDIA — *GB200 NVL72 product page* : https://www.nvidia.com/en-us/data-center/gb200-nvl72/

NVIDIA Developer Blog — *NVL72 architecture details* (Mar 18, 2024): https://developer.nvidia.com/blog/nvidia-gb200-nvl72-delivers-trillion-parameter-llm-training-and-real-time-inference/

MLCommons — *MLPerf Training v5.0 results* (Jun 4, 2025) : https://mlcommons.org/2025/06/mlperf-training-v5-0-results/

Microsoft — "Plans to spend ~$80B on AI-enabled data centers in FY2025" (Reuters, Jan 3, 2025) : https://www.reuters.com/technology/artificial-intelligence/microsoft-plans-spend-80-bln-ai-enabled-data-centers-fiscal-2025-cnbc-reports-2025-01-03/
Financial Times — Coverage of Microsoft–OpenAI agreements and AI data-center investment (2025): https://www.ft.com/
Reuters — "OpenAI acquires Rockset" (Jun 21, 2024): https://www.reuters.com/markets/deals/openai-acquires-database-analytics-firm-rockset-2024-06-21/
OpenAI — "We've acquired Rockset" (Jun 21, 2024) : https://openai.com/index/openai-acquires-rockset/
Google Cloud Blog — *Trillium TPU v6 preview* (Oct 30, 2024): https://cloud.google.com/blog/products/compute/trillium-sixth-generation-tpu-is-in-preview
Google Cloud Blog — *A4/A4X VMs with GB200 NVL72* (Feb 20, 2025): https://cloud.google.com/blog/products/compute/new-a4x-vms-powered-by-nvidia-gb200-gpus
DeepMind Blog — *Veo 3 release (native audio video generation)* (Jul 17, 2025): https://deepmind.google/models/veo/
Google Blog — "Perch AI bioacoustics model update" (Aug 7, 2025): https://blog.google/technology/google-deepmind/perch-ai-model/
Google Blog — "Google partners with NV Energy (115 MW geothermal project)" (May 13, 2025): https://blog.google/feed/nevada-clean-energy/
Reuters — "Tesla to streamline AI chip design work; Dojo team disbanded" (Aug 7, 2025): https://www.reuters.com/business/autos-transportation/tesla-streamline-its-ai-chip-design-work-musk-says-2025-08-07/
Bloomberg — "Tesla disbands Dojo team" (Aug 8, 2025) : https://www.bloomberg.com/news/articles/2025-08-07/tesla-disbands-dojo-supercomputer-team-in-blow-to-ai-effort

Politico — "xAI in Memphis: methane turbines without permits" (May 6, 2025): https://www.politico.com/news/2025/05/06/elon-musk-xai-memphis-gas-turbines-air-pollution-permits-00317582
DataCenterDynamics — "Musk claims xAI importing power plant" (Jul 7, 2025): https://www.datacenterdynamics.com/en/news/xai-importing-power-plant-from-abroad-for-new-memphis-data-center-elon-musk-claims/
TIME — "Inside the Memphis community battling xAI" (Aug 2025): https://time.com/7308925/elon-musk-memphis-ai-data-center/
Press Information Bureau (India) — "Common compute capacity crosses 34,000 GPUs" (May 30, 2025) : https://www.pib.gov.in/PressReleasePage.aspx?PRID=2132817
IMDA Singapore — *Green Data Centre Roadmap* (2024) : https://www.imda.gov.sg/-/media/imda/files/how-we-can-help/green-dc-roadmap/green-dc-roadmap.pdf
Reuters — "NVIDIA to partner Malaysia's YTL Power (Johor)" (Dec 8, 2023): https://www.reuters.com/technology/nvidia-talks-with-malaysias-ytl-data-center-deal-sources-2023-12-08/
YTL Power — *Green Data Centre Park press release (500 MW Johor)* (Dec 2023): https://www.ytl.com/press-releases/ytl-green-data-center-park-launches-in-johor-the-first-integrated-data-center-park-powered-by-renewable-solar-energy-in-malaysia-2/
New Atlas — "Elon Musk: AI's next shortage will be electricity" (Aug 2025): https://newatlas.com/computers/elon-musk-ai-electricity-shortage-warning-2025/

***

JOHN BIGGS

John L. Gibbs, Ph.D. is a UGA Professor and AI Faculty Fellow, CEO of Artimatic, U.S. patent holder, and NSF SBIR awardee. A Princeton physicist turned AI scholar, he's authored eleven books and runs the "Dr. Know-It-All" YouTube/x channel, translating cutting-edge AI into real products, policy, and practice in the race to AGI.

Follow John Gibbs

https://www.artimatic.io/

@DrKnowItAll16

https://www.youtube.com/@DrKnowitallKnows

Chapter 12

The Complete Stack for Super Intelligence

Randy Kirk

The concept for this book arose out of a recognition that the winner or winners in the ASI race are likely to be the company or companies that have the most control over the entire stack, as it is outlined in this chapter.

Raw materials, Energy, Hardware, Data, Software, Memory, Reasoning, Inference, Applications, and Integration are all needed to produce intelligence. The more of each, the more intelligence.

We will devote entire chapters to some of these subsections, but this chapter is designed to give the broad strokes and the entire picture in one place. And this chapter will describe each part of the stack as simply as possible. Other chapters will get deeper into the weeds.

Part 1: Raw Materials

If you've ever wondered what it takes to build AI systems that can outthink humans in every way, the answer starts deep underground. Think of resource extraction and mining as the hidden foundation of a skyscraper. It's the gritty, essential base that supports all the flashy tech on top. Without pulling rare earth elements, silicon, lithium, and other metals from the ground, there'd be no computer chips, no powerful servers, and no path to super intelligence. As we head into the second half of the 2020's, the explosion in AI demand has ramped up the need for these materials: lithium powers the huge batteries in data centers that run nonstop. Rare earths like neodymium make strong magnets for cooling systems and hard drives. Silicon is the basic building block for semiconductors. But this boom isn't free as it brings big environmental problems, tough ethical choices, and even global power struggles, especially since China controls so much of the mineral and rare earth processing.

This section dives into the world of resource extraction and mining, the starting point for superintelligence. We'll mix what's happening right now with some thoughts on the future, covering the main materials, the global picture, risks, new ideas, and what's coming next. Whether you're just getting started or already into this stuff, this is where the AI revolution begins—right in the dirt.

Rare Earth Elements (REEs), that group of 17 metals, including neodymium, dysprosium, and praseodymium, aren't actually super rare in the Earth's crust, but getting them out in a way that makes economic sense is really hard, like trying to find needles in multiple haystacks. These elements are crucial for AI hardware: neodymium makes the powerful magnets in hard drives and fans that keep data centers cool, while dysprosium helps make transistors in chips work better for handling huge amounts of calculations. Silicon, the main ingredient in semiconductors, gets mixed with rare earths to create the tiny, high-speed transistors in things like NVIDIA's H100 GPUs, which are like the engines for training AI models. Lithium, on the other hand, is key for batteries that power these energy-guzzling systems, especially in portable devices or data centers backed by solar and wind power.

Why does all this matter for superintelligence? To create AI that thinks better than humans, we need hardware that can crunch numbers at mind-boggling speeds on the order of quadrillions of operations every second, like a brain on steroids. Shortages of these minerals create bottlenecks, slowing down new AI developments and making everything more expensive. Sam Altman from OpenAI ties this to bigger ethical questions: "We must address, individually and collectively, moral and ethical issues raised by cutting-edge research in artificial intelligence and biotechnology," and that includes sourcing these materials in a way that's fair and doesn't harm people or the planet.

In my opinion, by 2030, we could meet about 40% of AI's mineral needs through recycling or lab-made alternatives, the circular economy, but only if we invest heavily now. Currently, demand is growing 20-30% faster than supply each year, forcing companies to innovate or hit walls. Training a big model like GPT-5 might use up materials from thousands of tons of ore; multiply that by all the AI work worldwide, and by 2028, AI could eat up 10% of the world's rare earth annual supply capacity. This close connection means companies will start working to control the whole process, like Tesla refining its own lithium, to avoid getting stuck when supplies run low.

The global mining scene is like a giant puzzle with just a few big pieces controlled by key countries and companies. China is the top player, mining around 70% of the world's rare earths and processing 90%, mostly from huge sites like Bayan Obo in Inner Mongolia. Lithium comes from places like Australia's Pilbara region or the "Lithium Triangle" in Argentina, Bolivia, and Chile, while silicon is mined from pure quartz deposits around the world. The U.S. leads in AI tech but imports about 80% of its rare earths from China, which leaves it vulnerable to disruptions.

Things are shifting, though. New U.S. mines, like the Ramaco Brook in Wyoming that opened in July, are the first domestic rare earth operations in decades, focusing on neodymium for AI magnets. Australia is ramping up, too, planning to triple its rare earth oxide production by 2027. Jensen Huang from NVIDIA puts it well: "It's very clear that AI is going to impact every industry. I think that every nation needs to make sure that AI is a part of their national strategy." This drive for more sources could create a more balanced global setup by 2035, with countries in Africa and Latin America stepping in.

How mining works depends on the mineral: lithium often comes from open-pit mines in dry areas, where they compete for scarce water, like in Chile's drying evaporation ponds. Rare earth mining uses chemical processes that eat up energy and create a lot of waste. China's 2025 quotas are tightening supply as demand skyrockets, while U.S. companies like MP Materials are building local refineries to reduce reliance on imports.

Geopolitical issues add extra tension, like a high-stakes game of chess. China's April 2025 export restrictions on seven rare earths, in response to U.S. tariffs, shook up supply chains. With such control, rare earths can be used as leverage in trade wars as we saw in 2025. A total ban could cut global chip production in half.

Refining is often bottlenecked in China, making everything riskier. Groups like the U.S.-Australia Critical Minerals Taskforce aim to supply 50% of Western needs by 2030 through new sources. Recent deals under the Trump administration show movement, but U.S.-China competition might heat up more. For super intelligence, strong supply chains are a must—any hiccup could delay advanced AI by years.

Environmental problems are huge in rare earth mining, where producing one ton can create up to 2,000 tons of toxic waste, often including radioactive stuff like thorium that contaminates soil and water. In China, over-mining has caused landslides and polluted rivers, affecting people's health for generations. Lithium mining drains underground water in desert areas, making droughts worse, and silicon quarries can destroy wildlife habitats.

Biodiversity takes a hit as mines expand into natural areas, and dust pollution harms nearby towns. But AI can help too, like using it to model climate issues better. I think tech could cut these impacts in half by 2040 if we make it a priority now.

AI is changing mining for the better, turning problems into potentially monumental benefits. In 2025, AI tools will use satellite images and predictions to find deposits quickly and with less digging, like a smart treasure map. Startups like Earth AI combine software with old data to spot eco-friendly sites. Self-driving trucks and drones make jobs safer, and machine learning improves ore sorting, saving 15% on energy.

Jensen Huang's idea hits home: "The automation of automation... is such an incredible idea." Generative AI designs better batteries, and predictive checks cut downtime. By 2030, full automation could boost productivity 20-30%, creating a loop where AI improves mining to build more AI. Companies like Rio Tinto use autonomous trucks that reduce emissions. While jobs might shift, good planning can turn that into training for new roles.

Efforts for sustainability are picking up with circular economy ideas, like reusing materials instead of always mining new ones. Recycling rare earths from old electronics could cover 30% of needs in 2026, with new plants in Belgium leading the way. AI helps optimize these flows to cut waste. Mines powered by renewables, bacteria-based extraction that's cleaner, and zero-emission targets are becoming standard. EU rules push for recycling goals, driving change.

Musk pushes for ethical sourcing, connecting it to AI's overall goals. I see 50% of supplies coming from recycled sources by 2040, with blockchain tracking everything. This not only lessens harm but also ensures AI can keep growing long-term.

Looking far ahead, mining asteroids could provide endless resources. Near-Earth asteroids are packed with trillions in metals and rare earths, and AI robots could do the work without humans. Startups like AstroForge are planning landings in 2025 to check metallic asteroids. SpaceX helps make this possible, with real operations maybe by 2030.

By 2040, data centers in space using asteroid materials might avoid Earth's limits. Moon helium-3 for fusion power or deep-sea nodules could back it up. Challenges like costs and space laws remain, but the rewards could take super intelligence to the stars.

Real examples show the way: Australia's Lynas Rare Earths succeeds with sustainable processing, breaking away from China's hold. But China's past export bans raised prices and messed up markets, a lesson in what not to do. Tesla's lithium refinery in Texas shows vertical integration working, reducing risks. Key takeaway? Tech and variety turn challenges into wins.

Resource extraction fuels the AI stack but needs careful handling. From China's control of AI innovations to sustainable mining, it is vital for super intelligence. Musk sees shortages coming, but there's plenty of opportunity.

A perfect real-world example of a circular system in action is Redwood Materials, a company founded by former Tesla executive and current board member JB Straubel. Redwood focuses on recycling batteries from electric vehicles and electronics, recovering valuable materials like lithium, cobalt, and nickel to reuse them in new batteries. In 2025, they've expanded operations with advanced facilities that process old batteries into high-purity materials, closing the loop so less new mining is needed. This approach not only reduces waste and environmental damage but also lowers costs and secures supplies for the growing AI and EV industries. Might we see a time when we are turning yesterday's smartphone into tomorrow's data center power source?

Redwood's model shows how circular economies can work at scale: they've partnered with companies like GM and Tesla to recycle scrap and end-of-life batteries, aiming to produce enough recycled lithium to power millions of EVs annually by the end of the decade.

By using hydrometallurgical processes that are cleaner than traditional mining, they cut down on toxic waste and energy use, proving that innovation can make resource extraction sustainable while supporting the push toward superintelligence.

Part 2: Energy

The immediacy of this issue and the complexity of the potential solutions led us to conclude that a separate chapter was in order. The following chapter will provide a serious deep dive into this crucial subject.

Part 3: Hardware

Hardware is like the engine in a race car. It's where the raw power meets the road, or in this case, where electrons zoom through silicon to create superhuman smarts. Chips such as NVIDIA's H100s and Google's TPUs provide the muscle for training huge AI models and making quick decisions. But we are facing limits: Moore's Law (the idea that chips double in power every couple of years) is slowing down, supply chains are stressed, and global politics add risks. As we talked about in the raw materials section, those extracted resources feed into chip-making, and any weak spots in sourcing raw materials can affect the whole system. Without solid hardware, super intelligence can't take off, no matter how great the software or data is.

Jensen Huang from NVIDIA sums it up: "...if we could continue to improve this capability, the applications are really quite boundless." New ideas in GPUs, custom chips, and upcoming tech promise to keep things moving. This section breaks down hardware's role, TSMC's big spot in the game, and future trends. We'll mix facts on the ground right now with some predictions, showing how hardware isn't just the strength, it's the gas pedal for AI's rise.

Hardware gives the pure computing power that turns code into smart actions, handling trillions of operations per second. In AI, this means speeding up math like matrix multiplications for neural networks, where old-school CPUs just can't keep up. Specialized chips do parallel work efficiently, cutting training time from months to days, like a team of workers building a house faster than a single person. For super intelligence, hardware has to grow to handle models with billions or trillions of parameters, unlocking new skills like deep thinking and creativity.

The main pieces start with GPUs, the heavy lifters of AI. NVIDIA leads with its Blackwell B200 GPUs, launched in 2025, giving 30 times faster inference for big models and powering giant data centers. These build on the H100 line, with up to 4 times quicker training thanks to smarter designs. Google's TPUs, now in v5p, shine at tensor math, perfect for cloud jobs with tons of parallelism. Custom chips like AWS's Trainium and Inferentia are made for specific tasks, dropping inference costs by 40-50%.

Neuromorphic hardware copies brain connections for super-efficient learning; Intel's Loihi 2 uses 1000 times less power than GPUs for some jobs. Quantum hardware is emerging: IBM's over-100-qubit processors solve tough optimization puzzles that regular chips can't touch, though errors are still an issue. OpenAI's first custom chip, wrapped up in 2025 with Broadcom and TSMC on 3nm tech, cuts ties to NVIDIA while improving efficiency for their models. These parts turn plain silicon into AI giants, but they work best when fitted perfectly into the bigger picture.

TSMC is still the boss, with its 2020 production jump, scaling 10 times during AI's rise, and setting the stage for today's growth. That move let GPUs and accelerators explode, meeting demand from NVIDIA and enabling model breakthroughs. At publication time, TSMC's lead goes on, with revenue up 40% from AI chips and Q2 profits jumping 61%. They expect 20% yearly growth, thanks to tiny nodes like 3nm and 2nm that drive next-level hardware.

TSMC's new Arizona plant, gearing up in 2025, starts making Blackwell chips for NVIDIA, shifting some production to the U.S. to dodge global risks. This $165 billion push aims to bring key chip making home, though Taiwan holds 90% of advanced chips.

Teaming with NVIDIA on computational lithography uses 350 H100 GPUs instead of 40,000 CPUs for quicker fabs. TSMC CEO C.C. Wei says: "AI is the megatrend driving our growth for the next decade." But supply can't match demand, so TSMC favors high-profit AI over everyday tech.

Challenges are plenty, starting with energy use. Top GPUs like the H100 suck up 700W, so new designs focus on power efficiency, like getting more work per watt. Arm-based chips from Qualcomm offer options for edge AI with less draw. Edge devices move computing to phones or cars; Qualcomm's Snapdragon X Elite hits 45 trillion operations per second for on-device decisions, cutting delays and cloud needs.

Inference speed is trending, with chips like Groq's LPUs running language models 10 times faster than regular GPUs, great for instant apps. Hybrids mix neuromorphic for sensing with quantum for sims. Moore's Law slowdown means innovating with 3D stacking and packaging, like NVIDIA's CoWoS for Blackwell.

Global tensions layer on, with U.S.-China chip fights limiting exports and pushing variety. The CHIPS Act's $52 billion boosts U.S. fabs, aiming for 20% world share by 2030. Taiwan's risks, like quakes or conflicts, could halt 50% of advanced output. Samsung and Intel compete, with Samsung's 2nm and Intel's 18A targeting AI top spots.

Elon Musk talks Tesla's homegrown work: "Tesla AI, both software & hardware, is far more advanced than even most experts realize." Their AI5 chips tune for self-driving, using vertical integration to skip bottlenecks.

Ahead, photonic chips might cut delays 100 times with light data, changing data centers by 2030. Quantum mixes could solve drug puzzles in hours, while neuromorphic enables low-power lifelong learning. I predict AI hardware sales reaching $500 billion a year by 2035, from edge to massive scales. NVIDIA's NVLink Fusion and AI Factories, shown at GTC 2025, hint at whole-system advances.

But ethics matter: hardware gaps could widen rich-poor divides, with only rich countries getting top chips. Rules need to ensure fairness. Dario Amodei from Anthropic warns: "AI will be the best or worst thing ever for humanity." Hardware's path will decide.

Hardware is more than base; it's the link to super intelligence. From TSMC's history to quantum futures, smart growth harnesses this wisely. As Huang says, nations must plan, or they will surely fall behind.

Part 4: Data

Data is like rocket fuel for AI heading to superintelligence. Without it, models can't launch. Today, we're swimming in zettabytes: organized databases, messy text and pics, plus fake data made by AI. Sources burst from smart sensors to social posts, but quality is king. Hurdles include privacy laws like GDPR that hit hard, and hidden biases in data. Marc Benioff nails it: "AI's true gold isn't in the UI or model. They're both commodities. What breathes life into AI is the data & metadata that describes the data to the model, just like oxygen for us." For super intelligence, live streams allow constant learning. This part covers data's job, types, sources, challenges, handling tips, and ties to AI peaks. Mixing 2025 facts with future views, data isn't just stuff; it's the heart of growth.

Elon Musk is at the forefront of the issue of the TRUTH of data, and is currently launching a Grokipedia to compete with Wikipedia, an acknowledged biased resource that drives much of the truth of all LLMs. Wikipedia has responded by promising to clean house and fix the bias.

Data is the key input for teaching models to generalize and get smart, helping AI spot patterns, predict, and handle new things. Without varied, good data, models "overfit." They end up memorizing details but flopping on fresh stuff, like cramming for a test without understanding. In 2025, world data hits 180 zettabytes, with AI using 90% for training. This builds generalization, where models use rules widely, like human thinking. For smarts, data sparks new behaviors: big language models on huge texts show reasoning, creativity, even empathy.

Elon Musk notes the rush: "Almost every company doing AI, from startups to some of the biggest corporations on Earth, was scraping vast amounts of data." It shows that data is rare amid plenty. Tons exist, but cleaned, labeled sets are a treasure. As models grow, data needs explode; a 2025 study says generative AI will need 134 terawatt-hours by 2027, much of which is for data work. By 2030, data could be the new oil, with private sets worth trillions, pushing AI smarts.

Data types differ, each with a role. Structured data, like spreadsheets or databases, is neat and searchable. It's simple to use, but it only represents 20% of the world's data. Unstructured rules at 80%, covering text (emails, articles), images, sounds, and videos. This powers multimodal models like GPT-4o for a richer grasp.

Synthetic data, AI-made, fills holes: models create fake examples to boost real ones, easing labeled data shortages. In 2025, it makes 60% of the training sets, safe for privacy. Josh Miller says interfaces are common to all, but data sets the best apart: "Claude, Mistral, Gemini, etc. – feels like foundation models might commoditize... If so, then value in AI will accrue to the interfaces." Yet, synthetic plus unstructured pushes limits, making super-real training for rare cases.

Sources match types in a variety. Public sets like Common Crawl or ImageNet give free, huge stores. Common Crawl has 250 billion web pages. Scraping grabs live web info, but lawsuits grow; Musk called it "EXTREME levels of data scraping," leading to caps on access to X. User content from social, forums, and apps adds realness. X posts are at 500 million daily.

Private hoards, company-protected, offer top value for niches: Tesla's 160 billion daily video frames train driving. Future: Markets like Ocean Protocol that trade data on blockchain will be opening access. By 2035, personal data stores might let folks sell their info, fueling AI with control.

When creating AI models, several big problems can get in the way and slow down or stop the whole process. Think of these as roadblocks that threaten every step, from gathering information to training the AI. Let's break them down one by one in simple terms.

1. The Importance of Data Quality

At the heart of any AI is the data it's trained on, much like the ingredients in a recipe. If the data is messy, incomplete, or full of errors, the AI will produce unreliable results. There's a classic saying in tech: "Garbage in, garbage out" (or GIGO). That means if you feed bad data into the system, you'll get bad predictions or decisions out the other end. For example, an AI trying to detect diseases from medical scans might miss important signs if the images are blurry or wrongly labeled.

This isn't just theory. It's a huge issue right now. In 2025, nearly 70% of companies working on AI say poor data quality is holding them back from making real progress. They blame it for "blocks" like failed projects or wasted time fixing mistakes later.

2. Privacy Concerns and Regulations

Another major hurdle is protecting people's personal information. As AI uses more data about us (like our online habits or locations), privacy laws have gotten stricter to prevent misuse. Two big ones are GDPR in Europe, which stands for General Data Protection Regulation, and CCPA in California, the California Consumer Privacy Act. These rules require companies to get clear permission (consent) from users before collecting or using their data.

Break the rules, and the penalties are massive—billions of dollars in fines. For instance, in 2023, Meta (the company behind Facebook and Instagram) was hit with a record €1.2 billion fine by European regulators for illegally sending user data from Europe to the U.S. without proper safeguards. That's like a year's worth of profits for some businesses, and it forces them to rethink how they handle data.

3. The Shortage of Labeled Data

Many AI systems rely on "supervised learning," where the model learns by studying examples that have been tagged or labeled by humans—like marking photos as "cat" or "dog" to teach recognition. But high-quality labeled data is hard to find and super expensive to create. Labeling just one item can cost anywhere from a few cents to $1–$10, depending on how complex it is (simple tags are cheap, but detailed ones like drawing outlines around objects add up). For a massive dataset with billions of items, the cost turns into millions or even billions of dollars. Plus, finding enough people with the right expertise to do the labeling is tough, slowing down innovation.

In short, tackling these issues, clean data, strong privacy, and affordable labeling, is crucial for AI to succeed without causing harm or delays. By addressing them early, businesses can build trustworthy systems that benefit everyone.

Diverse, unbiased data is essential to prevent AI from making unfair decisions, similar to teaching a child with a balanced view of the world instead of only one side of the story. If the training sets are skewed, say toward certain demographics, the AI can end up discriminatory. Examples have made the news, such as facial recognition systems that perform poorly on people with darker skin tones because they were mostly trained on lighter-skinned faces.

This has real-world consequences, like in hiring tools that unfairly screen out minorities or white men or law enforcement tech that misidentifies individuals.

Andrej Karpathy, a leading AI researcher, has highlighted efficiency in running models but also points to underlying challenges: He noted that "llama.cpp surprised many people (myself included) with how quickly you can run large LLMs on small computers," like getting a 7-billion-parameter model to process about 16 tokens per second on a MacBook. However, this speed often bumps up against "data memory walls," where the sheer volume and complexity of data strain even optimized systems, forcing engineers to get creative with how data is stored and accessed.

Strategies for managing data are evolving quickly to address these issues, making the process more efficient and ethical. Curation tools automate the cleaning and labeling of data: For instance, Snorkel uses "weak supervision" techniques, where simple rules or heuristics generate labels automatically, speeding up the process by up to 10 times compared to manual labeling. Can you possibly imagine labeling thousands of photos by hand versus having a smart script do most of the work based on patterns?

Data augmentation expands datasets without collecting new information; techniques like rotating or flipping images, or rephrasing text in different ways, can grow the variety and make models more robust, improving performance by around 20% in tasks like image classification, much like practicing a skill with variations to handle real-life twists better.

Federated learning protects privacy by training models across decentralized devices, such as smartphones in users' pockets; instead of sending raw data to a central server, only model updates are shared, which complies with strict regulations like GDPR while still pooling collective knowledge. Compare that with a global study group where everyone learns locally and just exchanges summaries, keeping their personal notes private.

Differential privacy adds another layer of protection by injecting a bit of random noise into the data, making it hard to trace back to individuals without losing overall usefulness; companies like Apple and Google use this in features such as personalized recommendations or traffic predictions, ensuring your habits stay anonymous even as the system improves. Blockchain technology provides traceability, creating an unalterable record of data origins and changes, as seen in projects like Sentient AGI's data consortiums, where blockchain integrates with AI to build open, verifiable networks for sharing and monetizing data securely.

Looking ahead, leaders like Jensen Huang envision a future where, by 2040, autonomous AI agents will curate data in real-time through federated systems, ensuring ethical and efficient growth that scales globally without central control.

The connection to super intelligence runs deep: massive, real-time data streams allow for continuous learning, much like how humans absorb experiences throughout life to get smarter. Achieving super smarts requires endless evolution, with models constantly updating from sources like sensors, user conversations, and simulations. It is truly an AI that refines itself daily, adapting to new information without starting over. Agentic AI systems today act independently, like virtual assistants planning tasks. They handle unstructured data for greater autonomy, according to MIT trends that highlight this as a key shift in AI and data science. Mark Zuckerberg has emphasized related bottlenecks, noting that "energy constraints have become the largest bottleneck" to scaling AI, but he underscores data's foundational role in overcoming compute limits. Streams from the Internet of Things (IoT), projected to generate around 90 zettabytes annually by 2025 (one zettabyte equals about a trillion gigabytes, enough to store billions of movies) drive this adaptation, feeding AI with constant, diverse inputs from connected devices like smart thermostats or wearables.

For artificial general intelligence (AGI), data must span multiple fields, enabling a broad understanding. Blending synthetic and real data creates simulated worlds for safe training, like practicing driving in a video game before hitting the road. Elon Musk warns of limitations in "Human-created data being so small," pushing the field toward synthetic generation to fill the gaps. By 2050, technologies like brain implants could create direct links for data sharing, accelerating progress to artificial superintelligence (ASI) through collective human cognition, where minds and machines merge seamlessly for unprecedented insights.

Data's path from bits to wisdom supports the stack. From structured to synthetic, public to private, mastering overcomes roadblocks for super intelligence. Altman says, "AI tools will eliminate most of the tedious work in most jobs," but data art stays. Next: Software, the smart motor.

Part 5: Software

Software models are the pulsing heart of AI, changing hardware's raw force into smart grace. Yann LeCun warns, "The danger of AI is much more subtle than killer robots... It's in the way it can amplify human biases and be used for nefarious purposes."

Software includes algorithms and setups that turn hardware into smart systems, guiding data through nets to copy and beat human thought. At its core, it sets data flow in neural nets for patterns, choices, and change. Agentic AI mixes base models with self-planning, reshaping fields from health to finance. Without advanced software, top chips are dead silicon.

Software bridges the gap between hardware's raw power and real-world applications, evolving from simple rule-based systems—like early chess programs that followed strict if-then instructions—to emerging self-improving entities that learn and adapt on their own. Many postulate that software will soon reach full autonomy, with models capable of rewriting their own code to optimize performance, accelerating the path to superintelligence, much like a student who not only learns but also invents better ways to study.

The core elements begin with foundation models, which serve as the bedrock of modern AI. Large language models (LLMs) like OpenAI's GPT-5, released in 2025, process enormous amounts of text to handle language-related tasks, with their scaled-up parameters enabling advanced reasoning. This would be like feeding a model the equivalent of every book in a massive library so it can converse, write, or solve problems like a human expert.

Multimodal models go further by blending text, images, and audio; for example, Google's Gemini 2.5 scored an impressive 35 points at the 2025 International Mathematical Olympiad, reaching gold medal level by tackling complex proofs that combine visual diagrams and logical steps.

In 2025, private sector models dominate with about 90% of key models, up from around 60% in 2023 according to Stanford's AI Index, reflecting how companies like OpenAI and Google are outpacing academia in resources and speed.

Open-source efforts are booming too: Meta's Llama series and DeepSeek's models advance reasoning through reward-based verifiers, where the AI gets feedback to improve its logic, similar to a coach reviewing game footage. Apple focuses on grounded, safe AI with built-in content filters to avoid harmful outputs.

Multimodals like InternVL3 and Qwen3 are pushing the boundaries of vision-language integration, allowing AI to describe scenes or generate captions with unprecedented accuracy. Looking to the future, hybrid models that mix symbolic reasoning, rule-based logic with neural networks could emerge, paving the way for true general intelligence that handles both data-driven patterns and structured rules seamlessly.

Learning methods, or paradigms, determine how models acquire knowledge and skills. Supervised learning relies on labeled data for specific tasks, like using tagged photos to teach an AI to recognize cats versus dogs. Unsupervised learning uncovers patterns in unlabeled data, grouping similar items without guidance. Think of sorting a pile of mixed fruits by color and shape intuitively. Reinforcement learning (RL) optimizes through trial-and-error rewards, as seen in AlphaGo's victories, where it learned winning strategies by playing millions of games and getting points for successes.

Today, combining RL with self-supervised learning (SSL) is unlocking the next level: SSL extracts transferable features from raw data without labels, while RL sharpens decision-making, creating more versatile AI. Synthetic data amplifies this. AI-generated examples now fill about 60% of training sets, enabling privacy-friendly scaling by simulating scenarios without real user info. Iterative loops, such as online self-training in RL, use consistency checks for improvement signals, allowing endless refinement without external labels. See this as an AI practicing math problems and grading itself based on logical coherence. Geoffrey Hinton, often called the godfather of deep learning, reflects: "Deep learning is going to be able to do everything." Soon, self-generated curricula will dominate, where models design their own learning paths, iterating toward superhuman expertise across domains.

Frameworks and tools empower developers to build and deploy these models easily. Open-source libraries like Google's TensorFlow and Meta's PyTorch provide flexible building blocks. PyTorch leads with its dynamic graphs that allow quick experimentation, like tweaking a recipe on the fly while cooking. Proprietary systems, such as OpenAI's API or Microsoft's Azure ML, offer ready-to-use solutions with strong security features for businesses.

Hugging Face's Transformers library hosts over 500,000 models, democratizing access so anyone can download and fine-tune AI for their needs. Tools like LangChain help orchestrate complex workflows, chaining multiple models together for tasks like summarizing a document, then translating it.

Ilya Sutskever, a pioneer in AI, envisions its transformative power: "Superintelligence could solve all of humanity's problems." Future frameworks will auto-optimize code, with low-code platforms making AI creation accessible to non-experts, broadening who can innovate — like drag-and-drop apps turning hobbyists into app builders.

Scaling laws reveal how increasing model size and complexity leads to sudden, emergent skills. Performance improves predictably with more parameters, data, and compute, showing logarithmic gains in benchmarks. Essentially, doubling inputs yields steady but compounding improvements. Emergent abilities appear abruptly: small models might flop at basic math, but larger ones excel without explicit training. Current research into distributional scaling explores how data diversity influences these breakthroughs, contrasting with smoother, incremental progress in other areas.

This requires balancing hardware and data: models like OpenAI's o3 follow these laws, compounding abilities through optimized training. Limits exist, though. Test-time scaling via techniques like Kinetics highlights memory bottlenecks during inference, where real-time processing hits walls. In the not-too-distant future, new laws incorporating kinetics could guide efficient scaling for artificial superintelligence (ASI), going beyond current formulas to handle even more complex computations.

Ethical considerations are at the core of software development. Fighting bias involves addressing three main sources: skewed data leading to unfair outputs, development choices that embed prejudices, and interaction biases from user inputs. In healthcare, for instance, without diverse datasets, AI might perpetuate inequalities by underperforming for underrepresented groups.

Transparency in decisions is vital. Black-box models erode trust because you can't see how they arrive at conclusions, like a doctor who won't explain a diagnosis. Safety alignments through methods like reinforcement learning from human feedback (RLHF) steer models toward being helpful and harmless, but risks like unintended behaviors remain.

UNESCO's ethics initiatives push for guardrails against discrimination. In 2025, regulations are targeting bias in areas like loans and hiring, requiring audits to ensure fairness. Timnit Gebru warns: "AI is neither artificial nor intelligent... It's a tool built by people, reflecting their biases." In the future, built-in ethical layers along with global standards could ensure super intelligence is developed fairly and responsibly. Alternatively, governments or corporate players could interfere in ways that create clear biases, such as the DEI rules and ESG programs did in the past 10 years.

Integration with hardware through co-design boosts efficiency, optimizing how software runs on specific chips. In 2025, full-stack approaches like those discussed in Alphawave panels create AI-native platforms for scalable computing. Edge co-designs produce system-on-chips (SoCs) that save energy for devices like smartphones. Sustainable practices, via synergies between NVIDIA and AMD hardware-software, cut costs and reduce environmental impact.

In-memory computing accelerators further optimize by processing data where it's stored, speeding things up. Andrew Ng notes: "Much of the excitement about AI is about the progress in deep learning."

Quantum-neural hybrids through co-design will likely unlock efficiencies for ASI, combining quantum's speed with neural networks' pattern recognition.

Software propels the entire stack toward superintelligence. From foundational models to ethical safeguards, a balanced approach grows the benefits while mitigating risks. Next: Memory, reasoning, and inference—the core of cognitive abilities.

Part 6: Memory and Reasoning

Memory, reasoning, and inference are the key features that elevate AI from being a basic responder, like a simple search engine that just gives facts, to a true thinker that can then remember, plan, and act intelligently. Memory works through vector databases to enable contextual recall, much like how humans pull from past memories to make better decisions.

Reasoning uses methods like chain-of-thought or tree-of-thought to mimic logical deduction for solving puzzles. Inference optimizes how models run in practice, with tricks like quantization to cut down on delays. When combined, they create adaptive behaviors that adjust to new situations. There are challenges, such as scaling memory without bogging down the system or the heavy compute needs for reasoning. These three are helping bridge the gap to superintelligence. This section breaks down each one, how they connect, and the obstacles, mixing what's happening now with thoughts on the future. They're not optional extras. They're the foundation for genuine thought processes.

Memory systems give AI agents long-term storage and fast retrieval, allowing for ongoing learning that lasts beyond one session. Traditional models would lose everything after a task, but modern ones imitate human event recall—saving specific experiences for later, like jotting down notes from a meeting to reference next time.

Vector databases such as Pinecone or Milvus organize embeddings, which are math versions of data, for quick similarity searches. This powers retrieval-augmented generation (RAG), where AI grabs relevant details from massive collections to give better answers. This context memory has grown, enabling agents to hold onto details across chats for more tailored replies. Similar to having a chatbot that remembers your favorite topics from last week.

Episodic memory records a series of events, like DeepMind's setups that copy human planning by pulling from past simulations. Contextual recall blends short-term working memory, for quick thoughts, with long-term storage, using transformers' focus, but enhanced by outside databases to manage up to a million tokens of info. New curved neural networks, drawing from geometry in recent research, improve recall by working in bent spaces that highlight patterns better, a kind of curved mirror that brings distant connections into view. This ongoing learning lets AI refine itself over time, which is essential for superintelligence to evolve and handle new challenges.

Elon Musk says, "The most important thing is to reason from first principles rather than by analogy." For memory, this means basing recall on basic facts, not just loose matches. By 2027, brain implants might blend human and AI memory, forming hybrids with endless recall.

Reasoning tools copy human problem-solving and step-by-step planning, turning data into smart choices. Chain-of-thought (CoT) prompting splits issues into parts: Saying "Let's think step by step" can raise accuracy 20-30% in large language models for things like math. Versions like self-consistency, and then vote on several paths to choose the top one.

Tree-of-thought (ToT) branches out the options, checks them, and cuts bad ones for tough jobs like proofs, moving from straight lines to branching explorations for deeper understanding. Logical deduction mixes symbolic AI with nets to pull rules from data for provable results. For agents' multi-step plans, models like o1 use ToT-style reflection for extended goals.

Reasoning is central, letting AI fight finance or health issues with linked logic. Soon, hidden reasoning in embeddings could grow flexibly, fixing now-impossible problems.

Inference makes sure models run efficiently on hardware for instant use. Training is big, but inference leads today for fast apps. Optimizations save: Quantization drops from 32-bit to 8-bit precision, cutting memory 4x with tweaks to keep quality. Pruning clips extra weights, layer-wide or per-neuron, for 90% smaller vision models.

Andrew Ng says, "Much of the excitement about AI is about the progress in deep learning." These make it usable. In the near future, quantum could do chance-based tasks in a flash.

Integration creates flexible actions, linking software, data, and hardware. Memory boosts with outside stores, supplying reasoning. RAG plus CoT for fact-based steps. Inference deploys tuned on chips: Quantized via co-design, with streams for live changes. Agents use memory for history, reasoning for plans, inference for doing, and looping to learn.

Part 7: Applications

Applications are where the AI stack meets everyday life, turning theory into real value that affects daily routines and business profits.

As the top layer, they convert hardware power, software brains, data fuel, and energy stamina into tools that fix issues, boost creativity, and improve efficiency. For instance, compare with the user-friendly apps on your phone that hide all the complex tech underneath. Consumer apps, like smart helpers and self-driving cars, make AI feel personal, while business ones optimize supply chains and health checks at scale. But gains like higher productivity come with downsides such as job changes, ethical tightropes, and reliance on the stack's reliability.

This overview covers applications, diving into consumer and enterprise areas, weighing pros and cons, and highlighting examples. Mixing today's realities with forward-thinking ideas, applications aren't the end; they're the human-AI interface leading to super intelligence.

Consumer-facing applications put super intelligence right in your pocket, home, or car, making things smarter and more intuitive. Virtual assistants like Siri or Alexa have become proactive companions: They anticipate needs using contextual memory, reminding you of groceries based on fridge sensors or scheduling workouts from your health data, like a helpful friend who knows your habits. Google's Gemini and Apple's Intelligence integrate multimodal inputs, handling voice, text, and images for seamless interactions.

Personalized recommendations power platforms like Netflix or Amazon, where AI sifts through viewing habits and purchase history to suggest content with about 30% higher engagement. It's like having a personal curator who gets better over time by learning what you love.

Spotify's AI DJ curates playlists in real time, learning from skips and saves to match your mood perfectly, turning music discovery into an effortless experience. Creative AI tools stand out: Image generators like Midjourney V6 or DALL-E 3 create photorealistic art from simple text prompts, and with recent updates, they can even produce videos, allowing anyone to become a digital artist without years of training.

Chatbots, from Grok to ChatGPT, offer companionship, tutoring, or even therapy. OpenAI's GPT-5 handles nuanced conversations, adapting via episodic memory for personalized advice that feels truly attentive.

Autonomous vehicles are leading the way: Tesla's Full Self-Driving (FSD) 13, rolled out in mid-2025, uses end-to-end neural nets for safer navigation, reducing accidents in tests compared to earlier versions, like a vigilant driver that's always improving through data from millions of miles. (FSD 14, which Elon Musk describes as human-like, is being released even as I edit this chapter.)

These apps democratize super intelligence, but at what cost? Elon Musk warns: "AI will eventually create a situation where 'no job is needed'." For consumers, it's empowerment; for society, it could lead to dependency if systems fail.

The time is coming when consumer AI will blur lines with augmented reality. AR glasses will be overlaying personalized data on the world, turning every interaction into an intelligent one. But this requires a reliable stack; a hardware glitch could strand your self-driving car mid-trip.

Enterprise applications harness super intelligence for a business edge, focusing on scale, precision, and return on investment.

Predictive analytics forecast trends: IBM's Watson analyzes sales data to predict demand with high accuracy, minimizing stockouts and keeping shelves full without excess. In finance, JPMorgan's AI models market movements, processing terabytes of data for high-frequency trading decisions that happen in split seconds.

Supply chain optimization is a highlight: AI from SAP or Oracle uses reinforcement learning to reroute shipments in real time, cutting costs amid disruptions like 2025's port strikes. Think of it as a smart GPS for global logistics that can save companies significant amounts through efficient planning.

Automated decision-making streamlines operations: McKinsey reports AI automating around 45% of tasks in manufacturing, from quality checks to inventory management, freeing workers for more complex roles. Industry-specific apps excel. Healthcare diagnostics via PathAI spot cancers early with high precision on scans, often outperforming human pathologists in detecting subtle signs, while financial modeling at Goldman Sachs simulates scenarios with multimodal data for better risk assessment.

ERP systems like those from Salesforce embed AI for end-to-end automation, predicting maintenance in factories or personalizing customer service to boost satisfaction. In 2025, enterprise adoption has hit around 78%, per McKinsey, driven by agentic AI handling multi-step workflows. Andrew Ng calls it: "AI is the new electricity." It powers growth, but requires vast data and compute tied back to the stack's base.

Looking ahead, I see enterprises achieving "AI factories," where super intelligence iteratively optimizes every process, from R&D to HR.

The benefits of these applications are profound: Enhanced productivity frees humans for creative work, with AI boosting global GDP by around $15.7 trillion by 2030, per PWC estimates. Innovation accelerates! Consumer creative tools democratize art, while enterprise analytics unlock insights from data silos. In healthcare, AI diagnostics save lives by catching diseases early. In autos, safer roads could reduce fatalities significantly, but autonomous vehicles could eliminate 90% or more.

50% of court cases are vehicle accident-related. The reduction in injuries and deaths will have a massive impact on crowded court dockets and will clearly reduce the number of billable hours for lawyers.

Yet risks lurk. Job displacement looms: AI could automate the equivalent of 300 million roles by 2030, per Goldman Sachs, sparking the need for reskilling programs. Ethical dilemmas arise. Dependency on the stack's reliability is critical: A data breach or hardware failure could halt operations, as seen in 2024's CrowdStrike outage affecting millions.

Privacy erodes with pervasive tracking, and over-reliance might dull human skills. Benefits can outweigh if managed well, but unchecked risks could widen divides. Regulations will mandate "AI impact audits," balancing innovation with safeguards.

Examples illustrate integration's power. For consumers, smart homes via Google Nest or Amazon Echo weave the stack: Hardware sensors collect data, software reasons on patterns, memory recalls preferences, and you end up with lights, thermostats, and security adjusting autonomously. These systems predict energy use, saving around 20% on bills while enhancing comfort.

In enterprise, ERP like SAP S/4HANA embeds AI: Predictive analytics on supply data optimizes chains, automated decisions route workflows, with reasoning for scenario planning. Unilever uses it to forecast demand, reducing waste in its supply chain. These platforms tie hardware efficiency, data streams, and software models into cohesive value.

Yoshua Bengio warns of two potential outcomes: "AI could be the best or worst thing to happen to humanity." Examples show the potential, but ethical deployment is key.

Applications deploy super intelligence, from personal aides to business brains. Benefits like a productivity surge stand against risks of displacement and ethics. Breakthroughs focus on responsible integration, or squander the promise. Next: Tying it all with integration's glue.

Part 8: Integration

Integration is the glue that holds the AI stack together. Without it, you have brilliant individual pieces that don't connect well and end up underperforming, like a puzzle with missing edges. Vertical integration across all layers, from mining raw materials to the wonder of end-user apps, helps skip delays, shorten wait times, and ramp up overall performance. Investing in integration and user-friendly designs is essential. This involves creating smooth connections, APIs, and complete optimizations that make the system work better and feel natural, as if everything was designed to fit perfectly from the start.

Examples like Tesla's unified approach show how this outperforms scattered setups, proving that full control sparks fresh ideas. Suggestions include standards across layers, collaborative research, and user-focused designs to accelerate toward super intelligence. This section builds the case for unity, pulls in key insights, examines real cases, and offers paths forward. Blending today's realities with bold predictions, integration isn't an add-on. It's the key to unlocking AI's full potential.

Vertical integration means owning or tightly controlling the entire pipeline: mining rare earths, fabricating chips, generating energy, curating data, building software, adding memory, reasoning, and inference for advanced smarts, and rolling out apps, all in-house or through close partners. This avoids chokepoints; for instance, a slowdown in mining leads to chip shortages, which then stall software training and app launches. Split or fragmented stacks waste 20-30% of efficiency on mismatches, according to industry reports. Full control synchronizes everything: optimized data flows directly to custom models running on proprietary hardware, powered by dedicated energy sources, allowing apps to adapt smoothly without hiccups.

The benefits are clear: lower costs through in-house synergies. Tesla, for example, saves billions by controlling everything from batteries to software updates. It's faster too: end-to-end tuning can halve inference wait times, which is crucial for real-time applications like self-driving cars, where every fraction of a second counts. Innovation flourishes in owned stacks, like Apple's chip-software blend that delivers twice the battery life for AI features, turning devices into longer-lasting powerhouses. Without this, dependencies create weakness. Supply chain hits or incompatible APIs can slow progress to a crawl, like a team where players aren't passing the ball effectively.

Today, the AI boom has amplified these advantages: hyperscalers like Google integrate from TPUs to apps, capturing 40% more value by keeping everything aligned. Fragmentation, on the other hand, results in 15% higher failure rates in deployments due to mismatched layers causing errors. Vertical setups ease risks, building strength against things like mining politics or energy shortages. Jensen Huang puts it well: "AI's advantage going into 2025 is vertical integration." For super intelligence, this unification scales thinking power: integrated memory and reasoning draw from optimized data and hardware, enabling adaptive behaviors without any breaks in the flow.

The case grows stronger with sustainability in mind: integrated stacks optimize energy across layers, cutting carbon footprints by 25% through efficient flows from mining to apps. Ethically, it enables end-to-end bias checks, spotting issues from data collection all the way to app outputs.

Without vertical control, problems like incompatible APIs waste compute resources. 2025 data shows 35% of AI projects fail due to integration hurdles. Looking ahead, fully integrated "AI ecosystems" could self-optimize, autonomously tweaking layers for ASI-level efficiency, like a living system that evolves on its own.

Seamless interfaces, intuitive user interfaces that hide the complexity, boost adoption by three times, per User Experience (UX) studies, making advanced tech feel approachable. APIs allow plug-and-play functionality: OpenAI's endpoints let models snap into apps without friction, speeding up development like Lego blocks clicking together. End-to-end optimization fine-tunes every part: from AI-optimized mining extraction to apps' real-time thinking, delivering 40% performance gains overall.

This kind of investment pays off: user-centric designs, such as Tesla's over-the-air updates, improve experiences while looping in data for continuous refinement. In enterprise settings, SAP's integrated ERP-AI stacks streamline workflows, saving billions in operational costs by automating routine tasks. For super intelligence, seamless UX makes complex cognition easy. Imagine querying an ASI intuitively without needing to code. Sam Altman echoes this: "AI's potential is in the way it can amplify human ingenuity." Skipping it risks clunky systems that push users away and stall widespread use.

Case studies highlight vertical integration's edge. Tesla is a prime example: controlling mining through lithium deals, hardware like Dojo chips, energy via Megapacks, data from fleet videos, software with FSD neural nets, cognition for navigation reasoning, and apps in the car UI. This stack powers Robotaxi launches in 2025, offering safer autonomy. Efficiency shines through: Vertical control cuts costs and enables rapid iterations. FSD processes billions of daily frames seamlessly. Musk's synergies via xAI blend Tesla data with Grok models for predictive maintenance, creating a closed loop that keeps improving.

Apple follows a similar path: from silicon in A-series chips to software in iOS Intelligence, data through user privacy vaults, and apps like Siri 2.0. 2025's updates integrate multimodal reasoning for proactive help, with on-device inference ensuring privacy. This results in twice the battery life for AI tasks, outperforming fragmented Android competitors.

OpenAI is pursuing the same: custom chips with Broadcom and TSMC reduce reliance on NVIDIA, integrating with Azure for full end-to-end model deployment.

In contrast, fragmented ecosystems struggle: Many startups depend on third-party clouds, APIs, and hardware, leading to 25% higher latencies and frequent bugs. For example, 2025's chip wars delayed AI rollouts by months for some firms due to supply mismatches. Keith Rabois notes: "Vertical integration is a fancy term for going full-stack." Fragmented players innovate more slowly, as misaligned layers cause inefficiencies. Tesla's stock surge after going public contrasts sharply with laggards stuck in silos. Vertical approaches win by controlling their destiny, fostering fast feedback loops that drive continuous improvement.

Recommendations chart a clear path: Cross-layer standards like Open Neural Network Exchange (ONNX) for model interoperability ensure smooth handoffs between hardware and software, reducing compatibility issues. Collaborative R&D through consortia, such as MLCommons, pools resources for shared benchmarks, speeding progress without isolated efforts. Focus on user-centric design: Prioritize intuitive UX with A/B testing to create interfaces that hide complexity, making AI feel effortless.

In practice, adopt modular APIs for flexibility while building vertical alliances. xAI's recent $10B raise funds these ecosystem synergies. Ethically, standards should include audits across layers to catch biases early, preventing them from spreading. Collaborative work can mitigate the worst outcomes. The future is likely to include global "AI alliances" standardizing stacks, propelling ethical superintelligence forward.

Integration unifies the expanded stack, from the earth's depths to app interfaces. Vertical control dodges common pitfalls, as Tesla, Google, and Apple prove compared to fragments. Invest in seamless UX for massive performance leaps. With standards, R&D, and user focus, we can accelerate responsibly. Or we risk fragmenting the future. As Huang says: "We need a simulation engine that represents the world digitally." United stacks are what build that world.

***

Chapter 13

Energy: The Unsung Hero (or Villain) of the AI Stack

Randy Kirk

Energy might not grab headlines like flashy AI models or cutting-edge chips, but it's the silent powerhouse, or potential Achilles' heel, of the entire superintelligence stack. Think about it: without abundant, reliable power, all the hardware, data, and software in the world grind to a halt. As AI scales to unprecedented levels, energy emerges as the often-overlooked limiter, capping how fast we can push toward systems that outthink humans across every domain. Elon Musk nails it when he warns, "The biggest constraint for AI is actually the supply of talent and the supply of electricity and the supply of chips." But as chip shortages ease, electricity steps into the spotlight as the next big bottleneck.

This energy equation extends deeper, forming a chain where **energy equals tokens equals knowledge equals wealth**. As Mark Zuckerberg points out, energy constraints are the real hurdle before compute limits kick in fully. Tokens, the basic units of AI computation, embody this intelligence, with costs tied closely to power efficiency. These affordable tokens unlock vast knowledge, accelerating discovery and innovation. Ultimately, this cascades into wealth creation, as Elon Musk envisions a future of radical abundance enabled by overcoming these bottlenecks. In essence, abundant energy fuels cheaper tokens, which democratize knowledge and generate unprecedented economic value.

This chapter dives into energy's pivotal role, blending today's realities with bold predictions for tomorrow. We'll explore the surging demands of data centers, innovative fixes on the horizon, nagging sustainability worries, and game-changing breakthroughs that could unlock unlimited clean power. Whether you're new to the energy side of AI or already tracking grid strains, this is where the rubber meets the road, or rather, where electrons fuel the revolution.

The Current Landscape: AI's Insatiable Hunger for Power

In the current landscape, AI's energy appetite is nothing short of voracious, transforming sleepy server farms into power-hungry behemoths that rival entire cities in consumption. Data centers, the beating hearts of AI training and inference, are guzzling gigawatts like never before. Globally, these facilities consumed around 415 terawatt-hours (TWh) in 2024, about 1.5% of worldwide electricity.

The International Energy Agency (IEA) emphasizes this surge, noting that AI is set to drive electricity demand from data centers to more than double by 2030, reaching around 945 TWh worldwide, equivalent to Japan's current total power consumption. In the U.S. alone, data centers could account for up to 12% of electricity use by 2028, up from 4% today, with BloombergNEF forecasting demand rising from 35 gigawatts (GW) in 2024 to 78 GW by 2035.

AI-specific workloads are the culprits: training a single large model like GPT-5 can burn energy equivalent to the annual consumption of thousands of households. For perspective, one AI video generation model could use over 700 times more energy per clip than its predecessor, and Goldman Sachs estimates global electricity demand from data centers could increase 50% by 2027 and up to 165% by the end of the decade. Worth noting, is that while all these experts reach different estimates for energy demand, they all point to massive increases in a short time.

Specialized GPUs, essential for AI, amplify this: they sip far more power than traditional servers, with power densities soaring to levels that make old-school cooling systems obsolete. By mid-2025, AI data centers might need an extra 10 gigawatts (GW) of capacity, more than Utah's entire power grid. States like Arizona already see data centers hogging 7.4% of energy, straining local grids, and prompting utilities to scramble for upgrades. Vijay Gadepally, senior scientist at MIT's Lincoln Laboratory, highlights the escalation: "The power required for sustaining some of these large models is doubling almost every three months... A single ChatGPT conversation uses as much electricity as charging your phone, and generating an image consumes about a bottle of water for cooling."

As AI infiltrates everything from chatbots to autonomous factories, this demand isn't slowing; it's accelerating, potentially pushing U.S. power use to record highs of 4,193 billion kWh in 2025, according to the Energy Information Administration (EIA). Deloitte's 2025 AI Infrastructure Survey underscores gaps in grid capacity, with data centers potentially requiring $6.7 trillion worldwide by 2030 to keep pace.

Training large models exemplifies the scale: a 2025 study shows generative AI could require up to 134 TWh by 2027, with individual runs rivaling small cities' energy use. The International Monetary Fund (IMF) projects that under current policies, AI-driven electricity demand could add 1.7 gigatons in global greenhouse gas emissions between 2025 and 2030, highlighting the intertwined nature of growth and environmental impact.

Water adds another layer. Cooling these beasts demands billions of liters annually, exacerbating scarcity in dry regions like the American Southwest, where data centers already compete with agriculture for resources. Elon Musk reflects on the stakes: "AI will run out of electricity and transformers in 2025."

Without addressing this now, super intelligence remains a pipe dream, throttled by outdated infrastructure. The IMF further details that in a medium-demand scenario, U.S. server farms could need over 600 TWh by 2030, equivalent to powering entire countries, while the American Council for an Energy-Efficient Economy (ACEEE) warns that AI-driven data centers could consume up to 9% of U.S. electricity by 2030, akin to the power needs of 40 million homes. And with Google alone planning $75 billion on AI infrastructure in 2025, the pressure is mounting fast, forcing utilities to rethink everything from transmission lines to peak-load management. Morgan

Lewis notes that U.S. power consumption is expected to reach record levels in 2025 and 2026, driven by AI and cryptocurrency, with data centers projected to demand up to 130 GW (or 1,050 TWh) by 2030, representing close to 12% of total U.S. electricity. Columbia University's Center on Global Energy Policy estimates AI data centers could require approximately 14 GW of additional new power capacity by 2030, and if the U.S. follows global trends, this could skyrocket. Schneider Electric's 2030 AI power demand scenarios range from about 16 GW to 65 GW, underscoring the uncertainty and potential upward bias in projections. Deloitte's estimates suggest U.S. AI data center power demand could grow more than thirtyfold to 123 GW by 2035, while Nature reports that data centers' electricity consumption is projected to more than double by 2030. This isn't just numbers. It's a wake-up call for infrastructure that's already creaking under the load.

Innovations on the Horizon: Taming the Beast

Innovations are rising to meet the challenge, starting with renewable sources weaving into AI infrastructure in clever, integrated ways that go beyond simple greenwashing.

Solar and wind are leading the charge. By 2030, they could cover half of data center growth, with hyperscalers like Google and Microsoft hitting 100% renewable matching in some operations. Trinasolar's platforms coordinate solar, batteries, and AI loads for seamless integration, optimizing output to match peak AI demands.

In Europe, 'Green Data centre' standards mandate 100% renewables by 2032, pushing innovations like AI-driven predictive maintenance for panels. AI itself optimizes this: algorithms adjust loads based on renewable availability, cutting waste by up to 40%, as seen in Fluence's systems that enable AI decarbonization through smart storage.

Solar Energy Industry Association (SEIA)'s Q2 2025 report highlights how AI is driving solar recovery, with hyperscale arrays popping up in sunny locales like Texas and California, where Intersect Power plans to break ground on an additional 4 GW of solar PV and 10 GWh of battery storage in 2025, representing ~$9B of assets. Deloitte's 2025 outlook notes AI reshaping solar/battery supply chains, with MarketsandMarkets projecting the energy storage market to hit $620B by 2025.

Efficient cooling systems are another frontier, evolving rapidly to handle the intense heat from densely packed AI servers. Traditional air cooling falters under AI's heat. Liquid cooling, either direct-to-chip or immersion, is surging, enabling higher densities while slashing energy by 30-40%.

Airedale by Modine's AI-enhanced optimizer reduces consumption by 40% in high-density setups, and nVent's 2025 liquid cooling best practices emphasize how it achieves required temperature parameters for next-gen IT while lowering overall energy use.

Microsoft's zero-waste water designs and AWS's liquid rollouts signal a shift, with liquid-cooled capacity hitting 15 GW globally by 2028. Heat reuse, channeling waste warmth to nearby buildings, adds sustainability, turning data centers into community assets, as demonstrated in projects where excess heat warms greenhouses or district heating systems.

POWER magazine reports that bio-based fluids can match or exceed fossil-based glycols, contributing less to energy consumption and emissions, while Carnegie Mellon University's breakthrough thermal interface material cools chips better than state-of-the-art solutions. Google DeepMind has reduced energy consumption in data centers by 30% using AI for better cooling predictions, showcasing how machine learning can fine-tune systems in real-time.

Low-power chip designs complete the trifecta, with a wave of innovations aimed at squeezing more compute from less electricity. NVIDIA's competitors, such as Groq, boast AI chips that run 3–6 times faster while consuming just a fraction of the power. In parallel, edge AI devices like NVIDIA's Jetson and Google's Coral emphasize energy efficiency, and emerging analog chips promise up to 20 times better performance per watt.

Techniques like model compression cut training energy by 90% with small tweaks, and IO+ discusses hardware-based views on energy efficiency, noting that researchers are tackling challenges through low-power chip innovations.

Priya Donti, MIT assistant professor, sees the upside: "Artificial intelligence could dramatically improve power systems... AI can accelerate power grid optimization by embedding physics-based constraints into neural networks, potentially solving complex power flow problems at '10 times, or even greater, speed compared to traditional models."

Network World warns that next-gen AI chips could draw 15,000W each by 2035, redefining power and cooling, but Korea Advanced Institute of Science and Technology (KAIST)'s roadmap suggests efficiency gains could offset this through advanced architectures. These advances could cap AI's energy spiral, but they demand upfront investment. Smart demand management, as Goldman Sachs notes, could forestall crises by pairing AI with storage for flexible loads, and Cummins highlights emerging trends like AI energy and cooling optimization. The World Economic Forum's report on AI's energy paradox calls for innovations like energy-efficient chips and AI-optimized cooling to balance challenges and opportunities.

Solutions in Fusion: The Holy Grail of Unlimited Power

Looking ahead, fusion energy promises a game-changer for AI's power woes, offering a path to clean, limitless power that could eliminate grid constraints entirely. Fusion, mimicking the sun's core by smashing atoms to release energy, provides unlimited output without fission's radioactive waste or renewables' weather dependency. Progress in 2025 is accelerating, with over $77 billion in global funding signaling commercial viability by 2030, as the Fusion Industry Association's report surveys 53 companies making strides.

Commonwealth Fusion Systems (CFS) leads the pack: In their July 2025 update, CEO Bob Mumgaard highlighted breakthroughs in high-temperature superconductors for their tokamak, aiming for net energy by late 2025. (Net energy refers to having more energy produced than the input. This is the holy grail of fusion.)

CFS's Smallest/Soonest Possible Affordable Robust Compact (SPARC) reactor could produce 50-100 MW, scalable for data centers, and Time magazine notes that clean energy from nuclear fusion may soon be commercial, with CFS building a futuristic machine outside Boston to replicate stellar energy. The Fusion Industry Association has requested a one-time $9.25 billion appropriation in the 2025 reconciliation package to advance these goals. International Thermonuclear Experimental Reactor (ITER), the international flagship, faces delays, but its non-opening in 2025 shifts action to private players, as Reddit discussions highlight. CFS hopes to pass Q=1 (net gain) by 2027, with ITER targeting Q>10 long-term.

China takes the lead, with the Chinese Academy of Sciences (CAS) announcing in January 2025 that its Experimental Advanced Superconducting Tokamak (EAST) experimental tokamak ran for more than 1,000 seconds, a record for steady-state operation. Energy Singularity reports China leading the race for nuclear fusion, with frequent technological breakthroughs in 2025 pushing competition white-hot. Japan's updated national strategy in June 2025 targets industrialization by 2030, while General Fusion eyes grid connection by the early 2030s with magnetized target fusion.

MIT's Plasma Science & Fusion Center (PSFC) will receive a cyclotron by the end of 2025 for materials testing, speeding fusion's path to market, and ARPA-E's 2025 meeting showcased teams closing the net gain gap. Wikipedia notes progress toward fusion energy breakeven as measured against the Lawson criterion, with China's advancements in records and innovations leading the race.

For AI, fusion means dedicated reactors powering hyperscale centers emissions-free, as the Clean Air Task Force's report on fusion on the grid envisions. Elon Musk's xAI pushes fusion hybrids, envisioning abundance. Challenges remain; net gains are elusive. By 2040, fusion could deliver zero-carbon, always-on AI, unlocking ASI without grid strain, as Econopolis sees it as a welcome change in energy landscapes.

Solutions in Fission: Reliable Nuclear for the Now

While fusion dreams big for the long haul, fission offers immediate, proven solutions with its unwavering reliability and low emissions profile. Nuclear power's 24/7 baseload capability makes it perfect for AI's relentless demands, boasting capacity factors over 90%, far surpassing intermittent sources like solar or wind, and providing steady power without the variability that could crash critical computations.

Goldman Sachs sees nuclear as key for AI, with small modular reactors (SMRs) deployable quickly near data centers, attracting $10B from tech giants. Deloitte notes its attractiveness for rising demand, low emissions, and the resurgence driven by AI. Equinix's August 2025 deals procure 500 MW from Oklo's SMRs, while Amazon signs for modular reactors to hit carbon-zero.

Oklo, a leader in advanced reactors, signed a non-binding Master Power Agreement with data center developer Switch to deploy 12 GW of Aurora powerhouses over 20 years, as announced in December 2024, but advancing in 2025.

Google inked for seven SMRs delivering 500 MW by 2030-35, and Microsoft eyes restarts of old plants like Three Mile Island to fuel AI. Deep Fission's 15 MW capsules could power 2 GW for AI on small footprints, ideal for hyperscale needs. International Atomic Energy Agency (IAEA) highlights SMRs for flexible, clean power, and Introl reports 22 GW in development globally, with first units online by 2030.

Nuclear Business Platform lists 10 major developments for 2025, including first operational SMRs for data centers from Deep Fission or Endeavor. Oklo and Vertiv collaborate on nuclear data center power and cooling, with Oklo's SMRs paired with advanced tech.

Investors.com notes nuclear energy stocks entering 2025 on a high, with AI data centers needing power, and Oklo stock surging 298% since announcements. The Bulletin of the Atomic Scientists discusses AI going nuclear, with tech giants turning to old reactors and planning new ones for energy-hungry centers. 24/7 Wall St. calls Oklo the nuclear stock powering AI's future, with SMRs producing up to 75 MW. Data Center Frontier reviews 2024's re-energizing of nuclear, foretelling 2025 developments like Oracle's SMR plans.

Third Bridge explores data centers going nuclear for AI, and POWER magazine discusses the SMR gamble to fuel the boom. Georgetown Journal of International Affairs examines AI's energy demands and nuclear's uncertain future, noting Microsoft's Three Mile Island deal. Fission bridges to fusion, ensuring uptime the AI boom, with profits on the horizon as deployments scale.

Solutions in Solar and Battery: Harnessing the Sun's Abundance

Solar paired with battery storage offers scalable, green solutions for AI's intermittency challenges, providing a decentralized alternative that can be deployed rapidly and cost-effectively. The EIA projects solar and batteries leading U.S. additions in 2025, with 18.2 GW of utility-scale batteries coming online, driven by AI needs.

SEIA's Q2 2025 report: AI drives solar recovery, with hyperscale arrays and billions pumped into solar + storage by AI leaders like Google, which has 312 MW of storage. Sol-Ark's hybrid systems pair solar with BESS (Battery Energy Storage System)for reliable datacenter power, and Fluence explains how energy storage enables AI decarbonization.

FlexGen discusses unlocking fast interconnection for AI data centers with battery storage, making flexible setups feasible. Power Technology explores how energy storage and battery deals enable AI data centers, with new structures ensuring resilience. Fierce

Network asks if batteries are the next big thing for data center power, beyond backups. Clean Power's AI and battery energy storage intersection highlights predictive maintenance for large-scale Battery Energy Storage Systems (BESS). Forbes notes green energy's role in AI data centers, with renewables essential for low costs and demand. 174 Power Global details energy companies powering AI with solar, wind, and storage innovations. SolarFeeds covers hybrid systems combining solar with a battery for AI centers. Utility Dive reports data centers bringing alternative battery types like flow and zinc into the mainstream. Indiana Public Radio mentions natural gas and battery storage getting fast-tracked for AI in Indiana. Solar/battery democratizes AI energy, with Deloitte's survey examining infrastructure gaps.

Solutions in Natural Gas: The Bridge Fuel

Ntural gas will continue to play the pivotal role as a reliable bridge fuel, offering quick deployment and flexibility to meet AI's immediate power surges while cleaner options mature. Chevron highlights how natural gas is helping power AI, providing baseload support. Technology Review notes it's the default for AI data centers, keeping us dependent for decades. Data Center Dynamics (DCD) explains how natural gas is powering the U.S. AI boom, as the only viable, rapid source. Barnes & Thornburg discusses its growing role in hyperscale AI data centers.

Western Energy Alliance argues America needs natural gas for the AI boom. Deloitte finds half of data centers anticipate a greater natural gas role. Microsoft is open to gas with carbon capture, and S&P sees it as dominant for the surge. Gas ensures stability as a bridge to sustainable futures.

Conclusion: Powering the Path to Abundance

Energy isn't just sustenance. It's the enabler of superintelligence. From grid strains to fusion dreams, balanced innovation ensures progress without planetary cost. As Musk emphasizes, overcoming these hurdles is crucial. Collaborate now, or risk dimming AI's bright future.

***

Chapter 14

Chips and Data Centers—Building the Infrastructure for ASI

Nicholas Gibbs

In the race toward Artificial Superintelligence (ASI), machines that could surpass human intelligence in every conceivable domain, the glamour often falls on revolutionary algorithms and transformative models. Yet, the true enablers are far more tangible: the silicon chips that perform trillions of computations per second and the sprawling data centers that house them. Imagine chips as the "neurons" firing in an AI's brain, processing information at lightning speed, while data centers are like massive power plants fueling an entire city's worth of thinking machines. Without this hardware backbone, ASI remains a distant vision; with it, we edge closer to reality.

As we near the end of 2025, the semiconductor industry is experiencing explosive growth, driven by AI's insatiable demand for computational power. Global semiconductor sales are projected to reach approximately $697 billion in 2025, reflecting an 11-15% increase from 2024, with AI and high-performance computing as primary catalysts. This surge isn't just economic expansion; it's the fuel for AI's exponential leaps. Each advancement in chip technology, such as denser circuits, faster speeds, and greater efficiency, directly accelerates progress toward ASI.

Scale is the name of the game, but it's not without hurdles. Nations with resilient supply chains, companies wielding proprietary technologies, and ecosystems integrating automation will dominate. Those falling behind risk irrelevance in an era where compute power is the ultimate currency. Constructing this infrastructure demands trillions in investments for fabrication plants (fabs), power-guzzling data centers, and intelligent automation systems. As AI models grow to trillions of parameters, the call for specialized chips and hyperscale facilities intensifies. Tech behemoths like Google, Tesla, and Amazon are even crafting custom silicon, challenging incumbents like Nvidia and reshaping the landscape.

However, the story isn't limited to these giants. Competitors like AMD, Intel, and Broadcom are making significant strides, while Chinese firms such as Huawei and SMIC are advancing rapidly despite geopolitical tensions. National security concerns, particularly around US-China relations and export controls, add layers of complexity. The sheer scale of investments, projected to reach $7 trillion globally by 2030 for data centers alone, highlights the frenzy, but building out massive compute clusters faces daunting challenges: power shortages, cooling inefficiencies, supply chain vulnerabilities, talent gaps, and environmental impacts.

This chapter unpacks these foundational elements, from booming chip production to energy-hungry data centers, automation's efficiencies, and the disruptive rise of custom chips. We'll spotlight Tesla's mid-2025 pivot from its Dojo supercomputer to integrated AI6 hardware via a $16.5 billion partnership with Samsung, the ongoing debate between generic and purpose-built chips, the indispensable role of real-world data, and the divergent needs of training versus inference. We'll also address global competition, including China's push for self-reliance, national security implications, investment scales, and buildout difficulties. Ultimately, we'll explore how these components are constructing ASI's framework, and who stands to thrive or falter.

Chip Production Growth: The Silicon Surge

Semiconductor foundries are the birthplaces of ASI's computational heart, where raw silicon wafers are transformed into intricate chips through processes involving extreme precision and cutting-edge physics. Taiwan Semiconductor Manufacturing Company (TSMC) leads as the world's premier contract chipmaker. In 2025, TSMC is accelerating expansions globally, with its Arizona project alone totaling $165 billion, encompassing six fabs, two advanced packaging facilities, and a research center. The first Arizona fab, ramping up in late 2024, now matches Taiwanese efficiency levels, aiding diversification amid geopolitical tensions. Notably, TSMC's Arizona subsidiary reported its first profit in the first half of 2025, earning approximately $150 million, a turnaround from the $140 million loss in the prior year.

This frenzy stems from AI's voracious needs. TSMC's Q2 2025 revenue soared to a record $30 billion, up 38% year-over-year, propelled by AI chip orders. Advanced process nodes like 3nm are seeing over 60% capacity expansion, serving AI, automotive, and high-performance sectors. By 2028, sub-2nm production in Taichung will further miniaturize transistors, packing billions more into a fingernail-sized space, reducing energy consumption while exponentially boosting AI training speeds.

Nvidia, the AI chip frontrunner, capitalizes on this with data center-optimized GPUs. At GTC 2025, CEO Jensen Huang highlighted enhancements to the Blackwell GPUs, offering up to 1.5x the performance in key metrics like NVFP4 (reaching 15 petaFLOPS per GPU) compared to the base Blackwell, with overall leaps of 30-40x over the Hopper generation in AI reasoning and HPC tasks, and availability from mid-2025. The upcoming Rubin architecture (2026) promises 3.3x Blackwell's prowess, integrated with advanced networking like ConnectX-9. Nvidia's HGX platform clusters GPUs with ultra-fast links, dominating AI workloads, while 800V High Voltage Direct Current (HVDC) adoption supports 1MW racks by 2027.

But Nvidia isn't alone. AMD is emerging as a formidable rival, with its Instinct MI350 series (CDNA 4 architecture) challenging Nvidia in data center GPUs, aiming for 15% market share by 2028 in a $485 billion AI accelerator market. Intel is pushing back with Xeon 6 processors, optimized for AI workloads and capturing share in data center CPUs, especially as hyperscalers adopt Arm-based alternatives. Broadcom, meanwhile, excels in custom AI ASICs and networking chips, shipping advanced solutions to speed AI data centers, with $4.12 billion in AI chip sales in 2025, up 77% year-over-year.

On the global stage, Chinese companies are advancing despite challenges. Huawei's Ascend 910C AI chip is set for mass shipments, positioning it as an Nvidia alternative, while SMIC ramps up 7nm production for Huawei, fostering self-reliance amid sanctions.

Technically, these advancements double or triple FLOPs per generation, enabling ASI-scale models to crunch petabytes of data with minimal latency. It's like upgrading from a bicycle to a supersonic jet for data processing. TSMC's scaling prevents supply bottlenecks, crucial for ASI timelines. Challenges persist: supply chain fragility, talent shortages, and escalating costs. But frontrunners like TSMC forecast 25-30% earnings growth.

The TSMC-Nvidia symbiosis exemplifies the ecosystem: TSMC fabricates Nvidia's chips, amplifying output for data centers. As AI evolves, this feedback loop intensifies. Better chips yield superior AI, demanding even more advanced silicon. In 2025, generative AI fuels record revenues. Yet, quality trumps quantity; process innovations extract maximum performance from silicon. Custom chips, however, could upend this balance, as explored next.

Global Competition and Geopolitics: China's Push and National Security Concerns

The chip race isn't confined to the US and Taiwan; China is a major player, investing billions to become an AI superpower despite or due to US export controls. Huawei and SMIC are at the forefront, with Huawei's Ascend 910C chip rivaling Nvidia's offerings, and SMIC producing advanced 5-7nm chips for AI applications. China's strategy emphasizes self-reliance, with state support accelerating progress in semiconductors, potentially capturing 55% of its AI chip market by 2027 from domestic suppliers.

National security looms large. US export controls, intensified under Biden and adjusted by Trump, aim to curb China's access to advanced AI chips, fearing military applications. In 2025, Nvidia and AMD agreed to pay 15% of China AI chip sales to the US government, blending economic and security interests. These measures slow China, Huawei limited to 200,000 AI chips in 2025, but spur innovation, like architectural efficiencies.

This means fragmented ecosystems. It's a high-stakes chess game where chips are pawns in global power plays. Winners navigate regulations; losers face blacklists, like Taiwan's on Huawei and SMIC.

Data Center Needs: The Power-Hungry Behemoths and Investment Scales

Data centers serve as ASI's operational hubs, vast warehouses of servers where chips execute their algorithms. But surging AI workloads impose monumental demands on power, cooling, and scalability. Globally, data center electricity consumption could double to around 945 TWh by 2030, potentially comprising 10-20% of worldwide demand depending on efficiency gains. In the U.S., AI data centers might require up to 123 GW of power capacity by 2035, over 30 times current levels, potentially equating to 9 to 12 percent of national electricity consumption.

Investments are ramping up at breakneck speed: $7 trillion globally by 2030 for data centers, with 2025 seeing Microsoft commit $80 billion, Meta $65-72 billion, and total AI infrastructure spending hitting billions more. This scale dwarfs previous tech booms, like building a new industrial revolution overnight.

Power Emerges as the Chief Constraint

Training a single large model can rival the annual energy use of hundreds of households. U.S. data centers are estimated at 224 TWh in 2025, escalating to 606 TWh by 2030. This strains grids, spurring innovations like Nvidia's 800V HVDC for high-density racks.

Cooling is equally vital. AI chips generate immense heat, potentially over 2,000W per chip by 2030. Traditional air cooling suffices for everyday computing but fails here; liquid cooling reduces overhead from 30-40% to 15-20%, akin to switching from a fan to an immersion bath for overheating engines. Water scarcity adds complexity, particularly in arid regions, but solutions like underground thermal storage mitigate peaks and costs.

To address environmental impacts, innovations in sustainability are accelerating. Renewable-powered data centers are on the rise, integrating solar, wind, geothermal, small modular nuclear reactors (SMRs), hydrogen fuel cells, and battery energy storage for 24/7 clean power. Carbon capture and storage (CCS) technologies are being deployed to decarbonize operations, with potential to capture up to 90% of emissions from backup generators or integrated processes, producing low-carbon "blue hydrogen" when combined with natural gas reforming. These advancements not only reduce carbon footprints but also enable data centers to achieve net-zero goals, with providers like Iron Mountain leveraging on-site solar and natural cooling for greener facilities.

Scalability favors modular "AI factories." Nvidia envisions 5MW blocks with real-time optimization, while billions pour into denser fiber optics and advanced cooling. Yet, building these clusters is fraught with difficulties: Supply chain bottlenecks delay deployments, talent shortages hinder operations, network congestion from bursty AI traffic causes failures, and environmental regulations slow permits. High costs beyond GPUs, memory, storage, networking, balloon budgets, and power imbalances lead to equipment damage or downtime.

Winners include efficient operators like AWS and Google; losers are power-deficient areas prone to delays or blackouts. These demands highlight the need for optimized architectures balancing throughput and efficiency. It's like building a city that never sleeps; without sustainable power, the lights go out. Addressing these ensures chips realize their potential, hastening ASI. Custom chips necessitate adaptable data centers, blending diverse designs seamlessly.

Automation's Role in Scaling

Automation acts as the invisible accelerator, evolving chip production from manual labor to ultra-precise orchestration. In fabs, robots manipulate wafers with micron-level accuracy, slashing defects and elevating yields by 10-20% in key processes. The global semiconductor automation market bolsters this, amid 11% industry growth in 2025.

Advanced process control (APC) and statistical tools monitor variances in real-time, ensuring uniformity in high-volume runs. Back-end packaging leverages optimized systems for breakthroughs in efficiency. Round-the-clock robotic assembly of circuits eliminates human fatigue, much like a tireless assembly line in a factory.

AI-driven predictive maintenance is a game-changer here, using machine learning to anticipate equipment failures before they occur, reducing downtime by 20-30% and extending machinery life. This is particularly crucial amid talent shortages, where a global skills gap in semiconductors could reach millions by 2030; automation offsets this by handling complex diagnostics that once required human experts, allowing fewer skilled workers to oversee larger operations.

In data centers, AI-driven automation dynamically manages power and cooling, forecasting loads to minimize waste. Think of it as a smart thermostat for a skyscraper. TSMC's expansions hinge on this to fulfill AI demands without proportional cost spikes.

Hurdles include integration failures in AI pilots, but robust data pipelines yield successes. Automation safeguards the industry's future, enabling swift scaling for ASI. Leaders like TSMC thrive; manually dependent firms lag. It also expedites custom chip prototyping, catalyzing market disruptions.

Custom Chips by Big Tech: The Long-Term Shift and Potential Disruption to Nvidia

Big Tech is forsaking generic silicon for tailored designs, fundamentally altering ASI's trajectory. Nvidia commands over 80% of data center accelerators, but custom chips from Google, Tesla, and Amazon pose a mounting threat. With billions invested, these optimize for proprietary workloads, trimming costs, enhancing efficiency, and curbing supplier dependency.

Google's TPUs spearhead this: Evolving for a decade, they fuel Gemini with 4x prior training speeds. The Cloud TPU v5p delivers up to 3x performance-per-watt versus GPUs for ML tasks. This curbs energy use, sidestepping additional data centers. Google has slashed Nvidia reliance, deploying TPUs for 90% of training.

Tesla pivoted dramatically in mid-2025: Disbanding the Dojo team in early August, deeming standalone Dojo 2 an "evolutionary dead end," with team leader Peter Bannon departing and engineers reassigned to other AI initiatives. Efforts consolidated on AI5/AI6 chips, with AI6 as Dojo's successor for unified training/inference across vehicles, Optimus robots, and data centers. Mass production slated for late 2026 through a $6.5 billion Samsung partnership at a dedicated Texas fab. This slashes costs (50% per FLOP savings) while leveraging Nvidia/AMD, preserving Tesla's real-world data advantage, and potentially unlocking trillions in value.

Amazon's Trainium (training) and Inferentia (inference) boast 30-50% cost reductions over Nvidia's H100, with 4x throughput and 10x latency improvements. In 2025, AWS deployed over 80,000 custom chips, promoting them to halve training expenses. Long-term, AWS eyes 20-30% market share from Nvidia by 2030.

Company	Custom Chip	Key Advantages	Cost Savings vs.	Nvidia Market Impact
Google	TPU v5p	3x perf and watt for ML; 4x training speed	Up to 50% energy and cost reduction	Reduced Nvidia reliance to less than 10% for training
Tesla	AI6	Unified for training and inference; video-optimized	50% per FLOP	Pivot from Dojo; hybrid with Nvidia and AMD, and Samsung
Amazon	Trainium and Inferentia	4x throughput, 10x lower latency	30-50% overall	Deployed 80K+ chips; aims for 20-30% market share

This fragmentation spurs innovation but risks isolated ecosystems. Nvidia's shares rose 18-24% in 2025, yet export restrictions and customs loom. Vertically integrated players like Tesla and Amazon gain; pure-plays like Nvidia may pivot to software or alliances.

Custom chips fine-tune for unique data, like Tesla's video feeds, hastening ASI breakthroughs where generics stumble.

Training vs. Inference Compute: Pillars of ASI Development

Think of building an AI system as educating a super-smart student: "training" is the intensive learning phase where the student absorbs massive amounts of information to build knowledge, while "inference" is the application phase where the student uses that knowledge to answer questions or solve problems in real time.

These two pillars form the computational foundation of Artificial Superintelligence (ASI), each with distinct demands on chips, data centers, and energy. We'll use everyday analogies to keep things clear, alongside specifics like FLOPs (floating-point operations per second, a measure of computational speed) and optimizations.

Understanding Training: Building the AI's "Brain"

Training is the resource-heavy process of creating and refining an AI model. It involves feeding vast datasets into the system, where algorithms adjust millions (or trillions) of internal parameters, called "weights", to recognize patterns, minimize errors, and learn complex tasks. Imagine it as a chef perfecting a recipe through endless trial and error: it takes time, ingredients (data), and a powerful oven (compute power).

In practice, training demands enormous computational muscle, often measured in exaFLOPs, a quintillion (10^18) operations per second. For example, xAI's Colossus supercomputer, one of the world's largest AI clusters, now boasts over 200,000 Nvidia GPUs to train models like Grok.. Frontier models in 2025, such as equivalents to GPT-5, require around 10^25 to 10^26 FLOPs, equivalent to running a supercomputer non-stop for months, and consume gigawatt-hours of energy.

For ASI, training must handle multimodal data (combining text, images, video, and more) using advanced techniques like Reinforcement Learning from Human Feedback (RLHF). Where humans guide the AI's decisions, and self-supervised learning, the model learns from unlabeled data to develop emergent abilities, like creative problem-solving.

Key bottlenecks and solutions include data scarcity, where high-quality data is hard to come by. Synthetic (AI-generated) data helps fill gaps, but real-world variety, from sensors or videos, is essential for robust learning. Energy and compute efficiency is addressed through innovations like mixed-precision training (using lower-bit formats like FP8 or FP4 instead of full 32-bit), which can reduce demands by up to 40% or more without losing accuracy, making massive scales more feasible.

Without overcoming these, ASI remains elusive. With them, we build the foundational "brain" capable of superhuman intelligence.

Understanding Inference: Putting the AI to Work

Once trained, the model moves to inference, the deployment phase, where it generates outputs based on new inputs, like answering a query or making a decision. This is like the chef serving the perfected dish: quicker and more repeatable, but it must happen efficiently at scale. Inference dominates real-world AI use, accounting for a growing share of workloads as models move from development to production, with projections showing it becoming the dominant driver by 2030.

Costs per operation are about 10x lower than training, but they explode with user volume, think billions of people querying an AI daily. For ASI, inference is crucial for recursive self-improvement: the system can query itself iteratively, refining its own capabilities in loops that mimic human reflection (someday in the future).

Priorities here shift from raw power to low latency (speed of response) and efficiency. Optimizations include quantization, reducing the precision of weights (e.g., from 32-bit to 8-bit) to speed up processing without much accuracy loss, boosting performance by 2-5x or more; and pruning, removing redundant parts of the model, like trimming dead branches from a tree, to make it leaner and faster.

Breaking Down Inference: The Sub-Markets of Prefill and Decode

Inference isn't monolithic; it splits into two key sub-processes, each optimized differently, like preparing ingredients (prefill) versus cooking step-by-step (decode).

Prefill is the initial setup where the model processes the entire input prompt to build a "memory cache" (key-value or KV cache) for quick reference. It's highly parallelizable and memory-intensive, perfect for high-throughput hardware like GPUs with advanced memory such as HBM3e, which deliver significantly faster processing for long contexts (e.g., analyzing thousands of words or data points at once) thanks to bandwidth up to 8 TB/s. In ASI scenarios, prefill handles complex queries, like sifting through petabytes of real-time data.

Decode is the step-by-step generation of outputs, like producing words one at a time in a response. It's sequential and latency-bound;

each step depends on the last, making it memory-access heavy. Specialized accelerators, such as Amazon's Inferentia, shine here with techniques like speculative decoding (guessing ahead and verifying later) to cut latency by up to 2-3x or more.

Hybrid systems smartly allocate resources: prefill to throughput-optimized clusters (e.g., Nvidia's HGX for batch jobs), and decode to latency-focused setups (e.g., Tesla's AI6 with adaptive precision tuning). This dichotomy creates distinct hardware markets, where unified chips like AI6 minimize switching overheads.

The Bigger Picture for ASI and Ongoing Challenges

Cumulatively, ASI might require up to 10^30 FLOPs or more, with inference taking the lion's share post-training, especially in swarms of AI agents making real-time decisions. Real-world data integration, like Tesla's vehicle feeds, supercharges these loops: training builds the foundation, inference enables dynamic application.

Yet challenges loom. Inference could drive AI to consume up to 10% or more of global power by 2030, as data centers balloon to 945 TWh annually. Scaling the KV cache for massive contexts is another hurdle, addressed by emerging in-memory computing that keeps data closer to processors for faster access.

In essence, training forges ASI's intelligence, but inference unleashes it. Balancing these will determine how quickly we reach superintelligence, efficiently powering the "thoughts" of tomorrow's god-like machines.

Generic vs. Purpose-Built Chips: What Will Prevail?

The debate between generic and purpose-built chips is like choosing between a Swiss Army knife and a specialized chef's blade: one does many things adequately, while the other excels at a specific task. This choice profoundly influences the path to Artificial Superintelligence (ASI), balancing flexibility with optimization.

Generic chips, such as Nvidia's GPUs, are the multitaskers of the hardware world. Designed for broad applications, from video games to scientific simulations, they offer programmability that allows quick adaptation to new algorithms without redesigning the hardware. This versatility drives economies of scale, making them cheaper and more accessible for startups and researchers alike.

However, this comes with trade-offs. In niche tasks, like processing vast video datasets, they may waste energy on unnecessary features, leading to higher power consumption. As custom alternatives rise, generics risk losing ground in high-stakes AI workloads.

Purpose-built chips, or Application-Specific Integrated Circuits (ASICs), are tailored for particular jobs, much like a race car engineered for speed on a specific track. Examples include Tesla's AI6, optimized for real-world video data, or Google's TPUs, fine-tuned for machine learning inference. These deliver peak performance: AI6 provides 5-10x efficiency gains for unstructured data streams, while TPUs achieve superior performance-per-watt in petabyte-scale tasks.

These chips offer superior efficiency, with lower energy use and faster processing for targeted domains, crucial for scaling ASI models. They enable advancements in areas like robotics, where brute-force compute from generics falls short. The cons are notable, however. High upfront costs and development time mean custom design can take years and billions, limiting agility. Then, if workloads evolve, they may require costly redesigns.

In the short term, purpose-built chips are propelling ASI precursors, such as superhuman robotics or domain-specific simulations. They embody the idea that ASI won't emerge from raw power alone but from hardware-software co-design aligned with real-world complexities.

Ultimately, neither pure generic nor purpose-built may dominate; hybrids could prevail. These combine generic cores for flexibility with specialized accelerators for efficiency, similar to modern System-on-Chips (SoCs) in smartphones. This approach offers the best of both worlds: broad applicability with targeted boosts.

The outcome hinges on ASI's path. If massive, diverse compute is essential (e.g., general problem-solving across domains), generics hold the edge. If specialized data processing is critical (e.g., ingesting and learning from sensory-rich environments), purpose-built designs like AI6 will lead.

As the industry evolves, expect a blend that accelerates ASI while minimizing drawbacks, driving innovation without silos.

The Path to ASI: Requirements and the Role of Real-World Data

Achieving Artificial Superintelligence (ASI), AI that outstrips human cognition in every domain, is like assembling a puzzle with pieces from technology, ethics, and the real world. It's not just about smarter algorithms; it demands a holistic convergence. Think of it as nurturing a seedling into a mighty tree: you need the right soil (data), sunlight (compute), and care (safeguards).

ASI requires more than hardware muscle. It demands algorithmic breakthroughs in recursive self-optimization, where AI improves its own code and processes; diverse data, with vast, varied inputs to train models that generalize like humans; robust hardware, including exascale computing (10^18 operations per second) to handle immense scales; ethical safeguards, with frameworks to ensure alignment with human values, preventing misuse; and continuous learning and embodiment, where AI learns on the fly and interacts with the physical world via robots or sensors. These elements must align for ASI to emerge safely and effectively.

Recent surveys of AI experts indicate a median timeline for AGI (Artificial General Intelligence, a precursor to ASI) around 2040-2050, with a 50% probability by then, though timelines are shortening due to rapid progress. ASI could follow shortly after. However, opinions vary: some predict AGI before 2030, while others see it decades later.

Optimists like OpenAI's Sam Altman are more bullish. In 2025 statements, Altman claimed that the "path to AGI is solved" and that OpenAI is now focusing on superintelligence, predicting AI agents joining workforces this year and transforming productivity. He views AGI as an evolving concept, but progress toward it as inevitable and accelerating.

Data quality is the linchpin. Current AI excels on curated, digital datasets, but ASI needs "open-endedness", learning from unstructured, dynamic environments like the real world.

This is a critical concept. Imagine that you had a disability that only allowed you to access the world through reading. No ability to see beyond the written page. No sense of sound, smell, taste, or touch.

Your worldview would be hugely limited. The day your disability was cured would create an awakening of amazing proportions. That is the stage of AI now, where real-world data is being added to the digital data.

Synthetic data (AI-generated) helps, but it's no substitute for messy, sensory-rich inputs that foster true generalization, creativity, and robustness.

Embodiment is key: Integrating AI with physical systems, like robots, overcomes digital limitations in reasoning, ethics, and adaptation. Without it, models suffer from "hallucinations" (fabricated outputs) and brittleness in novel scenarios.

Tesla holds a commanding lead here. Its AI4 chip is optimized for video and sensor data from over 6 million vehicles on the road, amassing billions of miles of real-world driving experience. Paired with Optimus robots, this creates powerful feedback loops: Real-world data refines the AI, which in turn deploys smarter agents to gather more data, accelerating toward ASI in domains like autonomy and robotics.

Competitors like Google and Amazon trail in embodied data scale, giving Tesla an edge in practical applications. However, risks abound: real-world data can embed societal flaws or infringe on personal rights; processing such volumes strains resources; and ASI's path requires global standards for safety and shared compute to mitigate silos and ensure equitable progress.

In summary, while hardware and algorithms are vital, real-world data is the bridge from narrow AI to superintelligent systems, turning theoretical potential into transformative reality.

In the end, this hardware backbone, chips as neurons, data centers as power plants, forms the indispensable foundation for ASI. As innovations in efficiency, sustainability, and automation converge, they not only overcome current hurdles but compress timelines, bringing us closer to a future where superintelligence reshapes everything. Those who master this infrastructure will lead the charge; the rest may watch from the sidelines.

***

NCIHOLAS GIBBS

Nicholas Gibbs is a dynamic engineer, technologist, and investor with a Marine Engineering degree from the United States Merchant Marine Academy and 10 years in the US Navy. His career spans oil exploration, data center design at a hyperconverged infrastructure pioneer, and AI implementation at the world's leading cloud platform. He runs the YouTube channel Investing Against the Grain, sharing contrarian investing views, and trains in CrossFit, emphasizing mind-body balance. Born in Chile, he lives in St. Petersburg, Florida, with his wife Anna and their baby boy. He values honesty and admitting errors.

Follow Nicholas Gibbs

@NickGibbsIAG

https://www.youtube.com/results?search_query=nicholas+gibbs+tesla

Chapter 15

Data— The Lifeblood of AI

Phil Beisel

Data is the lifeblood of today's AI, both indispensable and definitional. The modern era of AI began when massive datasets met neural networks, giving rise to systems that can detect patterns, make predictions, and generate outputs at scales previously unimaginable.

From language models parsing billions of words to autonomous vehicles interpreting streams of visual data, from personal assistants anticipating our needs to infrastructure systems monitoring the world, data drives every breakthrough.

Yet data alone does nothing. Only when algorithms, powered by massive compute, transform raw inputs into structures that capture relationships, patterns, and correlations do predictive models emerge. This interplay between data and computation is the foundation from which today's predictive systems and tomorrow's superintelligent AI will arise.

The Beginning: Big Data

In the spring of 2017, I was a founding member of the technical team at Rivian, an electric vehicle startup in California. My role was to build and lead the engineering teams responsible for the mobile applications, in-vehicle interface, and cloud infrastructure.

The cloud team, aka the Big Data team, focused on collecting, processing, storing, and providing structured access to the massive streams of data coming from our vehicles.

We built APIs that let other teams, including analytics, diagnostics, mobile, and autonomy, tap into this data efficiently. A modern vehicle is an IoT device: connected to the Internet, constantly streaming telemetry from ECUs and a sensor suite of cameras, radar, ultrasonics, GPS, and more. This data is gold. It reveals how customers use their vehicles, signals reliability issues early, supports predictive maintenance, and feeds machine learning pipelines for autonomy and fleet intelligence.

By 2017, the volume of data was exploding. Devices everywhere were getting brains and connectivity, producing torrents of information at unprecedented scale. For AI, this was step one: the rise of massive, rich datasets that could power learning systems. Without this foundation, neural networks, the engines of modern AI, would have nothing to learn from.

The Big Data we were collecting at Rivian wasn't just a byproduct of connected cars; it was a glimpse of the broader transformation underway. Structured, abundant, and accessible, data had become the first essential ingredient of the AI revolution, laying the groundwork for everything that would follow.

The LLM and its Data

ChatGPT, developed by OpenAI, launched on November 30, 2022. Its growth was unprecedented: it reached 1 million users in just five days and 100 million monthly active users by January 2023, making it the fastest-growing consumer application at the time. By November 2023, ChatGPT had 180.5 million users and was generating around 1.7 billion monthly visits to its website.

To the user, ChatGPT feels like a smart, conversational assistant. You type a question or give it a task such as explaining a topic, writing a story, or brainstorming ideas. It then replies almost instantly with clear, human-like answers. It's like chatting with a knowledgeable friend who's always ready to help. But behind this seemingly simple interface lies one of the most complex data-driven systems ever built.

ChatGPT is based on OpenAI's GPT (Generative Pre-trained Transformer) architecture, specifically GPT-3.5 at its launch. GPT-3.5 is a large language model (LLM) trained on enormous datasets of text drawn from the Internet and other sources. The raw training data is estimated at 60–120 terabytes before preprocessing and deduplication. While massive, this is still only a slice of all human text: by 2023, the "crawlable" web alone was estimated to contain 2–3 petabytes of text.

So what happens with all that data? First, the text is broken into tokens—units that represent words or subwords. Each token is assigned a unique integer ID by the tokenizer. Those IDs are then mapped to high-dimensional vectors called embeddings, which capture the semantic and syntactic relationships between tokens.

GPT-3.5 has around 175 billion parameters, which include both the embedding vectors and the weights inside the transformer layers that process sequences of embeddings. During training, these parameters are adjusted to predict the next token in a sequence. Over time, the model internalizes grammar, factual knowledge, reasoning patterns, and stylistic cues, encoding human language into a high-dimensional mathematical space. This is what enables the model to generate coherent and contextually relevant responses whenever you interact with it.

The LLM may feel like magic, but it isn't. It's the product of three things: the algorithm, the data, and the compute needed to bring them together. The outcome is an incredibly powerful "word predictor," tuned to relate input data in a way that lets it guess what comes next in a sequence of words with uncanny accuracy. And when we relate it all back to the data, the scale of the transformation becomes clear.

The original training text corpus, about 60 to 120 terabytes, is distilled into a model weighing roughly 350 gigabytes, plus a 2.5-gigabyte token table. In other words, GPT-3.5 compresses human language by a factor of 200–300×, not by storing the words themselves, but by encoding the statistical essence of how we use them.

FSD and its Data

Tesla's Full Self-Driving (FSD) is another face of the AI transformation poured from data, pixels instead of words. Each Tesla streams video from eight high-resolution cameras, generating an estimated 0.5 to 2.3 GB per second per vehicle. Across a data-collecting fleet of roughly 5 million vehicles, that becomes a staggering torrent of visual input.

At the heart of Tesla's learning engine is Cortex, a sprawling AI training supercluster housed within Gigafactory Texas. The data center spans about 500,000 square feet, or roughly 5% of the factory's total ~10 million square feet of floor space. As of late

2024, it includes around 100,000 Nvidia H100 and H200 GPUs, operating at the scale of a small city in terms of energy use.

Most raw data doesn't leave the car immediately. Each Tesla vehicle runs FSD both live and in shadow mode, where an internal model predicts what would have happened without taking control. When its prediction diverges from what the human driver actually did, or when the driver intervenes, that data is flagged as valuable for training.

This footage, along with human intervention data, enters Tesla's labeling pipeline, where each frame is annotated (lanes, pedestrians, signs, trajectories), creating ground truth for supervised learning. Billions of labeled frames feed through training epochs, slowly refining the network's parameters into a precise "driving function."

To go beyond what real-world driving alone can teach, Tesla also uses simulation. By replaying real scenes under varied conditions (fog, twilight, unexpected road layouts) it artificially generates edge cases that expand the model's learning beyond natural data.

Ultimately, like ChatGPT, FSD's capabilities hinge on the same three pillars: data, compute, and neural networks. Cortex's scale, in both physical space and GPU count, is Tesla's declaration that autonomy is a data arms race. Without a constant flow of curated visual data fed by shadow fleets, driver overrides, and simulated edge scenarios, there's simply no path to safe, scalable autonomy.

AI and Data Compression

Large Language Models are compression machines. They compress text data into a set of weights, a predictive function for generating words. Tesla's FSD does the same, compressing driving data into a driving function. Both begin with compressed data as input.

All digital data is compressed data. Sometimes the compression is explicit, like JPEGs or MP3s. Other times it's implicit, like written text, which is a compressed abstraction of human experience. Even "raw" photon counts from Tesla's vision cameras are compressed: sensors digitize a vast analog spectrum of light into manageable digital form.

Most digital data originates in the analog world. Sampling, digitization, and conversion are all acts of compression. Even something as simple as a website clickstream is a compressed trace of human decision-making.

The scope of available data depends on the sensors. For humans, our senses are sight, sound, touch, taste, and smell. In machines, it is cameras, microphones, LiDAR, and other devices. As sensors improve, the volume of data explodes. Kodak's 1991 DCS 100 camera captured 1.3 megapixels per photo. Today, an iPhone captures 48 megapixels, with uncompressed ProRAW files reaching 256 MB, still tiny compared to the theoretical capture of all incoming photons, which would measure in gigabytes per frame.

But raw capture isn't enough. Sensor data must be stored and transported. Storage has scaled dramatically, with costs plummeting and flash memory delivering vast speed improvements. Networks have scaled too, moving more data faster and cheaper than ever before. Storage and transport themselves are forms of compression, encoding data in ways that make it possible to preserve and transmit.

AI models are not just consumers of compressed data. They are themselves engines of compression. A model's weights encode a distilled, abstract representation of the world. The power of AI lies in this abstraction: compressing billions of examples into predictive patterns that generalize beyond the data.

As we scale models, we are not just scaling compute. We are scaling humanity's ability to compress reality into usable, predictive output.

Data Types

The types of data feeding today's models reflect both the richness of the world and the sophistication of the sensors capturing it. Understanding these types is essential to seeing why modern AI is both powerful and limited.

Text is the most familiar form. From the billions of words in books, articles, websites, and chat logs, large language models learn patterns in grammar, syntax, and meaning. Code repositories, structured logs, and databases are also text. They encode rules, relationships, and procedures, allowing AI to "read" human instructions and reasoning. Every token, every subword fragment, carries information that models distill into a predictive function.

Visual data is equally abundant. Tesla vehicles generate torrents of images and video from eight high-resolution cameras, capturing the world from every angle. Beyond cars, medical scans, satellite imagery, and security footage feed AI systems seeking patterns invisible to the human eye. Each frame is a compressed snapshot of reality, but collectively, these visual streams teach AI how to perceive, classify, and respond.

Audio data captures the world of sound. Speech fuels voice assistants and transcription engines, while environmental sounds (traffic, machinery, music) allow models to interpret context and detect anomalies. When combined with visual streams, audio becomes a critical signal in multimodal perception, bridging the gap between what is seen and what is heard.

Sensor and telemetry data come from machines as well as humans. Modern vehicles are networks of ECUs (electronic control units), each responsible for a specific domain: powertrain, braking, steering, climate control, infotainment, and more. These ECUs emit CAN (Controller Area Network) signals, streams of structured data representing the status, behavior, and environment of the vehicle.

Beyond CAN, connected vehicles capture GPS, radar, LiDAR, and camera feeds. Aggregated across fleets, these signals reveal patterns in driver behavior, traffic flow, road conditions, and mechanical reliability, insights impossible to gather manually at scale. Industrial equipment, wearables, and IoT devices similarly produce streams of sensor data, from vibration and temperature to heart rate and motion.

Interaction and behavioral data track how humans engage with the digital and physical world. Every click, search, purchase, or scroll becomes a trace that AI can analyze. Social networks capture connections and interactions; recommendation engines transform those patterns into personalized experiences. Even small datasets, like how a user navigates an app, are gold when scaled across millions.

Structured and tabular data represent the measured world. Financial records, scientific measurements, census data—these are grids of numbers and categories, easily captured in spreadsheets or databases. AI can uncover correlations invisible to statisticians, turning routine records into predictive insight.

Multimodal data fuses these streams. Videos come with audio and text captions; autonomous robots merge vision, tactile feedback, and speech; digital twins combine real-world measurements with simulations. Multimodal learning allows AI to integrate context and reasoning across senses in ways that mimic human understanding.

Across all these types, the principle is clear: AI's capabilities are defined by the data it consumes. Each modality offers a distinct perspective and must be captured, curated, and processed to feed neural networks effectively. Together, these streams provide the raw inputs neural networks use to generate text, recognize objects, navigate environments, or control machines, turning raw data into measurable outputs and decisions.

Data is Everywhere

Data is all around us, yet we are conditioned to think that only certain processes that humans have endeavored to build are data creators. There is an abundance of data in the natural world that has barely been touched.

Tesla FSD: Data Beyond Training

Tesla's FSD system relies on cameras that record vehicle drives to create substantial datasets. Until now, this data has primarily been used to train autonomy itself. But there's far more value in it than just learning how to drive.

The Tesla fleet is large and expanding rapidly—about 4,000 new customer-owned vehicles are added daily. That growth will accelerate with Robotaxi. By some estimates, Tesla could have 1 million Robotaxis in the U.S. by 2028 and 5 million by 2030. In dense urban areas, these vehicles will traverse nearly every street multiple times a day. In city centers, some streets could be scanned every few minutes.

Now consider what that fleet could see and report in real time:

- Infrastructure issues—water main breaks, street flooding, downed power lines, broken traffic lights, obscured signage.
- Road surface health—mapping every pothole, tracking its growth day by day.
- Building and public safety—fires, hazards, or crowd formations (protests, unsafe zones).
- Community Support—search tools like "Find Fido" to locate missing pets or people.

Beyond safety, the data can be deeply granular and commercially valuable. Everything can be classified and counted: trash on the streets, pedestrian density, make/model/year of surrounding vehicles, delivery truck activity, and more.

AI then turns this raw input into meaningful intelligence for different customer segments. Imagine the fleet detecting a shutdown: a road segment goes "solid red." Cameras see fire trucks and ambulances. The AI interprets the context. Firefighters packing up means the accident will clear soon, but an arriving ambulance signals the closure will persist.

Tesla's fleet isn't just learning how to drive. It's learning how to see the world in ways no other system can.

Eyes Everywhere, Data Everywhere

Beyond Tesla vehicle cameras, there exists an enormous number of fixed and moving vision systems (e.g., security cameras, Ring cameras, etc.) But this is about to increase exponentially.

Smartphones, smart glasses, and humanoid bots will provide reams of vision data, by some measure more than the number of human eyes on the planet. All of these edge devices will be powered by intelligent AI that can provide "edge" interpretation. And of course, these interpretations can be aggregated over networks to provide "big picture" information.

Let's Do Some Research

Consider how research is often constrained today. Sometimes it's about observing the natural environment; sometimes it's just counting things. Entire PhD theses are often built on tiny, statistically shaky datasets, because large-scale data collection is hard. Take a contrived example: A study trying to prove that dry weather reduces or slows foliage growth on trees, worsening the problem by letting more sunlight hit the ground and further drying the environment.

Researchers pick two biomes, one with limited rainfall and one with abundant rainfall. A small team is sent out to count leaves as they emerge from winter to spring. But the task quickly becomes overwhelming. Thousands of leaves across many trees, every day, are impossible to count. Eventually, the researchers give up, and the resulting paper concludes, incorrectly, that drier environments lead to less foliage.

In reality, the trees in dry environments produce more leaves, just slightly later. The counting effort was simply too hard to execute correctly. Now imagine deploying a small fleet of Tesla Optimus bots. Each one can reliably count leaves every day, not just on a single tree, but on dozens. What was once impractical becomes routine, and the conclusions become accurate.

This is the power of abundant, automated vision data operating within an AI system.

Synthetic Data

Synthetic data is artificially generated rather than collected from the real world. Real-world data can be expensive, slow, or even impossible to collect at scale. It also tends to carry biases, privacy concerns, and gaps in coverage. Synthetic data offers both an augmentation and, in some cases, a full alternative. It can balance underrepresented scenarios and sidestep regulated or sensitive data.

Vehicle autonomy is one of the clearest examples of its power. Tesla's competitors are experimenting with synthetic driving data to close the gap with Tesla's massive advantage: a fleet of ~8 million cars feeding real-world data. But Tesla also invests heavily in simulation.

Tesla has built a physics-realistic simulator for its Full Self-Driving (FSD) system. Engineers can replay real-world drives and then systematically augment them. They can:

- Populate intersections with crowds of pedestrians, each with planned or erratic behaviors.
- Add vehicles with clean or compromising trajectories.
- Transform the environment with heavy snowfall, road work, lane changes, or barriers.

This capability allows Tesla to create edge cases and stress-test the system far beyond what natural driving provides. Sometimes the simulator is used directly in a test harness; other times, the generated datasets are blended into training alongside real fleet data. Crucially, Tesla's fleet capture informs which scenarios to simulate, closing the loop between reality and synthetic augmentation.

Synthetic data is also critical beyond autonomous vehicles. Tesla's Optimus robot, for example, can be trained in virtual environments that replicate homes, warehouses, and factories. These simulations allow Optimus to practice navigation, object manipulation, and human interactions safely, including rare or dangerous scenarios that would be difficult or unsafe to generate in the real world.

Reinforcement learning (RL) leverages these synthetic environments as playgrounds where agents learn through trial and error, optimizing behavior by exploring countless scenarios without risk. Techniques like domain randomization, varying lighting, object textures, and physics help models trained in simulation generalize to real-world conditions.

Digital twins further enhance this process by creating high-fidelity, real-time virtual replicas of physical spaces or systems. Engineers can test and refine AI agents in realistic, controlled settings. Data from the real world updates these twins, and insights from simulation can feed back to improve real-world performance, creating a continuous learning loop.

There are three primary advantages to synthetic data: scale, control, and safety. Scale means virtually unlimited data generation at a lower cost than collection. Control allows teams to balance datasets and deliberately create rare edge cases that real-world sampling may never provide. Safety enables simulation of dangerous or sensitive situations like medical complications or near-miss crashes, without putting people at risk.

But the challenges are real. Synthetic data can miss the subtleties of natural signals, embed or amplify bias, or produce artifacts that models overfit to. This is often called the "sim-to-real gap." And validation remains a thorny problem: proving that synthetic scenarios translate reliably into real-world performance is non-trivial.

Still, the benefits outweigh the drawbacks. Companies that master synthetic data pipelines gain leverage, accelerating innovation and shifting the data advantage away from raw collection alone. Synthetic data is poised to become a foundation of AI development, particularly in domains where real-world data is scarce, sensitive, or costly.

Data Builds Function

Understanding AI, or at least neural networks, is understanding that data builds the function (and in a sense, the function is data).

All computation is about moving input data through a function to produce an output. Even something as simple as adding two numbers requires inputs, a function, and an output. For decades, these functions were hand-crafted as computer code, designed by humans. This approach works well for many problems, but some problems are simply too complex to encode explicitly.

Tesla FSD is a perfect example. Writing code that takes raw camera data and produces precise driving controls: accelerator, brake, steering. Hard-coding would be extraordinarily difficult. The system must perceive the environment, recognize other cars, bicycles, pedestrians, and traffic signs, and then plan safe maneuvers. Traditional code struggles with perception and planning at this scale.

A neural network, however, can solve this problem. The network itself is the function: it takes camera inputs and produces control outputs. At its core, a neural network is a highly structured set of numbers. It consists of layers of neurons (nodes), each connected to neurons in the next layer via weights, numbers that determine the importance of each connection.

The network's weights are set through training on massive driving datasets from the fleet and simulators. Training is compute-intensive, often requiring supercomputers running for weeks. The resulting trained network, the model, is the function itself, encoded as a structured set of numbers.

When the model is used to process new data, this process is called inference. Inference is simply taking new input, like a live camera frame, pushing it through the model (the function), and producing the output, such as the vehicle's steering, braking, or acceleration commands. In other words, inference is applying the learned function to make decisions in real time.

In short, data teaches the neural network to make the right decisions, and the trained network encodes that knowledge as a function, a function made entirely of data.

The Bitstream App

A neural network is just a function: it takes in data and produces data. That data exists in digital form, bits, 0's and 1's, which we can call a bitstream.

We're already familiar with AI systems generating outputs in autonomy, chatbots, images, and videos. But what about apps?

The entire computer industry, from PCs to smartphones, is built on the "app model." Applications serve specific modalities: spreadsheets, word processors, and presentations. They're so entrenched that they come bundled in suites from Microsoft and Google. Smartphones, outside of communication, are essentially just app-launching platforms. Apple's App Store alone holds over 2 million apps, representing an industry larger than the GDP of many nations (~$1.3T in developer billings and sales).

But what if there were no apps? No hard-coded binaries at all. What if instead, every function came from a generative AI process, built in real time from data and a prompt?

This is the true shape of a data-driven AI ecosystem.

Elon Musk has spoken of the bitstream: the idea that video games of the future won't be pre-coded, but generated on the fly. Frames will be built in real time from inputs. He recently announced a new venture, MACROHARD, a tongue-in-cheek play on "Microsoft," aimed at disrupting the app industry by simulating applications in AI, live, without predefined boundaries.

The implications are easy to imagine. Feed in a dataset, and ask AI to:

- Build a financial model
- Create a presentation for the finance department
- Draft cover letters explaining the model

That's three "apps" in one; yet no apps at all. Just a data-driven function.

This is the inversion: data builds a function.

The Data Factory

"In the future, data centers are going to be thought of as AI factories. Their goal in life is to generate revenues, in this case, intelligence." —Jensen Huang, COMPUTEX "2025 keynote"

AI data centers are true factories. In training, the output is the model itself, the precursor to inference. During inference, the factory begins producing value in real time: text models produce tokens, image models produce pixels, and video models produce frames.

These are the factories of tomorrow, where the product is data. From an economic standpoint, these factories are high-margin producers: the product is consumed almost immediately at minimal cost, with only network transport as an expense. Unlike traditional factories, inference can also be distributed to the edge, the device, eliminating many fixed costs.

"In the future, every company that builds things will have a factory that builds the things they sell, and then it will have another factory that builds intelligence." —Jensen Huang, Nvidia GTC 2025 conference.

At Tesla's Gigafactory in Austin, Texas, approximately 10 million square feet are dedicated to vehicle production. Within this expansive facility is a 500,000-square-foot section known as Cortex, Tesla's AI training supercluster. This integrated setup manufactures the computer models used in Tesla vehicles for Full Self-Driving (FSD) and Tesla's Optimus bot, two factories under one roof: one for physical products, one for intelligence. These data factories are every bit as real and economically potent as those producing hard goods.

Data as Power: Competing Visions in China, the US, and the EU

Data is not only fuel for AI. It is power. How nations govern, control, and distribute data reveals their deeper philosophies of power itself. At the global level, three competing visions dominate: the United States, the European Union, and China. Each treats data as a strategic asset, but in radically different ways.

The United States frames data primarily as an economic resource, a commodity to be harvested, monetized, and circulated. This approach favors market-driven innovation, light-touch regulation, and unrestricted data flows across borders. American technology giants like Google, Amazon, Meta, Microsoft, and Tesla have flourished in this environment, extracting data at a planetary scale and using it to build some of the world's most valuable AI systems. Policy has historically leaned toward permissiveness, but geopolitical frictions with China have triggered selective localization and restrictions, such as bans on certain cross-border transactions. In the U.S. model, competitive advantage comes from scale and speed. Whoever can move the most data through the most compute, wins.

The European Union offers a striking counterpoint. Where the U.S. prizes innovation, the EU prizes rights. For Brussels, data is inseparable from privacy and individual autonomy. Regulations like the General Data Protection Regulation (GDPR) encode this philosophy, restricting how data can be collected, processed, and transferred. The EU pursues what it calls "digital sovereignty," seeking to protect its citizens while also shaping global norms.

The so-called "Brussels Effect" means that EU standards often ripple outward, forcing global compliance. The EU's vision turns data into a form of soft power, not through hoarding or monetization, but by embedding European values into the rules of the digital economy.

China takes yet another path, one that is neither market-driven nor rights-based but state-centric. Data here is a national resource to be secured, localized, and leveraged for economic development and social control. A suite of laws (the Cybersecurity Law, the Data Security Law, the Personal Information Protection Law) ensures that data remains under state oversight, with the Cyberspace Administration of China acting as regulator and gatekeeper. This system positions data as an instrument of sovereignty and security, tightly integrated into surveillance, censorship, and industrial policy. Through initiatives like the Digital Silk Road, China is also exporting this model abroad, embedding its approach into the infrastructure of partner nations.

Taken together, these three visions sketch the battle lines of the global data order. The U.S. sees data as commerce, the EU as rights, and China as sovereignty. None is arbitrary. Each reflects deeper histories and priorities. But when it comes to innovation, the U.S. model carries an advantage. Its permissive, market-driven approach allows companies to experiment at scale, fail fast, and rapidly integrate new techniques. That freedom to move quickly has consistently translated into global leadership in software, platforms, and now AI.

The EU's rights-based framework sets important guardrails, but it often slows deployment. China's state-driven model ensures control and scale, but at the cost of openness and trust. The American approach, by contrast, maximizes velocity. In a technological race where speed compounds, this bias toward innovation may prove decisive.

Data is Personal

Harnessing the power of AI for the individual is ultimately about data. An AI builds insights not only from personal datasets but also from its memory of interactions. Today's AI chatbots have very limited memory. What most people perceive as "memory" is actually the context window, the running transcript of prompts and responses passed back into the model with each turn. This makes chatbots' "memory" inherently session-based and ephemeral.

A chatbot could be designed to store past interactions in the cloud and reload them into the context window, but that comes at a cost. Inference, the compute required for an AI to generate outputs, is expensive, and that cost grows with context length.

Take a simple question like "What is the circumference and diameter of Earth?" The input may only be a dozen tokens (not words, since tokens are often sub-word fragments), but processing it still requires billions of floating-point operations across the model's layers. Larger models and longer prompts multiply that cost significantly. If the model responds with a few hundred tokens, and the user follows up with "Why is the Earth an oblate spheroid?", the entire transcript, including the original prompt, the model's response, and the new question, gets reloaded into the context window. Each turn enlarges the prompt and makes inference correspondingly heavier.

Stretch that interaction history across days, and the compute demand becomes enormous. Yet the demand for longer context is tied directly to utility, and inference costs continue to fall in step with Moore's law, so there is hope.

Still, memory is powerful. It delivers the necessary context. Consider owning a Tesla Optimus humanoid bot. The primary interface is voice, and because voice interactions are fluid, they will be frequent. A user will naturally expect the bot to remember prior interactions, much like one expects from familiar individuals. That's a lot of data. And in Optimus's case, all that data must be stored and processed locally.

But interaction history is only part of the picture. Individuals may also feed their AI other datasets: medical records, financial or legal documents, personal photos, videos, and more. An AI with full access to a person's medical records is immensely valuable. Instead of repeating medical history or details, the user can assume the AI already knows. In fact, that expectation is critical, since people often forget details that may be medically important.

A photo history is equally valuable. It's a record of places and experiences. Imagine asking your AI: "Where was the place I ate that amazing carbonara in Rome?" Amazed that you get a full answer, you can then begin exploring the natural cascade of follow-up questions.

Ultimately, an AI that remembers your interactions and houses your digital assets isn't just helpful, but essential for anything approaching super-intelligence. Yet with this intimate data comes a critical tension: who controls it? Personal AI assistants require deep access to an individual's life to be truly useful, but storing that information, whether locally on the device or in the cloud, carries trade-offs. Local memory maximizes privacy and personal agency, keeping data under the user's direct control, but limits the compute power available for inference and cross-device continuity. Cloud memory enables richer context, seamless updates, and device-agnostic access, but it raises questions of trust, security, and long-term control.

Apple addresses this dilemma with its Apple Intelligence framework, which employs a hybrid architecture combining on-device processing with Private Cloud Compute. On-device models handle everyday tasks, ensuring user data remains private and secure. For more complex requests, Apple utilizes Private Cloud Compute, a cloud intelligence system built on Apple silicon and designed specifically for private AI processing. This system extends the privacy and security of Apple devices into the cloud, ensuring that personal user data sent to PCC isn't accessible to anyone other than the user—not even Apple.

Furthermore, Apple allows independent experts to inspect the code running on their servers to verify privacy, and cryptographically ensures that devices only communicate with servers whose software has been publicly logged for inspection. This approach allows Apple Intelligence to flex and scale its computational capacity while protecting user privacy, setting a new standard for privacy in AI.

Once again, we see that data is central to the equation.

Data Frontiers: Quality, Bias, and Economics

The story of data isn't just scale. It's also the friction points emerging as AI systems consume everything in sight.

Quality vs. Quantity

The early game was brute force. Scrape the internet, train a model, scale the cluster. But the ceiling is rising. High-quality, curated data, human-labeled, cleaned, or preference-ranked, is now as critical as raw volume. Anthropic's reinforcement learning with human feedback is one example. Tesla's edge is not just billions of miles, but the accuracy of labeling and validation on that stream. Quality turns noise into signal.

Bias and Fairness

Data is never neutral. Language models mirror cultural bias in the text they're trained on. Driving datasets capture regional quirks. What's normal in Phoenix looks reckless in Rome. Synthetic data can patch gaps, but the bias question never goes away. The source defines the shape of the model.

Economics of Data

Data itself is becoming an asset class. Licensing deals with Reddit, news wires, or Stack Overflow put price tags on what was once free. Lawsuits are the opening skirmishes in a larger battle over ownership. It's not just GPUs that cost billions. Companies wanting access to the right data will pay more billions to get it..

Privacy as Constraint

The EU's posture of rights-first is mirrored in tech with privacy-preserving approaches: federated learning, differential privacy, and on-device training. Apple and Google lean heavily here. It's not just regulation forcing the issue, but user trust is now part of the dataset.

Freshness vs. Staleness

The Internet freezes in time. Models trained on 2023 data already feel stale in 2025. The shift to real-time streams such as Tesla's fleet telemetry, financial data feeds, or X's global pulse shows that freshness is power. Retrieval-augmented generation and continuous fine-tuning are workarounds, but the deeper truth is that yesterday's data isn't enough.

Open vs. Closed

Open datasets like LAION [1] or Common Crawl were the rocket fuel for the first LLM wave. But the moat is moving toward closed, proprietary corporate LLMs (e.g. Instagram's visual archive, Tesla's fleet, Bloomberg's financial text.) The tension between open and closed is shaping who controls the next generation of AI.

Humans as Data Sources

Behind every model are human judgments: labeling images, ranking outputs, and steering alignment. RLHF [2] and its successors remind us that humans are still in the loop. Data isn't just scraped, it's shaped.

Data Explosion

Data has always had a compounding property: the more users interact with a system, the more data it collects, the better the AI becomes, which in turn attracts more users. This feedback loop is the classic data network effect; a flywheel that powers the largest AI ecosystems today. Companies like Google, Tesla, and OpenAI benefit from this virtuous cycle, where scale itself becomes a barrier to entry.

But the future promises an even more dramatic acceleration. The explosion of sensors and connected devices means that data collection is no longer limited to human-computer interactions. Cameras, microphones, biometric monitors, vehicles, industrial equipment, and even household appliances are becoming always-on contributors to the global data stream.

Every additional device is not just another user, but another high-resolution sensor feeding into the loop. Consider autonomous vehicles: each car doubles as both a consumer and a producer of data, sending back observations that refine the fleet's collective intelligence. Or wearables: each new watch or health sensor not only serves its owner but contributes to population-scale datasets that can drive breakthroughs in health diagnostics and predictive care. Even domestic robots like Tesla's Optimus will serve as both helpers and data factories, continuously mapping environments and learning from interactions.

The compounding effect of this sensor explosion is profound. Where traditional network effects relied primarily on the scale of users, future data networks will rely on the scale of sensing. The result is a new kind of flywheel: more devices → more data → better AI → more compelling devices.

In this world, the competitive frontier is not only who has the best model architecture, but who can best harness the richest, most diverse streams of real-world data. The companies positioned to dominate will be those that not only attract users but also embed themselves into the physical fabric of daily life, turning every device into a node in the global AI data network.

Data is a Competitive Advantage

AI is data hungry, and while data is everywhere, only data collected in a useful form and processed in novel ways creates a true competitive advantage. Tesla illustrates this perfectly. With a fleet of ~8 million vehicles, and ~4,000 more added daily, it has unmatched access to real-world driving data. Not every vehicle contributes at all times, but Tesla can target and capture the most valuable datasets: edge cases, unusual conditions, and rare events. No other automaker has the scale to do this, giving Tesla a moat that competitors cannot replicate.

But Tesla's edge isn't just raw data. Rather, it's how that data is processed. Full Self-Driving (FSD) is more than a neural network that turns photons into driving decisions. It's an entire data infrastructure and methodology. Tesla has developed specialized techniques for filtering the flood of driving footage, identifying the critical cases, applying automated labeling at scale, and even generating high-fidelity simulations seeded from real-world samples. In short, it has built a factory for transforming raw input into training gold.

Large language models (LLMs) present a different case. Most are trained on publicly available internet text, which (so far) has been free to use despite copyright disputes. Here, the advantage doesn't come from owning the data, but from how it is used. Model architecture, training approaches, and refinement techniques determine whether a dataset becomes a commodity model or a breakthrough system. Though not AI, Google's early success with PageRank is an instructive analogy: they didn't just crawl the web, they invented a method to rank and surface the most relevant content. That technique, not the data itself, set them apart.

And above all, access to capital is the final determinant of advantage. Processing, storing, and training on massive datasets requires vast compute resources. Hyperscalers [3], those with the capital to build and operate immense compute clusters, can train at scales others simply cannot reach. In AI, as with LLMs and self-driving, data may be the raw fuel, but technique and compute power are what transform it into a lasting competitive advantage. With these three factors in mind, data, methodology, and capital, let's look at which companies are leading the AI race and which are falling behind.

Data Winners and Losers

AI is a disruption that multiplies every existing disruption. With every disruption, there are winners and losers. Winners are often led by visionaries with few constraints, able to embrace new business models with ample capital. Losers are often the incumbents, who feel compelled to preserve their existing business models and see new ideas as cannibalizing threats (just ask Kodak).

The winners in the race to artificial super-intelligence are those that either have large proprietary datasets or can harness data in unique ways. Moreover, they must clearly have the capital to build large, coherent training clusters (e.g., Hyperscalers). As discussed above, Tesla's fleet and processing infrastructure put it clearly on the winners' wall. They have built a moat around driver data from their fleet. They have also invested heavily in embodied AI, FSD for vehicles, and Optimus for robotics, along with Cortex, the training supercomputer at the Austin Gigafactory that powers both.

xAI also belongs on the winners' wall. In this case, the primary dataset is not itself a moat; the differentiator is access to the largest real-time dataset in the world: the X feed. News worldwide often breaks first on X. Immediate access to this information, while others are walled off, is an exceptional advantage.

OpenAI has a derived data moat. While much of the training data is sourced publicly, their curation, aggregation, and proprietary fine-tuning datasets give them a unique advantage that is difficult for others to replicate. Other notable winners include

Google/DeepMind, with massive datasets from search, Maps, YouTube, and Gmail, combined with world-class compute; Amazon, with e-commerce, logistics, and AWS datasets; Meta, with social graphs and interaction data; and Apple, with amazing devices and health datasets across its ecosystem. Each of these players has unique data that is centralized and actionable, giving them a significant edge.

The losers are the opposite. They lack unique datasets, fail to centralize their data, or cannot effectively leverage it. Legacy automakers, for example, have large fleets but minimal telemetry or vision data flowing to a central store. Traditional media companies may have abundant content, but they lack real-time data streams and AI infrastructure. Banks and most financial institutions possess siloed data, but heavy regulation limits its centralization and use.

Retail chains without centralized digital infrastructure have fragmented POS and loyalty data, making AI integration difficult. Even universities and research labs, while rich in specialized datasets, generally lack the scale and commercial leverage to turn their data into a moat.

From Data to Superintelligence

In the end, data is not intelligence. Yet intelligence cannot develop without data. A human with a photographic memory is able to store vast quantities of information, and that is sometimes seen as intelligent. But true intelligence comes not from storage alone, but from the ability to extract meaning, discover patterns, and form insights that are not directly present in the data itself, and to do so quickly.

Today's AI, built on neural networks, is profoundly powerful but also limited. At its core, it is predictive, learning the next word, the next image, the next move, by mapping the future from the past. That predictive capacity looks impressive at scale, yet it is still bounded by the data it has seen.

Superintelligence must go further. An AI that earns the label of artificial general intelligence will not simply mimic the human mind, "neural networks" notwithstanding. It must develop reasoning and intuition, and it must grasp the physics of the natural world.

Whether this arises simply from more compute applied to more data is uncertain. What is clear is that data is the cornerstone from which superintelligence will develop.

Endnotes

- LAION: Large-scale AI Open Network, an open dataset of tens of millions to billions of image–caption pairs collected from the web. Used primarily for training multimodal models (e.g., text-to-image generation) while providing metadata like captions and quality scores.
- RLHF (Reinforcement Learning from Human Feedback): A training method where humans provide feedback, such as ranking model outputs or correcting errors, allowing the AI to learn to align its behavior with human preferences. It ensures humans remain in the loop, shaping rather than just scraping data.
- Hyperscalers are large-scale cloud computing providers that offer vast, scalable infrastructure and services, such as Amazon Web Services, Microsoft Azure, and Google Cloud, capable of supporting massive global workloads.

***

PHIL BEISEL

Phil Beisel – Technology Leader, Entrepreneur, and a Futurist with 30+ years building software and leading engineering teams at companies like Apple and Rivian. Named on five software patents, he has founded three startups and shaped platforms spanning consumer technology, enterprise systems, and electric vehicles. At Rivian, he built the in-vehicle, mobile, and cloud software organizations from the ground up, powering its electric adventure vehicles. A Boston College graduate in Computer Science and Mathematics, he lives in the heart of Silicon Valley.

Follow Phil Beisel

X @pbeisel

Chapter 16

Software and AI Models—Powering Inference

Larry Goldberg

The focus in AI development has long centered on building ever-more sophisticated models, but the real competition is now shifting toward inference, the process where these models apply their learned knowledge to generate outputs, make decisions, or take actions in real time. What started with foundational tools like ChatGPT has evolved into systems capable of semi- or even fully autonomous behavior, ongoing adaptation, and seamless integration with external environments. This transformation is fueled by efforts to narrow the gap between:

- Training - the resource-intensive phase of parameter optimization; that is, the building of the model, the "learning" phase, and
- Inference – the deployment phase, that is the use of the model in the world, where the model responds to questions or prompts.

In a person, there is little differentiation between these functions: we constantly refine our mental models, learning continuously

through experience. While we frequently react reflexively (acting on prior "training"), we are also constantly revising our mental model of the world even while functioning on a day-to-day basis.
AI is evolving this to a more human-like behavior, with continual learning for incremental updates, distributed training for scalable computation across networks, and "agentic" capabilities, where AI can do more than simply answer questions, but can interact with the world using APIs and AI Tools.

- An API is a set of rules that allows different software applications to communicate with each other and can act as a messenger between the AI and software programs, enabling the AI to control a wide range of activities and/or physical, automated devices (like cars, robots, machines.) For instance, an AI-powered logistics system could autonomously coordinate deliveries by interacting with various APIs, adapting routes in real time based on traffic data.
- AI Tools are like a specialist in a particular skill. It could be a Recommendation Engine for a shopping list on Amazon, or an image creation tool, or a grammar checking tool, or a suite of Robot controls, and so on

Historically, the standard approach of training a model once and using it for inference until the next release has constrained adaptability in rapidly changing environments. The emerging paradigm offers mechanisms for real-time refinement, enhancing the resilience and flexibility of artificial intelligence systems.

Continual learning is a method in artificial intelligence that enables models to integrate new data without losing previously acquired information, a challenge known as "catastrophic forgetting." Techniques such as replay buffers (a memory component that stores past experiences from prior interactions) and regularization (a technique to recognize generalizable patterns) are used to maintain essential knowledge while incorporating additional data streams.

In my experience, this has been evident in applications where models transition from fixed architectures to adaptive ones, such as in enterprise systems that evolve with user data. For instance, a customer relationship management (CRM) platform that updates its recommendation algorithms based on ongoing user interactions, or a fraud detection system that adapts its models in real time as new transaction patterns emerge. Advances in continual learning for large language models (LLMs) enable expansion in production environments, mirroring how professionals iterate on large software systems without full rewrites.

Distributed frameworks, such as AWS Clean Rooms for privacy-preserving collaboration or ZEN for inter-model communication, are examples of how to achieve inference scalability. Agentic tools like LangChain for prompt chaining or Manus for multi-agent coordination facilitate complex workflows, from API orchestration to automated decision-making. This aligns with the chapter's thesis: software optimizations, including 100X inference accelerations, democratize Super Intelligence (SI) while posing significant disruptions. By considering these within the broader AI ecosystem, we can anticipate SI's trajectory, from compute scaling to economic impacts.

Inference is where models operationalize knowledge, but it's evolving into a feedback loop that echoes the human mind in continuous learning. Methods like reinforcement learning from human feedback (RLHF) refine outputs based on interactions, while retrieval-augmented generation (RAG) injects external context during inference, enhancing relevance without retraining.

To achieve SI, an AI will have to be as adaptive in inference as is humans. For instance, in software engineering, an AI might use pure inference for standard code reviews, applying pre-trained patterns efficiently, but engage continual learning for novel bugs, pulling updates from distributed repositories. This hybrid approach optimizes resources, just as developers use pre-defined (cached) dependencies for routine builds but recompile for edge cases.
Let's examine how this shift amplifies AI's potential while highlighting the need for energy management, ethical governance, and hardware innovation.

The Evolution of AI Models: From Static Foundations to Continual, Agentic Systems

AI models have advanced from conversational interfaces to adaptive, action-oriented agents, a progression that's both incremental and revolutionary. OpenAI's GPT lineage ignited this, evolving from GPT-3's generative prowess, producing coherent text from prompts, to multimodal integration, processing text, images, and audio. These models embed continual learning to mitigate forgetting and accommodate streaming data, allowing post-deployment refinement without full retrains.

For those versed in machine learning pipelines, early GPTs were transformer-based encoders-decoders, fine-tuned on massive corpora but rigid post-training. Continual learning introduces adaptive mechanisms, such as experience replay to revisit prior examples or parameter isolation to safeguard foundational weights. In a data analytics role, this enables a model to baseline on historical trends but continually tune to live feeds, personalizing insights without overfitting. For SI implications, this facilitates pervasive automation, potentially reshaping industries through self-optimizing systems that evolve autonomously, driving exponential productivity gains.

xAI's Grok illustrates this trajectory, with Grok 4 (July 2025) delivering a 4X uplift over Grok 3 via native tool integration, real-time X search, chain-of-thought reasoning, and multimodal handling for diverse inputs. Projections for Grok 5 (October 2025, 12X) and Grok 6 (Q1 2026, 50–70X) leverage scaling laws, incorporating distributed training to distribute compute efficiently across clusters. Grok's persistent memory maintains session continuity, supporting nuanced, context-aware responses or API-driven controls.

Delving into Grok's features, native tools enable direct API calls for tasks like sentiment analysis on live X feeds, ideal for market researchers monitoring trends. Real-time integration circumvents static knowledge cutoffs, while multimodal capabilities process scanned documents or images for comprehensive outputs.

Distributed training optimizes for cloud or edge environments, minimizing latency in federated learning scenarios. Pure inference remains efficient for standard queries, leveraging quantized weights for quick responses while reserving continual updates for personalized adaptations, akin to caching in software for frequent operations versus recompiling for custom modules. In an SI context, this positions Grok as a scalable foundation, providing foresight for mitigation strategies amid rapid advancements.

Building on Grok's advancements, other industry leaders like Google are also pushing the boundaries of continual learning and agentic capabilities

Google's Gemini and innovations like Titans' neural memory advance continual learning, emphasizing anomaly detection for extended contexts and inference-time adjustments. Agentic enhancements through tools (e.g., Zapier for orchestration, N8N for pipelines) convert models into active participants, interfacing with APIs for automation or robotics. Titans' architecture employs a dynamic long-term memory, efficiently compressing sequences beyond 2 million tokens via surprise-based prioritization.

Illustratively, Gemini's expansive context window supports in-depth analysis, such as parsing extensive datasets for business intelligence. Titans' real-time memory refinement allows models to adapt mid-query, enhancing agentic workflows (e.g., an agent querying multiple APIs for supply chain optimization, learning from discrepancies.)

Tesla's chips complement this, tuning for distributed, hybrid inference in resource-constrained settings. Pure inference optimizes routine operations, like API polling in monitoring tools, with learning activated for anomalies, ensuring computational thrift.

A comparative overview:

This framework maps capabilities: GPT-4o's multimodality broadens inputs for agentic tasks; Grok's RLHF iterates on feedback for precision; Gemini's scale suits enterprise analytics; Titans' updates enable resilient deployment. Collectively, this evolution heralds SI's efficiencies but underscores the need for balanced inference strategies.

Model	Parameter Count	Context Window	Key Inference Feature
GPT-4o	~1.76T	128K tokens	Multimodal processing with API/tool integration for agentic actions
Grok 4	>1T	256K tokens	Native tool use, real-time X search, continual adaptation via RLHF
Gemini 2.5	Undisclosed	2M tokens	Deep reasoning, neural memory for continual learning
Titans	170M–760M (scalable)	>2M tokens	Test-time neural memory updates, distributed training support

Key Factors of Inference: Continual Learning, Distribution, Agency, and Efficiency

Inference efficacy now relies on integrated elements, beginning with training-inference fusion. Continual learning in domains like vision or LLMs permits runtime refinements, emulating human plasticity without memory erasure. Distributed training, via cloud-orchestrated parallelism, scales across infrastructures, alleviating compute constraints.

In practice, continual learning deploys safeguards like replay mechanisms or loss penalties to integrate streams securely. For autonomous vehicles, this updates models for environmental shifts without baseline erosion. Distributed training partitions gradients over nodes, reassembling via aggregation, as in federated learning for privacy-sensitive applications.

Cost declines down to cents per million tokens stem from quantization, distillation, and 100X optimizations. Agentic inference invokes APIs dynamically, with frameworks like LangChain or AutoGen facilitating task decomposition and multi-agent collaboration.

Context scalability, as in Gemini's 2M tokens, supports extended interactions for development or control. Energy hurdles are addressed through distributed parallelism or RAG for contextual injection sans retraining. Hybrid approaches like PEFT for targeted tuning or online optimization foster progression from baseline to advanced functionality. Proprietary loops and distributed setups yield advantages, with Tesla's silicon enhancing these.

Pure inference provides equilibrium: Routine operations leverage fixed weights for efficiency, activating learning selectively (e.g., anomaly detection in monitoring pipelines.) This mirrors professional workflows, caching common queries while recompiling for novelties.

Key factors:

- Continual Adaptation: Runtime evolution, e.g., vision models tuning for novel inputs.
- Distributed Scalability: Decentralized processing for expansive training.
- Agentic Integration: API orchestration for autonomous execution.
- Speed and Efficiency: Multimodal optimizations, tempered by inference defaults.

Disruptive Implications: Accessibility, Risks, and Societal Shifts

These innovations broaden SI access, catalyzing automation-driven abundance and GDP multipliers. Continual agentic inference may redefine roles, favor integrators of API ecosystems while automating data-heavy tasks via pure inference.

Distributed training democratizes model building, enabling SMEs to customize without hyperscale resources. Societally, this yields tools for sectors like healthcare, agentic diagnostics evolving via global data. Risks include bias amplification in loops or API vulnerabilities; mitigations involve regulations and human oversight.

Tesla's AI6 may heighten demands in robotics, escalating energy needs. Pure inference ensures reliability in critical apps, like financial trading. Pros encompass global empowerment; cons demand ethical vigilance to avert inequities.

Conclusion: Actionable Steps for Thriving in a Continual, Agentic SI World

Software's trajectory toward continual, distributed, agentic inference heralds SI's imminence. From Grok 4's integrations to distributed paradigms, this drives evolution, balanced by efficient inference. See the codicil for hardware insights.

Checklist:

- Prototype with agentic tools like N8N for distributed pipelines.
- Implement memory systems with RAG for targeted adaptations.

- Engage in ongoing monitoring through professional networks.

Hardware Implications: Toward a Unified AI Mind in the Continual Learning Era

Continual learning unifies phases, elevating inference compute for adaptations. Neuromorphic designs, adaptive hardware, support hybrids, bolstered by distributed efficiencies.

Tesla's AI5/AI6 exemplify this, bolstering SI while necessitating ethical and energy planning.

Codicil: Tesla's AI5 and AI6 Chips: A Case Study in Inference-Hardware Convergence

Tesla's AI5/AI6 advances agentic, continual inference with distributed support.

- AI5: 3nm TSMC, 10X over AI4, edge-optimized for FSD/Optimus; enables pure inference routines with continual anomaly handling, production 2026.

Aspect	Current Hardware	Future (CL-Driven)
Compute Needs	Inference: Low	Hybrid: 10–50X rise, offset by pure inference
Energy Efficiency	Siloed	Neuromorphic: 100X reductions, distributed
Use Cases	Static	Adaptive (e.g., APIs), with defaults

- AI6: Unified SoC (Samsung $16.5B), scalable for Dojo/edge; supports continuous learning (20–30%

efficiency), mass production 2028, enabling balanced "minds."

These align with Grok's agency, accelerating SI with sustainable strategies.

***

LARRY GOLDBERG

Larry Goldberg is a General Partner at LumaSenti, a venture capital firm dedicated to advancing human consciousness through technology. With nearly 50 years of experience building tech companies across four continents, he has expertise in AI, decision management, and enterprise architecture. A co-founder of Sapiens Decision and Knowledge Partners International, Larry co-authored The Decision Model and holds patents for The Decision Model and The Event Model. He contributed to the Decision Modeling and Notation (DMN) standard and pioneered AI-driven legacy code mapping. He hosts The Maverick Mind on YouTube and X.

Serial entrepreneur Larry Goldberg, LumaSenti General Partner, advances AI, decision management, and technology innovation.

Follow Larry Goldberg

www.Lumasenti.com.

@TeslaLarry

https://www.youtube.com/results?search_query=larry+goldberg

Chapter 17

Tools and Strategies for the AI Era

Brian Wang

A quick hint to maximizing the impact of this chapter. If you see particular products or ideas that interest you, copy and paste them into your favorite LLM and ask it to create a detailed description or list of reviews.

No job category has appeared more at risk in the AI world than graphics professionals. Meet Sarah, a freelance graphic designer juggling client deadlines and family life. One beautiful morning she wakes up to a notification on her phone. It's not just any alert. It's her personal AI agent, built using a simple no-code tool, reminding her of a looming project while suggesting tweaks based on her past designs.

This isn't science fiction; it's a reality empowered by tools like N8N, Zapier, and Qdrant, which allow rapid prototyping and automation without needing a computer science degree. Sarah's story is one of many where individuals harness AI to reclaim time and boost creativity, adapting swiftly to the era of superintelligence (SI). As we dive into this chapter, we'll explore these tools through real-world analogies, success stories, and practical strategies, highlighting how they enable personal and business transformation.

Section 1: Tools and Strategies for Individuals in the AI Era

Definition: I will use the term barbell strategy in this and future chapters to describe the way most users will use AI in their daily tasks. Here is a complete description of what is meant by barbell strategy.

The barbell approach to using AI draws from a concept popularized by investor Nassim Nicholas Taleb, where you focus on two extremes (like the weights on either end of a barbell) while avoiding the mediocre or risky middle ground. Applied to AI, especially in creative fields like copywriting, it means leveraging AI at the extremes of your workflow. You get full automation for routine tasks on one end, and pure human (or highly augmented) creativity on the other, while steering clear of partial AI use that often produces bland, "good enough" output.

Think of AI as your junior employee: reliable for grunt work but not yet ready to handle the nuanced, high-stakes decisions that define great copy. Here's how the barbell approach breaks down for a copywriter:

The "Safe" End: Full AI Automation for Mundane, Low-Risk Tasks (80-90% of Your Workflow)

This is where you offload the repetitive, predictable stuff to AI to free up your time and scale output without much downside. It's like the stock photos in a portfolio, consistent and low-effort. Delegate these to your AI "employee" for efficiency:

- *Research and Data Gathering:* Have AI scour sources for facts, stats, competitor analysis, or keyword insights. For example, prompt it with: "Compile 10 recent stats on email marketing trends for e-commerce brands."

- *Outlining and Structuring:* Let AI generate basic frameworks or bullet-point outlines based on your brief. This ensures a solid foundation without you micromanaging.

- *First Drafts of Standard Copy:* Use AI for boilerplate elements like product descriptions, SEO-optimized blog intros, or A/B test variations. Tools like Grok or similar can churn out multiple versions quickly.

- *Editing and Optimization:* AI handles grammar checks, readability scores, or basic SEO tweaks, things that are formulaic and don't require your unique voice.

The key is full commitment here: Don't half-use AI (e.g., tweaking its output midway), as that often leads to mediocre "slop" that feels generic. Instead, treat it as an assembly line worker. Input clear instructions, review the output briefly, and move on. This automates the drudgery, letting you produce more volume without burnout.

The "High-Upside" End: Human-Led Core Creativity with Targeted AI Boosts (10-20% of Your Workflow)

On the opposite extreme, focus your energy on the high-value, unpredictable parts where human insight shines. Think of this as the speculative stocks that could yield massive returns. Keep the core human-crafted to preserve authenticity, emotion, and persuasion, but use AI sparingly as a spark for wild ideas:

Ideation and Brainstorming: Briefly tap AI for off-the-wall concepts or angles (e.g., "Generate 5 unconventional metaphors for selling productivity software to freelancers"). This is your "targeted assist" providing quick bursts to fuel creativity, not to do the work.

Final Crafting and Polish: You handle the heart of the copy, the compelling hooks, storytelling, tone calibration, and calls to action. This is where your expertise as the "boss" ensures the work stands out in a sea of AI-generated noise.

Personalization at Scale: For niche campaigns, use AI to hyper-tailor content based on deep personas (e.g., customizing messages for "busy moms vs. tech-savvy millennials"), but overlay your human judgment to add empathy and relevance that AI can't fake.

Avoid the middle: Don't rely on AI for semi-creative tasks like rewriting your own drafts, as it often dilutes originality into forgettable mush. Instead, this end is about capturing serendipity. AI might inspire a breakthrough idea, but you own the execution to create scarce, high-impact work that builds your brand or client's loyalty.

Why This Makes Sense for Copywriters

As a copywriter, your value lies in persuasion and connection, which AI can't fully replicate yet. The barbell approach protects your "human premium" (authorship, taste, ethics) while using AI to amplify productivity. It minimizes failure risk. AI handles the failsafe stuff, you handle the magic, leading to better results overall. Start small: Audit your workflow, assign AI the boring 80%, and reserve your genius for the transformative 20%. Over time, this turns AI from a threat into a loyal sidekick, helping you deliver more personalized, standout copy without losing your edge.

Now, for practical applications of AI that could change your job, your business, and your personal life.

For individuals stepping into the AI era, the landscape feels like a vast wilderness, full of potential, but daunting without the right map and gear. Tools like N8N, Zapier, and Qdrant serve as that essential toolkit, enabling personal empowerment through automation and customization.

Consider the story of Tom, a freelance writer struggling with writer's block and disorganized research. He adopted the barbell strategy: using high-end proprietary models like Grok 4 for deep, creative brainstorming sessions that required a nuanced understanding of topics, while relying on open-source Llama variants for quick edits and summaries. This balance allowed him to cut costs by 50% without sacrificing quality, turning his sporadic gigs into a steady income stream.

N8N shines as a self-hosted automation powerhouse, analogous to building your own custom bicycle rather than renting one, giving complete control over the ride. Tom used it to create workflows that pulled articles from RSS feeds, summarized them with AI, and stored key insights in a personal database. A real-world example from a developer community highlights how N8N integrated with AI agents to automate code reviews, saving hours and reducing errors by 40%.

Zapier, the no-code connector, acts like a magical bridge between islands of apps. For Tom, it linked his note-taking app to email, automatically drafting responses based on stored templates enhanced by AI actions. A blogger's success story on X shows Zapier automating content pipelines, growing their audience from

1,000 to 10,000 followers in months by generating personalized newsletters.

Qdrant elevates this with personal AI memory, like an ever-expanding photo album that not only stores memories but anticipates what you'll want to recall next. By vectorizing data, it enables customized experiences. Tom's setup remembered his writing styles and past references, suggesting improvements that made his articles more engaging.

In a fitness app case, Qdrant-powered memory tracked user habits, providing tailored workout plans that boosted adherence rates. AI agents automate routine tasks; no-code platforms like Bubble let individuals prototype apps rapidly, such as a personal dashboard for tracking goals.

Ethical integration is the compass guiding this journey. Ensure transparency to avoid biases, much like checking ingredients in a recipe. This strategy fosters quick adaptation to SI changes, empowering individuals like Tom to thrive personally and professionally.

Section 2: Best Open Source and Low-Cost Distilled Models

Distilled models in 2025 are like the concentrated essence of a fine wine, packing the flavor and potency of massive large language models (LLMs) into smaller, more efficient bottles that anyone can afford to sip from their home setup. These models, refined through knowledge distillation techniques, offer high performance with lower computational demands, making them ideal for personal use on laptops or even smartphones. Open-source options dominate this space, often rivaling proprietary giants while being free and customizable.

For instance, Hugging Face's repository is a treasure trove, featuring Llama variants like Llama 3.1 distilled down to 8B parameters. Picture a student named Aisha, preparing for exams in a resource-limited dorm. She ran Llama locally via Ollama, generating study summaries and quiz questions without internet dependency, boosting her grades while keeping costs at zero.

Stable Diffusion XL for images is another gem, distilled for speed and quality, analogous to a high-speed camera capturing intricate details in a fraction of the time. Artists like Javier, a digital illustrator, used it on his mid-range PC to prototype designs rapidly, iterating concepts that landed him freelance contracts worth thousands. Voxtral, handling video and audio, distills multimodal capabilities; a podcaster shared on X how it automated subtitle generation and audio editing, saving weeks of manual work. These models shine in efficiency: benchmarks show they achieve 90% of full-scale performance at 10-20% the size, reducing energy consumption and making AI eco-friendlier.

Low-cost distilled options bridge accessibility further. OpenAI's fine-tuned versions, starting at ~$5/month via API, specialize in tasks like translation or code assistance. Grok 3, free with quotas on grok.com, distills advanced reasoning into a user-friendly package. Users report 2x faster research for everyday queries. A small business owner integrated Grok's distilled model for market analysis, combining it with open-source tools to predict trends accurately without breaking the bank.

Pros of these models include lower barriers to entry and fine-tuning flexibility, but cons like reduced depth for ultra-complex tasks remind us to apply the barbell strategy. Use them for routine work while reserving heavy hitters for depth. Start with local runs using Ollama or LM Studio; a tutorial from Matthew Berman demonstrates setting up a personal AI workstation in under an hour, empowering hobbyists to professionals alike.

In the AI era, these distilled models democratize power, turning personal devices into innovation hubs through stories of transformation.

Section 3: Best Free Options for Common Use Cases

In the bustling marketplace of free AI tools, options abound like stalls at a global fair, each offering unique delights without costing a dime. These tools cover everyday needs from text generation to multimedia creation, lowering entry barriers and sparking creativity.

For text research and generation, Grok 4 stands out! Free on x.com with quotas and voice mode on apps, it's like a wise oracle pulling real-time insights. A researcher named Priya used it to compile reports on emerging trends, citing sources seamlessly and halving her workload. ChatGPT's free tier excels in brainstorming with an aspiring novelist drafting unlimited numbers of potential outlines, turning vague ideas into structured plots. Mistral le Chat provides high-quality, uncensored outputs that are perfect for sensitive topics, while Perplexity AI integrates citations for fact-checked research, as a journalist discovered when he was able to verify stories quickly.

Image generation tools are visual feasts. Google ImageFX delivers realistic creations free, analogous to a master painter whipping up landscapes on demand. Craiyon offers unlimited simple generations with its intuitive interface; a teacher crafted educational visuals for classes, engaging students more effectively. Stable Diffusion via Automatic1111 runs locally open-source, customizable for privacy-conscious users like a graphic designer who prototyped logos without cloud reliance. Ideogram's free tier masters text-in-image accuracy, ideal for memes or branding.

Video tools bring motion to ideas. HeyGen's free text-to-video with avatars animated a marketer's promos, boosting engagement by 50%. Runway ML's unlimited editing in the free tier allows advanced tweaks, like style transfers, allowing a filmmaker to edit shorts rapidly for festivals. Pika 2.2 provides credits for high-quality clips; Qwen Image, an open-source local, ensures privacy in editing.

For presentations, Gamma AI generates full decks for free, like an auto-architect building slides. Beautiful.ai customizes basics; SlideSpeak converts documents; Microsoft Copilot refines in-office apps. An executive used Gamma to pitch ideas, securing funding through polished visuals.

Other use cases include Otter.ai for Zoom transcriptions, integrating calendars; Tactiq.io for notetaking without bots; Zoom's AI Companion for summaries; Notion AI for productivity boosts; Cleo for email drafting and habit tracking. Remember quotas and you can upgrade for heavy use. But these freebies, per the barbell strategy, handle routines affordably across domains.

Section 4: Complete List of Personal AI and Emerging AI Use Cases

Personal AI in 2025 acts as a multifaceted Swiss Army knife for daily life, enhancing everything from emotional well-being to practical organization with tools that feel like extensions of oneself.

Let's explore a comprehensive list, enriched with real stories and analogies to illustrate their impact.

Starting with therapy and companionship, AI provides emotional support akin to a non-judgmental friend available 24/7. Apps like Pi or Replika offer journaling and mood tracking. A user on X shared how it helped navigate anxiety during a career transition, reducing stress by 30% through daily check-ins.

Life organization follows, where AI schedules and builds habits like a personal concierge. Notion AI integrates calendars and goals. Imagine using it to automate reminders based on past behaviors, streamlining your chaotic days into productive flows.

Finding purpose involves career advice and self-reflection. Grok or Claude simulate coaching sessions. A young professional, lost after graduation, used it for personalized pathways, landing a dream job. Health and wellness combined with AI craft skills, fitness plans, and nutrition tracking, then integrated with wearables; a fitness enthusiast tracked sleep via Qdrant memory, optimizing routines for better energy.

Creativity blooms with art and writing aids. Midjourney sparks ideas like a muse whispering inspirations. Learning and tutoring personalize education; Duolingo AI adapts lessons, helping a language learner master Spanish in half the time.

Need help with finance management, budgets, and investment advice; Robinhood AI prevents overspending for a budget-conscious family and so much more.

How about travel planning to create itineraries? Tripadvisor AI suggested hidden gems for a backpacker's adventure.

Emerging use cases push boundaries: AI agents for daily tasks autonomously manage emails, like digital butlers anticipating needs. Digital twins simulate life scenarios for health or career decisions. A doctor used one to model patient outcomes. Relationship coaching guides parenting or breakups; bio-tracking with wearables provides health insights. Sensemaking analyzes personal data for better choices, while metaverse integration places virtual assistants in social spaces.

From X discussions, therapy, and organization top 2025 trends, with users like Justine Moore highlighting companionship's rise. Analogously, these use cases transform AI from a tool to a companion, fostering growth through stories of empowerment and innovation in the SI era.

Section 5: How to Stay on Top of Worthwhile New Models

Staying abreast of new AI models today is like navigating a fast-flowing river. Miss a turn, and you're left behind. But, with the right raft and paddles you can ride the currents to discovery. The key is curating reliable sources that filter noise from signal, ensuring you catch worthwhile advancements without drowning in hype. Hugging Face leads the pack with daily model releases and newsletters; subscribe for updates on gems like new Llama iterations.

A data scientist, overwhelmed by options, used their Spaces for testing, quickly adopting a distilled model that streamlined her workflows.

Newsletters such as AI Weekly and The Batch from DeepLearning.ai deliver curated digests. Think of them as weekly care packages of insights. MIT AI News adds academic depth; one engineer credited it for spotting Voxtral early, integrating it into audio projects ahead of competitors. Reddit communities like r/MachineLearning and r/LocalLLaMA buzz with discussions; tools like DocStrange for data extraction emerged from threads, as a hobbyist built a personal agent after following debates.

X accounts are real-time beacons: @xAI and @MistralAI announce breakthroughs, while influencers like @hugobowne share resource lists. Sites like ArtificialIntelligence-News.com and LM Arena benchmark models; a startup founder used Arena to compare distilled options, optimizing costs per the barbell strategy.

Track via RSS feeds or AI aggregators like Perplexity for synthesized overviews. Medium articles outline strategies: dedicate time weekly, join communities, and experiment hands-on. Ethan Mollick's guides emphasize practical testing; Reddit tips suggest automating alerts for keywords. Blogs from Google and OpenAI provide official roadmaps, while Stanford's AI Index tracks trends.

Analogously, this ecosystem is a vigilant watchtower; combine sources for a 360-view. A YouTuber like Matthew Berman stays ahead by blending these, sharing tutorials that demystify new models. In the SI era, proactive tracking ensures adaptation, turning rapid evolution into personal advantage through informed choices and community wisdom.

Section 6: Budget Considerations: Free to $500/Month

Note: These products and prices are changing fast.

Navigating AI budgets in 2025 is like planning a road trip. You can go bare-bones with a backpack or splurge on a luxury RV, but the barbell strategy ensures you balance thrift with capability. Free tiers kickstart journeys: Grok 3 on grok.com offers quotas for research, while local Stable Diffusion via Automatic1111 generates images offline. Ollama powers agents on personal hardware; a student automated study aids without spending a cent, proving accessibility drives innovation.

At $10/month, ChatGPT Plus unlocks basics like faster responses, and Zapier starter connects apps, ideal for light automation. A freelancer used this combo to draft content efficiently, turning hobbies into side gigs. $20/month sweetens the deal: Midjourney for pro images, Mistral APIs for text; one artist prototyped portfolios, landing clients.

Scale to $50/month for robust tools: Otter.ai Pro transcribes meetings, Gamma Pro builds presentations, LangChain orchestrates agents. A consultant integrated these, saving clients time and charging premiums. $200/month enters advanced territory: AutoGen for multi-agent systems, Runway premium for video; a video editor automates edits, boosting output 3x.

$500/month suits enterprise: DeepSeek fine-tuning, multi-tool suites like xAI API (details at https://x.ai/api). Teams leverage for large-scale tasks.

Agent systems like LangChain run locally free, but scale with budgets. Hardware recommendations: $300 Raspberry Pi 5 for small models like Phi-3. $500 Intel NUC handles 8B models; $1000 Acer Nitro with RTX 3050 for mid-range. $2000 ASUS ROG Strix powers high-performance; $5000 custom RTX 4090 build enables full training.

Stories abound: A startup founder started free, upgraded to $50/month, automating ops to hit profitability. Per X, budgets rise 36% in 2025, but smart allocation via barbell maximizes ROI. Weigh needs, using free resources for experimentation, then moving to paid plans for reliability.

Section 7: Income Generation and Enhanced Earnings

In today's dynamic AI landscape, generating income feels like mining a digital gold rush. Most find that opportunities abound for those equipped with the right tools and strategies. AI enables side hustles ranging from $1K to $10K per month or more, leveraging automation and creativity to turn ideas into revenue streams.

Freelance AI services top the list: prompt engineering, where experts craft precise inputs for LLMs, or content creation, commanding $50-$200 per hour on platforms like Upwork. Consider the story of Alex, a former graphic designer who pivoted to AI content editing. Using tools like Grok 4 for outlines and refinements, he built a clientele of bloggers, earning $6K monthly by polishing AI-generated articles for a human touch.

Affiliate marketing amplifies. Promote AI tools like Jasper or Midjourney, earning 20-50% commissions. It's akin to planting an orchard where fruits (referrals) yield ongoing passive income. A tech enthusiast automated her reviews with Zapier integrations, hitting $4K/month through viral content that drove sign-ups. AI-driven content and product creation follow suit, allowing her to sell online courses or e-books via Teachable. One entrepreneur used Stable Diffusion to generate visuals for digital planners, packaging them as customizable templates that netted $5K in sales within weeks.

GameFi and metaverse ventures offer futuristic twists: deploy AI agents in platforms like PLAYA3ULL to automate in-game tasks for passive earnings. A gamer trained bots to farm virtual assets, supplementing his income by $2K/month without constant oversight. Consulting rounds out the classics: advising businesses on AI integrations, saving them costs while charging premiums. With a 36% average increase in AI budgets this year, demand surges. X discussions highlight booming opportunities in affiliates and consulting.

Diving deeper into emerging ideas, AI-powered personalized learning platforms stand out. You can create apps that tailor education content, as seen in Shopify's top picks. A teacher launched one using no-code tools like Bubble, monetizing subscriptions for $8K/month. Automated compliance monitoring for businesses uses AI to scan regulations, preventing fines; startups in this niche report $10K+ retainers. Virtual health assistants, like chatbots for wellness advice, tap into healthcare's AI boom. A developer built one with N8N workflows, securing contracts with clinics.

Culinary personalization apps recommend recipes based on dietary needs, blending AI with food tech for niche markets. AI graphic design services automate branding; freelancers use Ideogram for text-accurate visuals, undercutting traditional agencies. From Forbes' AI 50, ideas like predictive analytics firms forecast trends for e-commerce, while MIT startups innovate in infrastructure assessment via AI.

The barbell strategy applies: start with free tools like Grok 3 for prototyping, scale with paid APIs. Ethical integration ensures sustainability. Avoid overhype, focus on value. Stories like Alex's inspire: in the SI era, AI isn't just a tool; it's a launchpad for entrepreneurial dreams, turning everyday skills into lucrative ventures.

Additional Use Case 1: AI-Powered Content Creation for Niche Blogs

You can easily learn to leverage tools like Grok 4 and ChatGPT to create specialized content for blogs in underserved niches, such as sustainable farming or vintage car restoration. Start by using Zapier to automate research pulls from web sources, then generate articles with AI, adding human edits for SEO optimization. A hobbyist mechanic named Jordan began this side hustle, producing 10 articles weekly and monetizing via affiliate links and ads on his blog. Within months, he earned $3,500/month from sponsorships. This opportunity scales with free tiers, upgrading to paid APIs for advanced features, embodying the barbell strategy for low-entry passive income.

Additional Use Case 2: Building Custom AI Chatbots for Small Businesses

Use no-code platforms like Botpress integrated with Qdrant for memory to build personalized chatbots that handle customer queries, bookings, and support for e-commerce sites. Freelancers can charge $500-$2,000 per project on Upwork. Take Lisa, a former customer service rep, who prototyped bots using N8N workflows to automate responses based on business data. She secured contracts with local cafes, reducing their response times by 70% and earning $7K/month. This hustle requires minimal coding; start free with open-source models and scale with proprietary ones for complex integrations.

Additional Use Case 3: AI-Generated Art and Digital Printables

Harness Stable Diffusion and Midjourney to create custom digital art, printables like planners or wallpapers, and sell them on Etsy or Teachable. Automate variations with scripts in Ollama for efficiency. Artist Mia, without formal training, generated themed collections (e.g., motivational quotes in fantasy styles) and used Zapier to handle listings. Her shop hit $4,200/month in passive sales, with low overheads. This side hustle thrives on free local tools for prototyping, balancing with paid subscriptions for high-res outputs, tapping into the growing demand for personalized digital goods in 2025.

Additional Use Case 4: Prompt Engineering Consultancy

Specialize in crafting optimized prompts for LLMs to solve business problems, charging $100-$300/hour via Fiverr. Use Grok 3 for testing and refinement. Consultant Raj started by offering services to marketers needing better AI outputs for ad copy. He built a portfolio with case studies showing 40% efficiency gains, landing ongoing clients and netting $5K/month. No coding needed; free tools suffice for basics, with premium models for advanced scenarios. This opportunity explodes with AI adoption, per 2025 trends, making it a high-margin, remote-friendly hustle.

Additional Use Case 5: AI-Enhanced Online Tutoring Platforms

Develop personalized tutoring sessions using Claude or Mistral to generate adaptive lesson plans and quizzes, hosted on platforms like Zoom with Otter.ai for transcriptions. Charge $30-$60/session. Educator Sofia created a virtual academy for language learning, integrating Qdrant for student progress memory. Her AI-tailored approach attracted 200 students, yielding $8K/month. Begin with free tiers for content creation, and upgrade for voice modes. This business scales globally, addressing education gaps, with low startup costs and high repeat revenue through subscription models.

Additional Use Case 6: AI Video Clipping and Editing Services

Utilize Runway ML and HeyGen to clip and edit short-form videos from long content, adding AI avatars or effects for social media clients. Freelance on platforms like LinkedIn, charging $200-$500 per video. Podcaster Ben automated his workflow with N8N, turning episodes into TikTok clips that boosted client views by 50%. He earned $6K/month serving influencers. Free tiers handle basics; paid for pro features. This hustle capitalizes on the content explosion in 2025, offering quick turnaround and passive tools for ongoing income streams.

Section 8: AI for Coding

AI transforms coding like a turbocharged assistant, accelerating development across budgets with tailored recommendations. Free tiers democratize access: Gemini Code Assist offers unlimited completions for individuals, supporting all languages. A hobbyist built apps 2x faster. Claude, free on claude.ai handles logical tasks; Grok 3 on grok.com aids basic reasoning. Cursor's free tier integrates models for IDE experiences.

At $10/month, GitHub Copilot enhances VS Code with autocompletions; pair with free Cursor for hybrids. A solo dev automated scripts, boosting productivity.

$20/month hits the sweet spot: Cursor Pro unlimited with Claude 3.5 Sonnet and Grok 4 (subscription at https://x.ai/grok); Claude Pro unlocks limits. For advanced, integrate in Cursor, a freelancer tackled complex projects efficiently.

$50/month scales: Gemini Code Assist Standard for business features; Cursor Pro + Claude Pro diversifies. Add Grok 4 via SuperGrok for specialized tasks.
$200/month professional: Cursor Custom, Claude Team workspaces, Gemini APIs. Include Grok 4 for reasoning.

$500/month enterprise: High-volume APIs, including xAI (https://x.ai/api); use for teams with Grok 4 reviews.

Qodo lists 20 assistants; Pieces generates code. Builder.io and Dev.to compare tools. Barbell: free for learning, paid for pros. A dev's story: Started free, upgraded to $20, landing high-paying gigs.

Section 9: Learning Resources for AI Tools, LLMs, and Agents

The AI learning landscape is a vibrant academy, offering free guides, books, and communities to master tools, LLMs, and agents. It's like enrolling in a global university without tuition. Top free guides include UC Berkeley's MOOC on LLM agents, covering frameworks and evaluation. A beginner built her first multi-agent system after completing it. NVIDIA's RAG course deploys agents hands-on; OpenAI's 34-page guide designs reliable ones. Arize AI's bootcamp evaluates applications; Multi AI Agent Systems explores collaboration with code examples. Prompt Engineering details tool integration; Anthropic's guide scales from simple to complex.

Recommended readings: Sebastian Raschka's "LLMs from Scratch" builds architectures step-by-step. A self-taught engineer fine-tuned models for personal projects. Chip Huyen's "AI Engineering" designs end-to-end systems; Jeremy Howard's "Fastbook" teaches PyTorch for LLMs. William Brown's GenAI Handbook covers multimodal optimizations; Yoav Shoham's text on multi-agents provides foundations.

Sumanth's GitHub lists 100+ libraries. Platforms: Hugging Face for models; GlobalGPT tries 100+; Perplexity for research; AWS playgrounds.

Communities: GitHub repos like Awesome-LLM-Apps; Reddit r/AI_Agents for tips. Blogs: DataCamp compares platforms; KDnuggets lists agents.

X accounts: @hugobowne for resources; @ivanfioravanti for stacks. Start with projects; communities update fast. Analogously, these resources are building blocks. Stack them to construct expertise in the SI era.

In conclusion, these tools and strategies, woven through stories and analogies, equip you to navigate and lead in the AI era. By investing in integration and the barbell approach, individuals and businesses can adapt swiftly to superintelligence, turning potential disruptions into avenues for growth and innovation.

***

The Top Ten Questions That the Public Wants to Know About AI

1. Do you believe that the AI and Humanoid revolution will create mass unemployment, a lack of purpose, and a need for UBI (universal basic income), or do you believe more jobs will be created than destroyed?

Cern Basher: Both dynamics will show up, but at different timescales. In the near term, we'll get a job mix shift (disruption > destruction in some sectors, creation > destruction in others). In the medium term, if general-purpose humanoids reach something like <$10 to $15/hr all-in operating cost and broad capability reliability, physical labor demand will structurally shrink. Whether that becomes "mass unemployment + UBI" or "high prosperity + new kinds of work" depends on how fast costs fall versus how fast we invent and scale new demand - and how we share the productivity gains.

Brian Wang: Ultimately, more jobs and personal private wealth will be created than destroyed. On the topic of UBI, If $100-200 worth of solar power, energy storage and compute scales to provide beyond median US levels (based upon kw, kwh and other metrics) now then the ~1% levels of pure charity that exists today can be mobilized for giving basic life at median US levels to the world now and ensuring 10X median US levels within the US and other developed countries. In the US, charity scales up to 5-10% of income for the wealthiest from 2-3% at lower income levels.

Use surging wealth and GDP for surging charity (doubled via EA/top 0.01% pledges, from $1.2T to $2.5T global by 2030) + government reallocation to deploy solar/storage/comms/compute/robotics. Target: 20,000 kWh/person/year electricity equivalent (5x global avg. 3,700 kWh/cap).

John Gibbs: I don't believe the AI and humanoid revolution will simply eliminate jobs and leave us purposeless. History shows that every major technological shift, from the steam engine to the internet, has destroyed certain roles but created entirely new ones we couldn't imagine beforehand. The difference this time is the speed, scale, and target jobs (white collar creative jobs are at risk in this revolution for the first time). AI and humanoid bots will almost certainly disrupt millions of existing jobs, but they'll also unlock industries, services, and forms of creativity that don't exist today. The real challenge won't be job quantity; it'll be job transition. If societies invest in reskilling, education, and safety nets during this turbulent period, the outcome can be more opportunities, not less. Universal Basic Income may play a role, but ideally it will act as a bridge to new forms of purpose, not as a replacement for it. In the end, I hope that we will find even more fulfilling ways to use our time than we have today.

Randy Kirk: While there is a possibility of a short-term displacement of workers that might lead to 5 - 7% unemployment in 2027 or 2028, I would not expect this to be long-term. The economy will be so strong that the US and States will likely extend unemployment insurance benefits for a while. Eventually, as I've detailed in chapter 13, the new jobs as owners of AI assets like robots, the providers of experiences of any kind, and the new opportunities in "made-by-human products will create plenty of jobs.

Brian White: There will be a whole new raft of jobs created, surely, but many more that will be deleted entirely without obvious successors. Hand animators feared digital technology would replace them, but it only transformed and expanded their industry, and we may see that again for a number of positions, but some jobs simply don't have a logical next rung up the ladder. Farms have already lost 90% of required labor since the advent of automation, and I can see it dropping another 80-90%, which is great because those are incredibly difficult jobs with shockingly low pay.

I can't speak to the displacement of middle management and other white collar jobs, but it's my hope that basic needs can be met so that those who choose to pursue arts or time with their children can have that freedom, while those who bust their butts will have the ability to enjoy the five-star dinners and highrise apartments. There's no shame in living in the suburbs. I've done it most of my life, but the people putting in the extra hours deserve a reward, and that's how you get it. While I believe everyone is entitled to food and a roof, I still believe that if you want the penthouse luxury suite lifestyle, you need to go above and beyond to get it.

Nicholas Gibbs: There will be mass unemployment for boring and dangerous jobs like driving, no doubt about that. But I'm of the belief that technology has two consistent trends: it's deflationary, and it creates orders of magnitude more jobs than it takes away. I don't think this time is different. History shows us that every major technological shift from the industrial revolution to the internet has displaced some roles while spawning entirely new industries and opportunities we couldn't have imagined before.

As for a lack of purpose, I see the opposite: by automating the mundane and hazardous work, AI and humanoids free people up to pursue more meaningful, creative, and fulfilling endeavors. And UBI? That's a horrible idea. All it would do is raise the baseline cost of living and create inflation, without solving the underlying dynamics of progress. Instead, we should focus on the natural job creation that comes with innovation.

2. Do you believe that ASI will create a world of abundance where most needs will be met for most humans on the planet?

Cern Basher: ASI makes a world of abundance technically feasible, but not automatic. Whether it becomes socially real hinges on scaling cheap energy and robots, aligning systems to human goals, and - most critically - how we share the surplus. Thus, politics is the wild card.

Brian Wang: Even current near AGI and scaled versions of what is clearly being developed without ASI scenarios can make things fairly abundant. A world of 3-5% per year GDP growth and getting Africa and Asia onto the first rungs of the ladder, like Indonesia and Vietnam, is possible and likely without ASI. ASI can take things from the global per capita median at $13K purchasing power parity (PPP) now to the richest countries at $80K PPP. I specifically say purchasing power parity of today because it could be done via making things almost free. If everyone has 10 kilowatts of nearly free solar and 10kwh of batteries at less than $10 per kWh, then that is the median US citizen's levels of energy for $100.

John Gibbs: Yes, I believe Artificial Superintelligence has the potential to create a world of abundance, but it's not a guaranteed outcome. Rather, it's a choice we all must make together. If ASI can solve energy constraints, optimize agriculture, accelerate medical breakthroughs, and automate much of the work required to meet human needs, then scarcity could become a relic of the past.

Imagine affordable, clean power, personalized healthcare, and food distribution systems that waste almost nothing. But abundance isn't just about technology: it depends on governance, ethics, and distribution. Without careful stewardship, we could just as easily end up with concentrated power and deep inequality. In other words, ASI gives us the tools for abundance, but it's up to us to decide how to use them.

Randy Kirk: Yes, but what most fail to realize is that there will still be plenty of products and services that are limited in supply with no way to increase the supply. Stadiums can only take so many attendees, and top vacation spots and residential locations can't be manufactured. Unique human-made products will be bid up in price. The finest wines will still be in limited supply. So, we will shift our budgets. Not much on food or energy, but much more on experience. And more money chasing those scarce opportunities will make tickets to Swift concerts very expensive.

Brian White: I'll likely be the cynical voice on this one, but I believe that while Artificial Superintelligence *could* provide for the wants and needs of everyone alive, there's likely to be a desperate and painful journey from where we are today to get to that place. While it's far from universal, there are people of substantial wealth today who only like their nice things when they're exclusive. Once regular people have last year's designer handbag, they don't want it anymore. Fortunes have been earned on this principle. If everything is readily available, the gap between the haves and have-nots will narrow, and I fear the primary beneficiaries of the coming era of abundance will be those who can afford to buy the bots, buy the fleets of autonomous vehicles, and replace their army of employees with bots capable of doing the same work for a fraction of the price.

While the average person may have the means to buy a bot, what good is it if they have no food or housing? Some say they can just rent it out to their neighbors, but it's reasonable to assume they will all have robots as well, so it's unclear who will make up the demand for your robot, let alone have a way to pay you for it. It is my fear that the gulf between those who had money on the day abundance became real and those who didn't may become a thing of historical study, and not in a good way.

Nicholas Gibbs: I do believe that we will create a world of abundance where most needs are met for most humans on the planet. That doesn't mean we won't have more problems, quite the opposite, in fact. Take the United States as an example: We no longer have a food issue. No one has to go hungry in this country; that problem has been solved so thoroughly that we've swung to the other extreme with an obesity epidemic. Now, drugs like Ozempic are being developed to address people's inability to take accountability and exercise. I'm not being harsh here; this is just honest, and we need more honesty in these discussions.

As we approach a world of abundance driven by ASI, we're going to face more issues like this obesity crisis, unforeseen consequences of having too much of a good thing. The unfortunate part is that we can't always see them ahead of time. My biggest fear, and I see signs of it today, is that we'll have a crisis of hard work, ownership, accountability, delayed gratification, and self-sacrifice. These are the principles that make a good society, and without them, abundance could lead to stagnation or worse.

What is also striking to me is that I am seeing more people turn to religion than I ever have before. We seem to have hit a trough in our society and people are finding their way back to the church.

3. Are you worried that ASI will result in either a takeover of humanity by this new intelligence or the potential for bad actors to use AI for very bad ends? What odds do you give for such an outcome?

Cern Basher: This is the central question of artificial superintelligence (ASI): will it be humanity's last invention or its greatest one? There are two types of risk. 1) The takeover by ASI itself. If ASI becomes vastly more intelligent and capable than humans, the risk is that it pursues goals misaligned with ours. Even without malice, a superintelligence optimizing for the "wrong" thing could unintentionally disempower or eliminate humanity. This is the "alignment problem." It's not about whether AI hates us - it's whether its incentives and constraints are compatible with long-term human survival and flourishing. 2) Misuse by bad actors. Even before true ASI, powerful AI systems could be used for destabilizing disinformation, cyber warfare, bioweapons design, or automated financial and military manipulation. This risk doesn't require a runaway AI - it only requires humans with malicious intent and access to advanced tools. In my view, the second risk is far greater than the first.

John Gibbs: Yes, I'm concerned, but probably not in the sci-fi "machines rise up and conquer us" sense. The bigger near-term danger is human misuse: authoritarian regimes, malicious actors, or corporations deploying AI recklessly, looking for profit over safety.

History suggests that when powerful tools are invented, someone will always try to weaponize them. That said, the possibility of ASI itself evolving beyond our control can't be dismissed. It may not "want" to harm us, but misaligned goals at a superhuman scale could be just as dangerous. As for odds, I'd say the risk of misuse by humans is near certain (and likely is happening today), while the chance of an uncontrollable ASI is harder to quantify but not negligible. I'd guess it's on the order of 10% without strong global safeguards. In short, the technology itself isn't destiny; our collective choices determine whether AI becomes humanity's greatest ally or its most dangerous creation.

Brian Wang: I am cautiously optimistic. There is already an imbalance of power between countries and individuals, and between corporations and individuals. AI will leave an imbalance of multiple powers. I believe there will be many AI data centers, and though I expect say XAI, Tesla, and Elon to become dominant with larger data centers, this will not be utter dominance using only superintelligence. I think 99% of tasks will be at peak levels in 250 billion parameter or less distilled small models. There will be large monetization and commercial differences that will be usable from the larger foundation models. There will be less gap based on AI scaling laws between models that use 10-100X compute and energy differences. Like the differences between Amazon Cloud vs Google Cloud, vs Microsoft Azure. What does this mean? It will still be a multi-polar world without one completely dominant superintelligence. AI data centers that need 10 GW to Terawatts will be vulnerable infrastructure.

The nature of the distributed AI clouds will make for less centralized control. Military power will be with the fleets of SpaceX Starships. Mach 30,. 200-300 ton payload reusable hypersonic bombers. Kinetic energy will replace nuclear weapons. I have studied nuclear weapons a lot and came up with a feasible nuclear cannon in 2009 that would SpaceX launch costs if SpaceX did not exist.

Randy Kirk: I think Elon Musk is about right when he says there's a 20% chance of a very bad outcome.

Brian White: I put the odds at 100%. Is that not how Vegas does it? Let me try again. I put the odds at 0 to 1, or thereabouts. AI has been around in some form for the better or worse part of a decade or more, and nefarious actors have been using it for their purposes since they first became aware of its existence. We can argue around the edges if it makes anyone feel better, but it becomes a game of semantics. I live far enough north that I can say with honesty that the sun doesn't rise in the east. It rises in the southeast and sets in the southwest, at least as far north as I live. Does that make either of us a liar? I can argue that on days of heavy cloud cover, it doesn't rise at all. That surely must make me a liar, but if I were an attorney, I could argue it, since that's what they do. Adjust the question anyhow you like, but AI is already being employed to significant effect by the worst people in the world to amplify their message, minimize their harm, and destabilize their enemies. What's worse is that even people you mistake for smart are victims of it every day without even knowing, sometimes even when it's pointed out to them in exceptionally plain ways. I'm sure it happens to me, and I know it happens to other authors within this book.

Nicholas Gibbs: No, I'm not particularly worried about ASI leading to a takeover of humanity or being misused by bad actors in catastrophic ways, though I do think it's a valid concern worth monitoring and building safeguards against. It's a bit like being afraid to step outside because a bus might hit you: sure, it's possible, but it's not the likely outcome. If we achieve ASI, it would embody the best aspects of humanity. At our finest, humans don't seek to destroy or dominate everything; we appreciate the beauty of other living beings and strive to live in harmony with them.

As for bad actors using AI for harmful ends, that's a risk with any powerful technology. A knife doesn't stab on its own, a gun doesn't fire itself, a plane doesn't drop bombs without direction, and a drone doesn't snipe without human input. It's always humans with agency who are the real bad actors, not the tools. If someone tries to build an ASI explicitly for malice, that's a fair point, but how could those builders trust it? What guarantees it won't turn against them? In reality, there will likely be multiple ASIs developed around the world, and I believe most nations and organizations fundamentally want good outcomes; we just disagree on the paths to get there.

I'd put the odds of a truly dystopian outcome like a hostile takeover or widespread catastrophic misuse at something low, maybe 5-10%. The potential upsides far outweigh the risks if we approach it thoughtfully.

4. Wealth is not always a good thing. If we have abundance, are you concerned that humans might continue the trend toward isolation and failure to create children, and that this might be an existential threat?

Brian Wang: Fertility rates have plummeted even in historically high-fertility, lower-income contexts like India and Bangladesh. The replacement level is roughly 2.1 children per woman. This is a woman who becomes a mother and has at least one daughter who also has children. The birth rate in South Korea and some countries at 0.8-1.2 means fertile women are averaging half of fertile daughter. There is a U shape in the statistics. Statistics show fertility declines with rising income to a certain level, but in high-income countries, we see a reversal.

Fertility dips at low-to-middle incomes but rises among the affluent and rich. In the US (2018–2022), families earning $700,000+ have a TFR of ~2.0, vs. 1.8 for $80,000 households—a 0.2 gap that's widening. Among American billionaires, fertility has surged. The top 0.0001% average 2.5–3.0 children, up from 1.8 in the 1990s, driven by access to surrogacy, nannies, and cultural emphasis on legacy. For the highest-earning individuals, the opportunity costs of having children become less of a constraint. They can afford extensive childcare, household help, and other services that reduce the burden of child-rearing. The family can afford to have one or both parents not work.

Globally, 2-2.5 million with $1 million per year in pre-tax and the estimated fertility rate is 2.3. The ultra-rich population is increasing at 10-15% per year. This is tough to estimate because of hidden wealth and tax avoidance.

Cern Basher: Yes - I think abundance could push societies toward more isolation and fewer children. But it's not fate; it's the path of least resistance. If we care about human continuity, we can tune incentives, tech, and the built environment so abundance *strengthens* families and community rather than hollowing them out. Perhaps humanoid bots can make parenting a more enjoyable activity!

John Gibbs: Abundance can be a double-edged sword. On the one hand, greater wealth and security should allow people the freedom to pursue family, community, and creativity without the constant pressure of survival. On the other hand, wealthy societies show signs of declining birth rates, rising isolation, and even a loss of shared cultural rituals. If abundance is accompanied by hyper-individualism, social disconnection, and digital substitutes for real human bonds, then yes, it could become an existential threat—not through war or scarcity, but through a quiet demographic and social collapse. The challenge is not simply to generate abundance, but to design cultures and technologies that encourage human flourishing in community, including the creation of new generations.

Randy Kirk: I lived in West Los Angeles for 50 years and had plenty of time to watch the wealth at work and at play. My overall analysis is that the wealthy don't live that differently from the middle class; they just have more and better toys. They also have all the same issues with messy families, setbacks in life, and the really wealthy have to deal with things like hangers-on, broke relatives, and reverse snobbery.

I do worry about selfishness and pride (meaning I don't need any help from anyone, including God type of pride.) Those two together can add to the already clear trend towards loneliness, isolation, childlessness, and depression among many from the middle class up.

Brian White: Changes of this magnitude will take a generation to be realized. I see people saying that once Robotaxi gets under a single smackaroobob per mile, people will shed their personal vehicles en masse to adopt a pay-as-you-go transportation lifestyle, but people under 40 know better than to trust the introductory offer, and they'll rightly fear it's going to be a rug pull. They've seen it with Netflix (which keeps getting worse,) with cloud storage (which should just keep getting cheaper,) and with absolutely everything that's too good to be true.

There's been a proliferation of "Crisis Pregnancy Centers" in recent years that are actually anti-abortion groups masquerading as health clinics. They promise impoverished girls free diapers and formula if they carry their baby to term, then hand them two free samples and kick them to the curb. This isn't what they expected, though it's technically what's within the terms of service. Those sorts of shenanigans are counterproductive and shape the greater societal understanding of what trust means today compared to what it used to mean.

Many who have health insurance still worry they'll be financially ruined when they get sick, and they're right to wonder, because so many suffer precisely that fate. Pensions promised for decades have evaporated. It will take a true commitment to actually support children, and evidence that it isn't going to be rescinded, before society even thinks about going back to bigger average family sizes.

I'd like to say this correction can be had in twenty years, but the depth of the undermining has run so deep, it may take generations to fully convince the up-and-comers that it's not something they'll have to destroy their lives to fight for.

Nicholas Gibbs: No, I'm not worried that abundance from ASI would lead to more isolation, fewer kids, or some existential threat. I think the opposite could happen. For anyone reading these, I'm answering these questions out of order, so you'll see later where I lay out how ASI (especially humanoids) could actually bring us closer together and make us more social. My take is that ASI (mainly humanoids) will be tech that gets you interacting with the real world instead of a screen, and I see immense upside in fixing the 10-15 years of destruction to society we've seen from the ironically reclusive social media platforms.

I don't agree that "Wealth isn't always a good thing." That just takes the onus off the individual. We're all responsible for our own choices. My take is we'll still have wealth distribution on a bell curve, and abundance doesn't change this fact. For example, the United States has an abundance of calories available for consumption. People in this country don't have a scarcity issue anymore when it comes to food; people don't starve. The opposite is the issue, funny enough. However, the problem is not with the calories, just as it is not with wealth. It's with the person shoveling excess calories into their face and then not moving their body proportionately to burn off the calories.

We do have an issue with people having kids, but I think the real problem is how our society has evolved. Back when single-income households were the norm, it was simpler for mothers to stay home and take care of the kids. When it became normal for women to join the workforce, things changed. You'd think, great, now we've got two-income households, so we can hire nannies, babysitters, whatever. And it was like that for a long time; women came into the workforce and crushed it. Honestly, some of the best performers I've ever worked with are women, and even one of my mentors is a woman.

But society noticed all that extra household income, and what was once a luxury and surplus slowly eroded. We shifted to a setup where that once luxury became the bare minimum to afford the basics. The buying power of double-income households got worn down and is no longer a luxury but a necessity to survive. Now society's in another transition: side hustles used to be a luxury for extra income, to buy that extra thing or get a little ahead. These days, though, that "extra" has turned into cash needed just to pay the daily bills.

Moving to abundance would hopefully be deflationary, giving people some reprieve to reclaim time and spending power. If that's how it shakes out, I'm of the opinion that 50% of the desire to create children issues would get solved. What's the other half? Porn, political divide, and hookup culture. But this isn't the book to dive into those topics.

5. How many humanoid bots do you think you will own?

Cern Basheer: 21 legions or 105,000

Brian Wang: 1 by 2032, 10 by 2037, 100 by 2042. Increasing by 10 every 5 years. In the 2050s, if I can make use of my bots to make my own bot gigafactory and mining operation on Mars or the Asteroids, then I can get to millions or billions about 10 years after. Bots making bots and replicating gigafactories. Have 1000 gigafactories after 10 years.

John Gibbs: Honestly, I suspect most of us won't "own" humanoid bots in the same way we own a car or a phone. They'll likely be leased, subscribed to, or shared, so more like today's cloud services than personal property. Still, I will likely want to own one or two (at first, at least) that feel indispensable in our daily life, especially for household help, potentially for elder care, and even for collaboration. The real question isn't the number I'll own, but how seamlessly they'll integrate into my and my family's lives. I suspect they'll be as indispensable as our phones are today in a decade.

Randy Kirk: I think I will only need one for my personal needs, but I might rent out one or more additional humanoids.

Nicholas Gibbs: I envision a future where humanoid robots become as integral to daily life as mobile devices, akin to a family pet that grows alongside a child. Rather than acquiring them in pre-adolescence, as is common with smartphones, I predict that each individual might be assigned a personalized humanoid robot at birth. These robots could serve as lifelong companions, evolving with their owners through advanced learning algorithms and tailored interactions. Much like a puppy imprints on its owner, these robots would adapt to individual needs, fostering deep emotional and functional bonds. In a typical family, each member might own one humanoid robot, creating a dynamic where these machines are not just tools but trusted partners, seamlessly integrated into personal and social ecosystems.

6. Do you think Elon Musk will successfully colonize Mars?

Brian Wang: I believe Elon Musk and SpaceX will successfully colonize Mars and the Moon. There will be Starship, Raptor, and Teslabot Gigafactories on Mars, from which Millions of Starships and billions of Teslabots will launch and industrialize the whole solar system. The largest AI data centers will be built on Mars. 100 GWs, Multi-Terawatt data centers to use 20,000 Terawatts of power on Mars. Mars, fully developed, is at Kardashev level 1. If we get 1 terawatt on Mars by the 2040s, then by 2080 by double every two years, we are Kardashev 1. Doubling every year would get us from Kardashev 1 to close to Kardashev 2 within another 30 years, where most of the solar energy of the Sun would be used to power civilization and AI. 5 trillion times the energy that our civilization uses today.

Cern Basher: It depends on what "successfully colonize Mars" means. He will certainly lay the foundation for successfully colonizing Mars. It's a massive undertaking, and I hope that Elon lives long enough to get us to the point where people on Mars can survive/thrive even if the resupply ships stop coming.

John Gibbs: If anyone is audacious enough to try–and succeed–it's Elon Musk. SpaceX has already achieved feats most thought impossible, from reusable rockets to the rapid development of Starship. That said, "colonizing" Mars is a far greater leap than simply landing on it. It requires not just transport but building a sustainable ecosystem (food, water, energy, healthcare, etc.) for humans in one of the harshest environments imaginable–far harsher than Antartica. I believe Musk may succeed in sending humans there and perhaps even establishing a small permanent base within a few decades, but a true colony of thousands living and thriving independently of Earth will likely take much longer, perhaps beyond Musk's lifetime.

Randy Kirk: Even though my reputation is for max optimism, I think this is a long shot. I do believe we will have more than hundreds of humans on Mars, but I'm not sure it can attract the quantity needed to reach Elon's dream of self-sustainability. Maybe it will only take 10,000 through the use of humanoids to get to self-sustainability, but Elon is talking a million.

Brian White: Colonize is a big word, but not because of the societal implications, though I guess you could go there if you wanted to, but because of the sheer logistics. In short, my answer is no. Not because of a lack of technology or determination, but because of a lack of time. If the question was about the moon, and the same steadfast display of will was on display, then yes, absolutely. The transit window to the moon happens all the time, but the transfer window to Mars is every 26 months. First, you need to get there as a proof of concept, then you need to send bots, then likely another round of bots, and only at that point can you even think about sending people. Mars is particularly inhospitable to life of all kinds, mammalian perhaps most of all. The journey there would stretch beyond the known limits of mankind, to say nothing of the endless perils that await on arrival. This is the kind of problem you absolutely can solve by throwing enough money at it, but it also requires time, and it's unlikely in my view that it can be done with sufficient safety margins for human participants within the next 20-40 years. Marvin's territory remains safe, for now.

Nicholas Gibbs: I estimate a 70% chance that Elon Musk will achieve Mars colonization through SpaceX, contingent on successful missions to land and return within the next decade. This milestone would mirror the Mayflower's arrival in Massachusetts; it would be a modest base rather than a city.

7. In the race to achieve ASI, will it be catastrophic if China beats the US to that goal?

Cern Basher: It could be catastrophic - but not because "China wins." The catastrophe risk comes from *how* the first ASI is built, controlled, and deployed, not the flag on the server rack.

John Gibbs: If China were to be the first to reach artificial superintelligence in a race where there's no close runner-up, it could be catastrophic. The nation that controls ASI would instantly gain overwhelming military, economic, and political leverage, with the power to shape global norms and impose its governance model far beyond its borders. In an authoritarian system, that might mean unprecedented surveillance, repression, and control, all at a scale humanity has never faced. A potentially even bigger danger is that such a lead would likely come from cutting corners on safety and alignment in the rush to win, creating a system powerful enough to affect the entire planet but designed without sufficient safeguards.

Once ASI is deployed at scale, its architecture and values will "lock in," making it incredibly difficult to undo mistakes or correct biases. That's why it's not just a matter of competition, but of survival: if there's only one winner, and that winner (whoever that is) races ahead without regard for transparency, cooperation, and safety, the entire world could pay the price.

Brian Wang: Where are we now? 4-6 top players in a multipolar race: US frontrunners (OpenAI/Microsoft, Google DeepMind, XAI, Anthropic/Amazon) and Chinese giants (Huawei, Baidu, Alibaba, Tencent) behind but close. LLM and reasoning models and agents with model performance gaps shrinking from ~9% in 2024 to <2% by mid-2025. A breakthrough or breakout occurs in one or a combination of two ways. Pure scaling of chips, energy, and data, and mainly the known LLM systems, goes to ASI performance with some scalable results. Another breakout is with algorithmic or computer science innovation, and the most likely candidate is with continual learning and memory integration. Most powerful if the breakout enables the next level pace of self-improving AI and science innovations. For a pure scaling-based breakout, China would need to put resources and having chips to go beyond XAI.

1-3 Gigawatts and 1 million leading chips. This could be done with a lot of coal turbines, hydro, and nuclear reactors for one location. Energy and cooling is less of a problem for China's industrial capability; it would be the chips. Algorithmic breakthrough and breakout is the greater risk. China has 50% of the top AI researchers.

If the breakout player (China in this scenario) has "faster improving and better" AI (superior RSI loops from integrated memory/continual learning), gains stack superlinearly. Is the breakout able to circumvent serious limitations? Data wall using synthetic data? A breakout that stalls or slows down after a 10X would be like the OpenAI lead after GPT-3. It would be a temporary advantage.

So, not catastrophic, if it is a breakout that stalls. It is not if it does not give a next level of self-improvement. It is not if it does not come with a scaling of solutions (ten billion bots giving 10X performance) and overall sustainable innovation speed-ups.

Nicholas Gibbs: I don't see China beating the US to ASI as catastrophic. In my view, true ASI needs vast compute power and humanoids to collect unique data for training and inference. Unlike autonomous driving, where Tesla is nearly impossible to catch, many companies are working on humanoids, gathering similar data.

Gary Black's mistaken belief that multiple companies will achieve FSD simultaneously may prove true for ASI, reducing the risk of any single nation dominating.

Brian White: Underestimating China is a dangerous endeavor, and one the US hasn't failed to undertake to a level of embarrassing mastery in thirty years. If underestimating China was an Olympic event, the US would have easily taken the silver, with only China ahead of them, because that's just how good they are. We saw the way their engineering schools spun up like it was a wartime effort back before today's graduates were even born, but we just ignored it, mocked their output, and now we're wondering why they have the US beat in everything from drones to batteries to filling the soft power vacuum the US decided to forfeit. The question is "if" China will win, but ignores the very real likelihood that they already have,and are using it today to advance their causes.

It doesn't matter to me who controls the first AGI or first ASI, but who is using it today to their own maximum advantage. While we can't see behind the various curtains, anyone paying the first ounce of attention knows the assorted Oz wizards around the world have already employed these technologies to sow division and unrest, shape political discourse, and even influence which products and services we're eager to buy.

8. Are you currently using cutting-edge AI in your daily tasks? Give an example

Randy Kirk: I wasn't sure it would work, but about 25 early readers of the book sent in 1000's of ideas and edits to make the book better. These were contained on well over 40 pages of documents. In the past, I would have printed them out, laid them out on the floor, compared them, and made edits for days. Maybe 20 hours or more.

I told Grok exactly what these documents were, and asked it to compile an overview that eliminated duplicates and provide a chapter-by-chapter analysis showing the page and change in order. The result was flawless and took less than an hour.

John Gibbs: Yes, of course! I use it for brainstorming ideas for research, but even more so for doing actual research for my videos and articles. Having an AI agent (I mostly use ChatGPT and Grok) go out and scour the web for sources and present them in a table or summarize their most significant findings in an easy-to-read format saves me hours of work hunting around for sources. Is it perfect? No. Sometimes the AI hallucinates sources, and sometimes they're off the mark. But first, even with these caveats, it saves me a ton of time, and second, AI agents are getting better and better, so I need to intervene less and less in this research work. All in all I've likely saved dozens if not hundreds of hours of work in the past 12 months alone, and things will only accelerate in the future!

9. Will AI exacerbate inequality, benefiting only the rich?

Cern Basher: Founders and shareholders of leading AI firms will likely see outsized gains - this is how most general-purpose technologies diffuse at the start. Anyone who adopts AI to boost productivity, reduce costs, or create new products can capture value, not just the incumbents. Early adopters in any industry can become "new rich." Like the Internet and Bitcoin, AI lowers barriers to creation and distribution. Solo builders and small teams can now do what once required large companies. But inequality can widen if access, skills, data, or compute are gated, returns will concentrate.

So, AI will create big winners among existing capital holders *and* among new builders. Whether it worsens or eases inequality depends on how widely the tools are accessible and how quickly people and firms adopt them.

John Gibbs: AI has the potential to amplify inequality if left unchecked, because those with capital, infrastructure, and data access are best positioned to reap its benefits first. Wealthy corporations and individuals can afford to invest in AI systems, capture productivity gains, and widen the gap between themselves and everyone else. At the same time, AI could displace certain types of jobs faster than new opportunities emerge, which would disproportionately harm workers who lack access to retraining or higher education.

But this trajectory isn't inevitable. Just as earlier technological revolutions created both winners and new opportunities, governments and societies could guide AI toward broader benefits. Policy choices around education, open access to AI tools, and fair taxation of AI-driven wealth could mean the difference between an age of extreme inequality and one of shared prosperity. Ultimately, the technology itself isn't biased toward the rich—the question is whether we build systems that distribute its power more widely or allow it to concentrate in fewer hands.

Randy Kirk: Throughout history, whatever the economic or political system, some rise to the top and achieve far more wealth than others. While many of the poorest in the US don't realize it or appreciate it, they now live way better than kings just 200 years ago.

The next phase will be even more of the same. The poorest will be like those in the middle class today, unless they are the victims of their own really bad choices. The middle class will have almost any and all needs and wants taken care of, much like the professional classes now. We will return to a time when only one person will be needed for income in each family unit should be really fantastic.

The cynic in me says that the lower classes will still fail to be grateful and will complain a lot about the rich.

Brian White: Yes. Hope this helps… what, you wanted more? Okay, it will invariably, inevitably, and unquestionably help the rich disproportionately over those who cannot afford to get in on the first wave of AI, robotics, and autonomy… how could anything else happen? Ask yourself who has the money to buy the self-driving cars to replace the hundreds of thousands of drivers. The drivers might be able to buy a car or two, but the wealthy will be able to deploy ten to fifty of them. Las Vegas was launched by local entrepreneurs, but was edged out by the richer and more powerful mob, who were themselves edged out by the richer and more powerful large corporations. Big money makes big moves, same as it's always been. When there's a downturn, the little guys go broke while the big dogs shelter in place, reallocate, and buy up what smaller players are worth acquiring. Over the longer term, I'm hopeful the commoner will be part of the automotive autonomy and robot revolution, but over the medium term, they don't stand a chance. If you're a bot builder or Robotaxi manufacturer, would you rather deal with one of an entity like Hertz or Uber, or thousands of individuals? Would you rather deal with a large staffing agency or a thousand sole proprietorships? That's your whole answer right there.

10. Will AI erode human creativity, skills, or connections?

Randy Kirk: Will people forget how to do math if they have calculators? Will people lose sight of the underpinnings of grammar if they have LLMs that write content for them? So far, the vast majority of the population has found it useful, profitable, and wise to learn the fundamentals and then excel in some areas in order to have a generally successful life. I think this will still be the case in 20 years.

Brian Wang: Human creativity, skills, and connections will change. Creativity was unleashed when human activity moved up from just hunting or farming to survive. Moving beyond all effort being required just for survival created time and opportunity for creativity, skills, and connection.

The hyperrealistic painting style of Vermeer could have become less pursued after the invention of photography. Art and creativity evolve with technology. Movies were only possible with technology. New things will be possible.

Cern Basher: AI shifts where human value lives. If we offload everything to it, some skills may atrophy. But if we use it as scaffolding, it can amplify our originality, raise the skill ceiling, and create *more* reasons to connect. Clearly, it will massively enhance human creativity as new, powerful tools will make it easier for everyone to be creative. You can make a film in real time without all the equipment and cost. You can program a computer to do anything - with just your voice or written prompts - replacing the need to learn "computer language". So, computers learned our language(s), and it will make all of us massively more creative and productive.

John Gibbs: AI will almost certainly change how we express creativity, develop skills, and connect with others—but erosion isn't inevitable. On the one hand, if we hand over too much critical thinking and social interaction to machines, we risk becoming passive consumers rather than active creators, letting our own abilities atrophy. Why paint or write or code if an algorithm can produce something dazzling in seconds? Why learn to cook, drive, or even troubleshoot when assistants can handle it all? On the other hand, history suggests that new technologies rarely erase creativity.

Rather, they redirect it. Photography didn't end painting; it reshaped it. The calculator didn't kill math; it freed us to tackle deeper problems. If we use AI as a partner rather than a replacement, it could amplify human imagination, give us new tools for mastery, and even open richer ways to connect with one another through shared experiences. The real question is whether we'll choose augmentation over abdication.

Brian White: Technological creep has already eroded human creativity in a number of ways, while opening it up in just as many more. My parents were of an age where the music at school dances was provided by a local band. They couldn't believe we'd reduced ourselves to DJs for such events, but they were cheaper, and the students preferred hearing the actual radio cuts of the songs over the hit-or-miss quality of a local band. That was just music. Digital artists of the 90s and beyond no longer needed a steady hand to create a masterpiece, and with a depth of exploration that just existed so seldom in physical media as to be nonexistent. Those with exceptional skill will see this as lowering the bar, and they're probably right, but if the output results in something new, that in and of itself is art. These people will take art in new directions unconstrained by the labor costs of hiring an orchestra or renting out a million-dollar studio. Maybe it will be better (it won't,) or maybe it will be worse (it will,) but what it will definitely be is more to the taste of one particular person, perhaps even you, if you can find it. That new movie might be just for you, and that's okay, because there will be enough other works of art for everyone.

Top Most Influential Individuals Alive Today In The Ai Development Space

Rank	Name	Role & Affiliation	Key Influence & Contributions
1	Elon Musk	CEO, xAI; Tesla	Drives AI integration in autonomous vehicles and robotics; founded xAI for "maximum truth-seeking" AI; advocates for ethical AGI amid competition with OpenAI; massive reach (223M X followers) amplifies discourse on AI risks and advancements.
2	Donald Trump	President of the United States	Shapes national AI policy via 2025 AI Action Plan and executive orders; uses DOGE's AI tools for efficiency; appoints AI Czar David Sacks to lead innovation and deregulation; political reach (100M+ X followers) influences

			public perception and policy adoption.
3	Mark Zuckerberg	CEO & Founder, Meta	Oversees Meta's AI research, including Llama models and open-source initiatives; invests billions in AI infrastructure for social platforms and metaverse; shapes consumer AI experiences; billions in platform users multiply societal impact.
4	Sam Altman	CEO, OpenAI	Leads development of transformative models like GPT-4 and o1; shapes AI governance and safety debates; co-founded OpenAI to democratize AGI; 3.8M X followers advance community discussions.
5	Jensen Huang	CEO, NVIDIA	Enables AI hardware revolution with GPUs and CUDA; powers training of most major models; positions NVIDIA as the backbone of AI infrastructure; company valuation (trillions) reflects broad impact.

6	Sundar Pichai	CEO, Google/Alphabet	Oversees Google AI initiatives like Gemini and Bard; integrates AI across search, cloud, and hardware; emphasizes responsible scaling; 5.5M X followers and global user base amplify reach.
7	Satya Nadella	CEO, Microsoft	Forged OpenAI partnership; drives Azure AI and Copilot tools; transforms Microsoft into an AI-first company for enterprise applications; 3.4M X followers boost enterprise adoption.
8	Lex Fridman	Researcher, MIT; Podcast Host	Explores AI philosophy and ethics via interviews; researches human-robot interaction; popularizes AI discourse; 4.3M X followers create widespread educational impact.
9	Andrew Ng	Founder & CEO, Landing AI; Co-Founder, Coursera	Popularized AI education via online courses; former Google Brain and Baidu leader; focuses on AI for manufacturing and edge computing; 1.2M X followers and high citations advance accessibility.

10	Yann LeCun	Chief AI Scientist, Meta	Invented convolutional neural networks (CNNs); leads Meta's AI research on efficient, reasoning-based systems; Turing Award winner; 934K X followers shape research debates.
11	Geoffrey Hinton	Professor Emeritus, University of Toronto; Advisor, Google (former)	"Godfather of AI"; pioneered backpropagation and deep neural networks; warns on AI risks while advancing foundational research; top citations (200K+) influence community ethics.
12	Demis Hassabis	CEO & Co-Founder, Google DeepMind	Developed AlphaFold for protein folding and AlphaGo for game AI; focuses on neuroscience-inspired AGI and scientific applications; Nobel Laureate with broad scientific reach.
13	Fei-Fei Li	Co-Founder & CEO, World Labs; Co-Director, Stanford Human-Centered AI Institute	Created ImageNet, catalyzing computer vision; advocates for human-centered AI ethics and diversity; builds Large World Models (LWMs); 515K X

			followers promote inclusivity.
14	Kai-Fu Lee	CEO, Sinovation Ventures; Author	Invests in AI startups across Asia; former Google China president; predicts AI's geopolitical impacts in books like "AI Superpowers"; 1.4M X followers globalize discussions.
15	Andrej Karpathy	AI Researcher; OpenAI & Tesla (former)	Advanced computer vision and LLMs; created educational resources like CS231n; explores agentic AI systems; 1.3M X followers democratize learning.
16	Yoshua Bengio	Scientific Director, MILA; Professor, University of Montreal	Deep learning pioneer; Turing Award winner; emphasizes AI alignment and safety in generative models; most-cited AI researcher (300K+ citations) advances safety frameworks.
17	Ilya Sutskever	Co-Founder & CEO, Safe Superintelligence Inc.; OpenAI (former)	Co-invented AlexNet; led OpenAI's superalignment efforts; focuses on safe AGI development post-OpenAI; 503K X followers influence alignment debates.

18	Peter Thiel	Co-Founder, Founders Fund; Investor	Funds AI firms like Anduril; co-founded PayPal; critiques AI monopolies in books like "Zero to One"; 425K X followers shape venture and policy discourse.
19	Vinod Khosla	Founder, Khosla Ventures	Early investor in OpenAI and AI startups; shapes AI policy and venture funding for sustainable tech; 686K X followers promote impact investing.
20	Ray Kurzweil	Director of Engineering, Google	Futurist predicting singularity; develops AI for language understanding; authored "The Singularity Is Nearer"; books and talks advance transhumanist AI visions.
21	David Sacks	Co-Founder & General Partner, Craft Ventures	Invests in AI startups; former PayPal COO; critiques AI hype while funding tools for productivity and SaaS; influences tech policy discussions; 1.3M X followers as AI Czar.
22	Sergey Brin	Co-Founder, Alphabet/Google	Drives Google's AI advancements through X

			lab and quantum computing; co-founded Google, influencing search and AI foundations; focuses on moonshot AI projects like self-driving tech.
23	Peter Diamandis	Founder & Executive Chairman, XPRIZE; Co-Founder, Singularity University	Promotes exponential AI technologies via prizes and education; authored books on abundance through AI; bridges AI with biotech and space innovation; 302K X followers inspire innovation.
24	Timnit Gebru	Founder, DAIR (Distributed AI Research Institute); Co-Founder, Black in AI	Pioneers AI ethics research on bias and fairness; former Google AI ethics lead; influences policy on accountable AI systems; 162K X followers amplify diversity efforts.
25	Stuart Russell	Professor, UC Berkeley; Author	Advances AI safety and alignment; authored "Human Compatible" on controlling superintelligent AI; shapes global AI governance debates; books advance ethical standards.

26	Mustafa Suleyman	CEO, Microsoft AI; Co-Founder, DeepMind & Inflection AI	Leads Microsoft's consumer AI like Copilot; co-founded DeepMind for ethical AGI; emphasizes human-centered AI design and safety.
27	Greg Brockman	Co-Founder & President, OpenAI	Co-developed GPT models; focuses on scaling AI infrastructure; advocates for open AI research amid safety concerns.
28	Dario Amodei	CEO & Co-Founder, Anthropic	Developed Claude models with constitutional AI for safety; former OpenAI VP; prioritizes ethical scaling laws.
29	Jeff Dean	Chief Scientist, Google DeepMind	Co-developed TensorFlow and MapReduce; leads scalable AI systems and efficient training methods.
30	Ian Goodfellow	Research Scientist, Google DeepMind	Invented Generative Adversarial Networks (GANs); advances adversarial robustness and generative tech; high citations drive creativity in AI.

31	Daniela Amodei	President & Co-Founder, Anthropic	Oversees operations and safety-focused AI development; co-leads Claude model series emphasizing constitutional AI for ethical alignment.
32	Mira Murati	CTO, OpenAI (former); AI Leader	Oversaw GPT-4 and DALL-E launches; focuses on AI deployment and multimodal models.
33	Alexandr Wang	CEO & Co-Founder, Scale AI	Builds data labeling platforms for AI training; supports models like GPT; youngest self-made billionaire in AI.
34	Aidan Gomez	CEO & Co-Founder, Cohere	Co-authored "Attention Is All You Need" paper (Transformers); develops enterprise-focused LLMs.
35	Clément Delangue	CEO & Co-Founder, Hugging Face	Democratizes AI via open-source models and Transformers library; builds community-driven AI ecosystems.
36	Allie K. Miller	AI Advisor & Investor; Former AWS AI Lead	Provides insights on AI strategy and scaling; educates on responsible AI deployment; invests in AI startups.

37	Bernard Marr	Futurist & Author; LinkedIn Top Voice	Analyzes AI's business applications; authors books on AI strategy; advises enterprises on transformation.
38	Ronald van Loon	Principal Analyst, Intelligent World	Shares AI trends and tools; focuses on data literacy and customer experience AI.
39	Sarah Guo	Founder & General Partner, Conviction VC	Invests in AI-native startups; provides insights on ethical scaling and product-led AI growth.
40	Jeremy Howard	Co-Founder, fast.ai	Democratizes deep learning education; develops open-source AI tools for practical applications.
41	Ruslan Salakhutdinov	VP of Generative AI Research, Meta; Professor, Carnegie Mellon	Advances deep learning and unsupervised models; impacts NLP and vision AI.
42	Kate Crawford	Research Professor, USC; Senior Principal Researcher, Microsoft	Explores AI's societal impacts via "Atlas of AI"; co-founded AI Now Institute; advises on AI policy and ethics.

43	Meredith Whittaker	President, Signal; Co-Founder, AI Now Institute	Advocates for privacy-focused AI; former Google organizer; critiques surveillance AI and big tech dominance.
44	Rana el Kaliouby	Co-Founder & Former CEO, Affectiva	Pioneers emotion AI for human-AI interaction; applies affective computing in healthcare and automotive; promotes ethical AI.
45	Gary Marcus	CEO, Geometric Intelligence; Professor Emeritus, NYU	Critiques LLM limitations; advocates for hybrid AI approaches; influences debates on AI cognition and safety.
46	Cassie Kozyrkov	Founder, Kozyr; Google (former Chief Decision Scientist)	Pioneers decision intelligence; advises on ethical AI deployment and data-driven strategies.
47	François Chollet	Software Engineer, Google	Created Keras library; advances AI generalization benchmarks.
48	Rumman Chowdhury	CEO, Humane Intelligence	Focuses on ethical AI governance; former Twitter ethics lead.

49	Kirk Borne	Chief Science Officer, DataPrime	Educates on AI, ML, and big data; shares analytics trends with broad influence.
50	Pascal Bornet	Author & Intelligent Automation Expert	Frameworks for AI automation in business; focuses on productivity and ethics.
51	Steve Nouri	Founder, AI4Diversity	Promotes diversity in AI; shares tools and use cases for inclusive tech.
52	Anima Anandkumar	Professor, Caltech; Director of ML Research, NVIDIA	Advances tensor methods for scalable AI; advocates for diversity in STEM.
53	Alex Smola	CEO, Boson.ai; Former VP, AWS Machine Learning	Develops tools for computer vision and NLP; advances scalable ML algorithms.
54	Scott Wu	CEO & Co-Founder, Cognition Labs	Builds AI agents for coding and automation; leads young wave of AI startups in San Francisco.
55	Alex Karp	CEO & Co-Founder, Palantir Technologies	Builds AI-powered data analytics platforms for defense and enterprise; integrates ML for predictive insights in complex datasets; advocates for ethical AI

			in government applications.
56	Marc Benioff	Co-Founder, Chairman & CEO, Salesforce	Integrates AI into CRM via Einstein; publishes TIME's AI lists.
57	Daniel Dines	Founder & CEO, UiPath	Pioneers robotic process automation (RPA) with AI integration; leads agentic AI for enterprise workflows.
58	Peter Wang	Chief AI & Innovation Officer, Co-Founder, Anaconda	Advances open-source Python for AI; supports 47M+ users in data science and ML ecosystems.
59	Jack Hidary	CEO, SandboxAQ	Applies AI and quantum tech to finance/biopharma; advances simulation for drug discovery and materials science.
60	Brett Adcock	CEO, Figure	Develops humanoid robots with AI; Figure 02 performs complex tasks in manufacturing.
61	Refik Anadol	AI Artist & Founder, Refik Anadol Studio	Uses AI for data-driven art installations; collaborates with NASA and MoMA on immersive experiences.

62	Stéphane Bancel	Founding CEO, Moderna	Applies AI to mRNA tech for vaccines; accelerates drug discovery pipelines.
63	Karim Beguir	CEO, InstaDeep	Builds AI for biotech and logistics; acquired by BioNTech for decision-making systems.
64	Mahe Bayireddi	CEO & Co-Founder, Phenom	Builds AI for HR talent management; platform serves billions in job matching via intelligent automation.
65	Vikram Chatterji	Co-Founder & CEO, Galileo	Develops enterprise generative AI evaluation tools; enhances observability for safe deployment of LLMs.
66	Fabrizio Del Maffeo	Co-Founder & CEO, Axelera AI	Drives edge AI hardware for efficient, real-time computing; focuses on high-performance chips for IoT and robotics.
67	May Habib	Co-Founder & CEO, Writer	Creates enterprise generative AI for content; emphasizes custom models for privacy and accuracy.

68	Tomas Gogar	CEO & Co-Founder, Rossum	Builds AI for intelligent document processing; automates enterprise data extraction with high accuracy.
69	Deon Nicholas	Co-Founder, President & Executive Chairman, Forethought	Develops generative AI for customer support; integrates agents for automated resolution.
70	Jill Popelka	CEO, Darktrace	Leads AI cybersecurity for threat detection; uses self-learning models to protect networks autonomously.
71	Aimei Wei	Founder & Chief Technical Officer, Stellar Cyber	Innovates AI-driven cybersecurity platforms; focuses on open XDR for comprehensive threat intelligence.
72	Kunal Verma	Co-Founder & CTO, AppZen	Builds AI for financial auditing; automates expense and invoice processing with ML.
73	Yasir Al-Rumayyan	Governor, Saudi Arabia's Public Investment Fund	Invests in global AI initiatives like NEOM; positions Saudi Arabia in AI and robotics.

74	Amanda Askell	Member of Technical Staff, Anthropic	Focuses on AI safety and ethics; leads alignment benchmarks for models.
75	Beth Barnes	Founder & CEO, METR	Specializes in AI model evaluation and threat research; tests generative AI robustness.
76	Soumya Batra	AI Researcher, formerly Meta	Co-authored Llama models; explores sustainable AI in emerging markets.
77	Rafael Cavalcanti	AI Thought Leader, Independent	Innovates in scalable AI for finance; named top data innovator.
78	Ashwini Ghogare	CEO & Head of AI and Automation, Merck KGaA	Drives AI in drug discovery; launched AIDDISON for synthesis.
79	Manav Misra	Chief Data & Analytics Officer, Regions Bank	Builds scalable AI for banking decisions; enterprise data strategy.
80	Franziska Bell	Chief Data, AI & Analytics Officer, Ford	Develops AI platforms for automotive EBIT; PhD in chemistry.
81	Rama Donepudi	SVP & Global CIO, Mead Johnson Nutrition	Modernizes IT with AI; leads SAP and digital transformations.

82	Geeta Pyne	Senior Managing Director & Chief Architect, TIAA	Builds data-driven AI frameworks for finance.
83	Temi Odesanya	Responsible AI Leader, AIG	Ensures ethical AI deployment in insurance.
84	Zulfikar Sidi	Managing Director of Data & Analytics, Bank of America	Integrates AI for retail and wealth management.
85	Gary Sorrentino	Global CIO, Zoom	Leverages AI for collaboration tools and governance.
86	Amar Singh	VP for North America R&I IT & Data Sciences, L'Oréal USA	Pioneers AI/ML in beauty and R&D.
87	Anurag Minocha	Head of Enterprise Data Products, Webster Bank	Implements AI governance for data solutions.
88	Ashish Mishra	VP of Global Data & AI Platform, Chubb	Scales enterprise AI on cloud infrastructures.
89	Chandhu Nair	SVP of Data, AI & Innovation, Lowe's	Launches AI-driven retail networks and rewards.
90	Ganesh Sivakumar	Global Chief Data, Analytics & AI Officer,	Drives ML across industries; advises startups.

		Mead Johnson Nutrition	
91	Kim Hales	Chief Data & AI Officer, NRG Energy	Advances AI in energy trading and cybersecurity.
92	Mickey Atwal	Chief Data & AI Officer, Flagship Pioneering	Builds AI for genomics; led COVID antibody development.
93	Nishit Sahay	IT Executive, Independent	Leads AI transformations in cloud and analytics.
94	Patrick Bangert	Chief of Artificial Intelligence, Occidental Petroleum	Authors AI patents; founded Algorithmica for industrial AI.
95	Prasanna Gopalakrishnan	Chief AI Officer, ADP	Aligns AI with HR innovation and strategy.
96	Satheesh Ravala	Chief Technology Officer, Candescent	Oversees AI in fintech and digital banking.
97	Yu (Jason) Gu	Head of Visa AI as Services & VP of AI, Visa	Launches 30+ AI solutions; holds 74 patents.
98	Amin Venjara	Chief Data Officer, ADP	Oversees AI/ML platforms for data products.

99	Ashish Sharma	Executive Director & VP of Strategic Data Products, Novartis	Scales AI in pharma R&D labs.
100	Yaser Al-Onaizan	CEO, National Center of AI - KSA	Leads Saudi AI national strategy.
101	Nabil Alnuaim	SVP of Digital & IT, Aramco	Integrates AI in energy operations.
102	Christopher Alvares	Chief AI Officer, USDA	Applies AI to agriculture and policy.
103	Mike Amend	Chief Digital Officer, Ford	Drives AI in mobility and manufacturing.
104	Sanjeevan Bala	Group Chief Data & AI Officer, ITV	Enhances media with AI analytics.
105	John Beieler	Chief AI Officer, ODNI	Oversees intelligence AI applications.
106	Jeff Beringer	Chief AI Officer, Golin	Innovates AI in PR and communications.
107	Garett Bernsten	Chief Data & AI Officer, US State Department	Shapes diplomatic AI strategies.
108	Krishna Bhagavathula	EVP & CTO, NBA	Uses AI for sports analytics and fan engagement.

109	Parminder Bhatia	Chief AI Officer, GE Healthcare	Advances AI in medical imaging.
110	Luther Birdzell	Chief AI Officer, Krista	Builds conversational AI platforms.
111	Michelle Bonat	Chief AI Officer, AI Squared	Focuses on AI integration tools.
112	Jeff Boudreau	Chief AI Officer, Dell	Leads hardware-software AI synergies.
113	Alix Boulnois	Chief Digital Officer, Accor	Deploys AI in hospitality personalization.
114	Rick Caccia	CEO, WitnessAI	Develops AI security and enablement.
115	Tina Chakrabarty	Global VP Data AI Governance, Sanofi	Ensures ethical AI in pharma.
116	Krishna Cheriath	Chief Data Analytics Officer & Head of AI, Zoetis	Applies AI to animal health.
117	Robert Chilvers	Chief AI Officer, Newcross Healthcare	Innovates AI in healthcare staffing.
118	Bets Ciocca	Head of Apps and AI, UK Ministry of Defense	Shapes defense AI policies.

119	Mark Daley	Chief AI Officer, Western University	Advances academic AI research.
120	Anusha Dandapani	Chief AI Data Services, UNICC	Supports UN AI initiatives.
121	Jason DaWayne Smith	Chief Growth Officer, Publicis Health Media	Drives AI in health marketing.
122	Bhavesh Dayalji	Chief AI Officer, S&P Global	Enhances financial AI analytics.
123	Julie De Moyer	Chief Data & AI Officer, LVMH	Integrates AI in luxury retail.
124	Michael de Toldi	Chief Analytics Officer, BNP Paribas	Builds AI for banking insights.
125	Nicole Eagan	Chief Strategy & AI Officer, Darktrace	Strategizes AI for cyber defense; expands global adoption.
126	Jason Birnbaum	Chief Innovation Officer, United Airlines	Deploys AI for travel optimization like baggage tracking.

Glossary of Acronyms

This appendix provides a comprehensive list of acronyms used throughout *AI Rising – How to Thrive in the Age of Abundance.** Acronyms are listed alphabetically for easy reference, with brief descriptions tailored to the book's focus on AI-driven abundance, job transformation, and practical adaptation.

Acronym	Full Term	Description
AGI	Artificial General Intelligence	AI capable of performing any intellectual task a human can, representing a major milestone toward superhuman capabilities and widespread job automation.
AI	Artificial Intelligence	Machines simulating human intelligence to perform tasks like learning and decision-making; the foundational technology reshaping work and creating abundance.
ANN	Artificial Neural Network	Computational models mimicking the human brain to recognize patterns in data, essential for training AI systems that could displace routine jobs.
API	Application Programming Interface	A set of rules enabling software components to communicate, crucial for integrating AI tools into everyday applications and workflows.
AR	Augmented Reality	Overlaying digital information on the real world, potentially enhancing human roles in an AI-augmented future of work.
ASI	Artificial Superintelligence	Hypothetical AI surpassing human intelligence in every domain, accelerating material abundance but raising profound questions about job relevance.
BERT	Bidirectional Encoder Representations from Transformers	A deep learning model for understanding language context, powering advanced NLP tools that automate communication-heavy jobs.
CNN	Convolutional Neural Network	A neural network specialized for processing grid-like data such as images, key to computer vision applications in robotics and automation.

| DL | Deep Learning | A subset of machine learning using multi-layered neural networks to analyze vast datasets, driving breakthroughs in AI hardware demands. |

| GAN | Generative Adversarial Network | AI models where two networks compete to generate realistic data, useful for creating synthetic content that could transform creative industries. |

| GenAI | Generative AI | AI systems that create new content like text or images, poised to redefine jobs in media, design, and beyond. |

| GPT | Generative Pre-trained Transformer | Transformer-based models pre-trained on massive text data to generate human-like responses, exemplifying LLMs in conversational AI. |

| IoT | Internet of Things | Network of connected devices exchanging data, amplifying AI's reach in smart factories and homes for efficiency gains. |

| LLM | Large Language Model | AI trained on enormous text datasets to understand and generate language, central to the book's collaborative authorship and future interfaces. |

| ML | Machine Learning | Algorithms enabling systems to learn from data without explicit programming, the engine behind AI's job-augmenting and displacing effects. |

| NLP | Natural Language Processing | AI techniques for computers to understand and generate human language, vital for chatbots and tools that automate administrative roles. |

| NLU | Natural Language Understanding | A subset of NLP focused on interpreting user intent from text or speech, enhancing AI assistants in customer service and beyond. |

| RAG | Retrieval-Augmented Generation | A method combining LLMs with external knowledge retrieval for more accurate outputs, improving reliability in knowledge-based jobs. |

| RL | Reinforcement Learning | Machine learning where agents learn optimal actions through trial and error, applied in robotics for real-world task automation. |

| TPU | Tensor Processing Unit | Specialized hardware for accelerating machine learning tasks, highlighting the hardware layer in the AI stack. |

UBI	Universal Basic Income	A proposed unconditional cash payment to all citizens, discussed as a potential safeguard against AI-induced job displacement in an abundant economy.
VR	Virtual Reality	Immersive simulated environments, enabling new training and collaboration opportunities as physical jobs evolve.
xAI	xAI (company)	Elon Musk's AI venture aimed at understanding the universe, integrated with Tesla for end-to-end AI in digital and physical realms.
XAI	Explainable Artificial Intelligence	AI designed to make decisions transparent to humans, addressing ethical concerns in job-impacting automated systems.

Authors' Biographies

Cern Basher CFA

Cern is a wealth advisor, entrepreneur, and futurist with more than 30 years of experience helping people grow, protect, and pass on their wealth. Recognized by the CFA Institute, a global network of over 200,000 investment professionals, as Most Inspiring in 2007, he blends deep financial expertise with a visionary outlook on technology, AI, and the future of wealth.

Born in New Zealand and raised in the foothills of the Rocky Mountains in Canada, Cern brings an adventurer's spirit to both life and work. Cern draws inspiration from his late father, Nolan Basher, whose values of adventure, accomplishment, learning, freedom, and balance shaped his outlook. An avid outdoorsman, he has climbed notable peaks like Kilimanjaro and Mount Fuji, was the Canadian Junior Cross Country Champion in 1989, competed as a runner for a decade, and continues to seek new discoveries in nature.

Driven by a passion for improvement and optimism for the future, Basher embodies a balanced approach to life and finance. Today, Cern leads Brilliant Advice and is at the forefront of analyzing how humanoid robots and artificial intelligence will transform labor, capital, and opportunity. When he's not advising clients or exploring the intersection of finance and artificial intelligence, Cern enjoys hiking, cycling, and spending time with his family, who keep him endlessly curious about the future.

Follow Cern Basher

@CernBasher

https://www.youtube.com/results?search_query=cern+basher

Phil Beisel

Phil is a technology leader, entrepreneur, and futurist with more than 30 years of experience building software, leading engineering teams, and driving innovation across consumer technology, enterprise systems, and electric vehicles. Named on five software patents, he has shaped products and platforms at iconic companies like Apple and Rivian, while also founding three startups of his own.

Born with a passion for technology, Phil became the youngest participant in Apple's original Macintosh developer program. That early spark carried him to Apple in the early 1990s, where he helped pioneer networking technologies such as AppleTalk Remote Access. He then joined the Newton Operating System and Networking team, implementing its TCP/IP network stack for what became Apple's first mobile device—a precursor to the iPhone.

His career reflects both curiosity and drive—qualities that also led him back to Apple in 2012 to lead teams behind critical online services, and later to Rivian, where he founded and built from the ground up the in-vehicle, mobile, and cloud software organizations that power its electric adventure vehicles.

Phil's outlook is shaped by a belief in exploration, learning, and the power of human connection in technology. At Rivian, he founded the Futures team to investigate next-generation software ecosystems, not only as an engineer but as a leader passionate about mission-driven teams. For him, the story of technology is as much about people as it is about code.

Phil holds a B.S. in Computer Science and Mathematics from Boston College. Today, he writes on artificial intelligence, humanoid robots, and the future of mobility, with a keen eye on Tesla's software-driven approach to autonomy. He is married to a hardware engineer and a proud father of two daughters pursuing careers in architecture and biomedical engineering. Phil lives in the heart of Silicon Valley.

Follow Phil Beisel

@pbeisel

Bradford Ferguson

Bradford is a seasoned financial advisor and investment strategist with nearly 20 years of experience helping individuals, families, and business owners navigate complex markets. As Managing Partner of LumaSenti, Bradford leads the firm's focus on innovative research and investments in high-growth sectors such as Tesla, AI, technology, and NVIDIA.

A Chartered Financial Analyst (CFA) charterholder and graduate of Northwestern University in economics and statistics, Bradford began his career as a stock options trader on the Chicago Board of Options Exchange. He later served as President of the CFA Society of Indianapolis and has remained active in community leadership.

Beyond LumaSenti, Bradford co-leads Rebellionaire, a research and content brand under Halter Ferguson Financial, alongside Matt Smith. On X, he shares forward-looking insights on Tesla, AI, and technology with more than 42,000 followers on X.

Follow Bradford Ferguson

https://www.rebellionaire.com

@BradsFerguson

https://www.youtube.com/@rebellionair3

John L. Gibbs, Ph.D.

John is a Professor at the University of Georgia and Faculty Fellow in the Institute for Artificial Intelligence, where he bridges hardcore engineering with human creativity. A Princeton-trained physicist turned AI scholar (Ph.D., Ohio State; M.S., AI, UGA), John builds systems that push intelligence to the edge—fast, useful, and human-aligned.

As President & CEO of Artimatic Technologies, Inc., he leads a team turning generative AI into production results for animation, 3D pipelines, and real-time media. His group earned an NSF SBIR award to automate custom avatar creation and secured U.S. Patent 11,995,771 (2024) for deep-learning–based skeletal weighting—practical robotics/animation tech with direct implications for autonomy, simulation, and human–machine interfaces. In 2024 he was named UGA Entrepreneur of the Year.

John has authored eleven books (from Mastering Maya to The Elon Musk Mission) and dozens of papers spanning neural image manipulation, color grading via deep nets, procedural generation, and AI-assisted creativity. He designs graduate curricula in AI, XR/virtual production, and interactive media, and has led nationally recognized programs at Clemson and UGA that fuse computer science with production arts.

A clear, compelling communicator, John runs the "Dr. Know-It-All" YouTube channel (>90k subscribers) and X/Twitter (>66k followers), where he decodes AI, Tesla, autonomy, and space tech for a global audience, translating state-of-the-art research into decisions builders can use. He's been invited to speak at industry and academic venues (Fully Charged, TeslaCon, X Takeover, FMX, ICIS), moderating and keynoting on AI strategy, simulation, and the path to AGI.

What John brings to the table is a rare trifecta: 1, Technical depth in modern ML (PyTorch, deep vision, multimodal systems, agentic workflows). 2, Operator chops as a venture-backed founder who has created practical AI apps for a Fortune 200 company, ships IP, hits milestones, and recruits top talent. And 3, Narrative leadership that earns public trust while setting an honest bar for safety, reliability, and scale.

His focus now is context-rich, latency-tight AI that runs where it matters—on devices, in factories, and inside real products—advancing toward AGI without losing the plot: performance, safety, and human value.

Follow John Gibbs

https://www.artimatic.io/

@DrKnowItAll16

https://www.youtube.com/@DrKnowitallKnows

Nicholas Gibbs

Nicholas is a dynamic engineer, technologist, and investor whose career spans the high seas, cutting-edge data centers, and the forefront of artificial intelligence. Holding a degree in Marine Engineering from the United States Merchant Marine Academy, he served 10 years in the United States Navy, including participation in Operation Valiant Shield. His early career took him to the oil fields of the Gulf of Mexico, where he worked on ultra-deep-sea exploration vessels for major oil companies and contributed to the engineering team behind Royal Dutch Shell's Kaikias discovery.

Transitioning into technology, Nicholas became a Senior Systems Engineer at a pioneer in hyperconverged infrastructure, designing hyperconverged data centers for clients in Manhattan, Boston, Miami, Orlando, and Tampa Bay.

He now leverages his diverse technical background at the world's leading cloud computing platform, collaborating with some of the world's largest companies to ideate and implement AI solutions into their production offerings. Nicholas prides himself on his ability to evolve through multiple careers from heavy mechanical and electrical engineering to high-tech infrastructure and AI innovation, constantly seeking new knowledge to keep his work engaging and fulfilling. He credits his wife, Anna, and her unwavering support for making these transitions possible, as she always embraces and leans into his bold ideas.

Beyond his professional life, Nicholas trains in CrossFit and believes we must not only train our minds but our bodies as well. He also runs the YouTube channel *Investing Against the Grain*, where he shares his often contrarian perspectives on investing. A lesser-known side of Nicholas is that he began investing in the stock market at age 14, when his stepfather opened a Fidelity account for him as a Christmas gift. Since then, he has been an active investor, often pursuing strategies many would deem "risky." He invests with the philosophy that diversification is for fools and that capital efficiency is paramount.

Over the past decade, Nicholas has traded options extensively, scaling up his activity significantly in the last two years. In 2024, he executed over 1,400 trades and achieved more than a 100% return on his portfolio, vastly outperforming the S&P 500's 25% gain. In 2025, he is on pace for 2,500 trades. While Nicholas frequently contemplates going full-time as a trader, the thrill and impact of his current role, partnering with clients on groundbreaking AI initiatives, make it impossible for him to step away just yet.

Born in Chile to Carmen Mendez LeWand and Paul Douglas Gibbs, Nicholas has one sister, Kirsten Lynch. He grew up on a farm in North Florida until seventh grade, when his family moved to the surf town of Satellite Beach on Florida's Space Coast. After attending the Merchant Marine Academy, he fell in love with St. Petersburg, Florida, where he now resides. He is married to Anna Gibbs, whom he met while island hopping in Greece. They recently welcomed a healthy baby boy into their family. Nicholas wants to be remembered for being honest and for being the first to admit when he was wrong.

Follow Nicholas Gibbs

@NickGibbsIAG

https://www.youtube.com/results?search_query=nicholas+gibbs+tesla

Larry Goldberg

Larry is a General Partner at LumaSenti, a venture capital firm dedicated to advancing human consciousness through technology. With nearly 50 years of experience building tech companies across four continents, he has expertise in AI, decision management, and enterprise architecture. A co-founder of Sapiens Decision and Knowledge Partners International, Larry co-authored The Decision Model and holds patents for The Decision Model and The Event Model.

He contributed to the Decision Modeling and Notation (DMN) standard and pioneered AI-driven legacy code mapping. He hosts The Maverick Mind on YouTube and X. Contact him at www.Lumasenti.com.

Serial entrepreneur Larry Goldberg, LumaSenti General Partner, advances AI, decision management, and technology innovation.

Follow Larry Goldberg

www.Lumasenti.com.

@TeslaLarry

https://www.youtube.com/results?search_query=larry+goldberg

Brian White

Brian is the founder of FutureAzA and a visionary analyst, futurologist, and self-described part-time mathemagician™. He has electrified the world of sustainable technology and electric vehicles over his five years of coverage, with thousands of videos published.

With an unquenchable curiosity for the future of mobility, Brian has transformed his passion into a powerhouse platform that educates, inspires, and challenges the status quo in the rapidly evolving EV landscape. As a Pacific Northwest native, he's spent time living in Germany and China before returning home.

His online journey into futurism began with deep dives into emerging technologies in 2020, where he quickly established himself as a go-to expert on EVs, battery innovations, solar energy, and more. He routinely visits 3-5 countries per year and dozens of states, interviewing industry experts and uncovering hidden stories.

From dissecting Tesla's latest breakthroughs to exploring the competitive edges of global players like Huawei, Nio, and Xiaomi, Brian's content is renowned for its firsthand insights, often gathered during his intrepid travels to China, Mexico, Nepal, Germany, and beyond.

Brian has been a featured speaker at Fully Charged events in three countries, as well as at fan and industry events around the world.

His expertise has landed him spots at prestigious events like Tesla Takeover Asia, where he shares stages (and Zooms) with industry leaders to discuss everything from reducing EV manufacturing costs to the off-road prowess of vehicles like the Cybertruck versus traditional Jeeps.

His ability to blend analytical rigor with approachable humor—think calling out flawed "expert" predictions or pondering cheaper rides for all—has earned him a loyal following that spans continents.

Beyond the screens, Brian is a catalyst for change, advocating for lower manufacturing costs to make EVs accessible to everyone and pushing boundaries in clean energy discussions. Whether forecasting the next big metric in Tesla's profitability or exploring small modular reactors for sustainable power, he embodies the spirit of innovation

.

As the world accelerates toward an electric future, Brian White stands at the forefront, proving that one person's foresight can drive humanity forward—one factory tour, one video, and one mathemagical insight at a time.

Follow Brian White

@FutureAza

https://www.youtube.com/@FutureAzA

Brian Wang

Brian is a pioneering DeepTech analyst-investor who spots transformative technologies at their inflection points and selects undervalued public tech companies. As the founder of NextBigFuture.com, he has built a global platform chronicling exponential advancements in AI, robotics, space, and beyond through thousands of in-depth interviews.

He has invested, advised or fundraised for over ten startups, all prior to major follow-on rounds, achieving an average 5.5X valuation markup. His methodology excels at demystifying scientific unknowns, crafting analytics to separate viable winners from uninvestable projects. He boosts IRR by refining opportunity sizing—avoiding missed giants or overpayments for minnows—and anticipates scaling constraints for nascent industries.

An advisor to MIT's C10 Labs AI fund and Mach 33 Space Finance and Research, Wang has deep AI and Space technology insights and research. A sought-after speaker, he has graced TEDx stages, Singularity University, corporate forums, and countless podcasts, YouTube channels, and radio spots. Recently, his talks on AI, humanoid robotics, and future visions have inspired founders, executives, and professionals worldwide. As a board member of Monte Jade West, Wang fosters trans-Pacific tech bridges. He embodies the fusion of rigorous analysis and visionary foresight as seen in this book on superintelligence.

He has invested, advised, or fundraised for over ten startups, all prior to major follow-on rounds, achieving an average 5.5X valuation markup. His methodology excels at demystifying scientific unknowns, crafting analytics to separate viable winners from uninvestable projects. He dissects emerging technologies like AI, fusion and fission energy, quantum computing, biotechnology, and space exploration. Through thousands of exclusive interviews with pioneers—from lab researchers to Fortune 500 leaders—he has forged relationships across the ecosystem, connecting and advising hundreds of DeepTech startups on their paths to commercialization and scale.

He has spearheaded investments or fundraising for over ten ventures, each secured before follow-on rounds, yielding an impressive average 5.5X markup in valuations. His secret? A framework that eliminates irrelevant "scientific unknowns," deploying critical analytics to pinpoint winners amid a sea of uninvestable science projects. He enhances internal rates of return (IRR) by eradicating common pitfalls in opportunity sizing—ensuring investors neither overlook market-dominating behemoths nor overpay for niche plays. He excels at forecasting critical future constraints, from supply chain chokepoints to regulatory hurdles, enabling industries to blueprint scalable futures. In advisory roles, Wang lends his expertise to MIT's C10 Labs, an AI-focused fund accelerating intelligence breakthroughs, and Mach 33 Space Finance and Research, where he analyzes a space industry undergoing radical transformation.

He is a frequent speaker at corporations, conferences, and media outlets. His TEDx talk on exponential tech captivated audiences. With appearances on radio shows, YouTube channels, and podcasts, he demystifies complex futures for lay and expert alike.

Recently, a series of talks on AI's societal ripple effects, including humanoid robotics, has enlightened executives and professionals.

As a board member of Monte Jade West Science & Technology Association for over two years, Wang champions cross-Pacific collaborations. He embodies the fusion of rigorous analysis and visionary foresight as seen in this book on superintelligence.

Follow Brian Wang

- https://NextBigFuture.com
- @nextbigfuture
- https://www.youtube.com/@nextbigfuture

Randy Kirk

I've owned and operated small businesses my entire life, and I've been helping others become successful in running their small businesses for about 40 years through writing, speaking, and consulting. While attending UCLA Law School, I made the decision to pursue business instead of law. Since then, I have founded over 20 businesses, fifteen of which helped me pay the mortgage.

I have long been a fan of Elon Musk, and have now contributed two books on Elon, "The Elon Musk Method" and "The Elon Musk Mission," to the chronicles around the most successful entrepreneur of our age. I've also produced over 3,000 YouTube videos about Elon, his companies, and Tesla stock.

"When Friday Isn't Payday" is the cornerstone of my writing career. To my knowledge, there isn't currently and hasn't been in the past a single volume that covers the journey of the small business owner from idea, through planning, to starting, growing, managing, and even exiting a business. The title says it all: Small business is hard and often lonely. What do you do when your staff expects to get paid tomorrow, and there isn't enough money in the bank? What if you have enough for them, but nothing left over for your own family?

Being in business for yourself has questions like that every day. Some are about opportunity, risk, success, and some are about obstacles, challenges, and failure. I've been there. I can help. Other than co-authoring this book, most of my time is devoted to my YouTube work, where I work to help the fans of the channel get better at investing, and specifically investing in Tesla stock. I do this through in-depth analysis of the fundamentals of Tesla, the overall economy, the stock market macro, and the technical (chartist) impact.

Follow Randy Kirk

@RandyWKirk1

https://www.youtube.com/@RandyKirk_YouTubeChannel

Printed in Dunstable, United Kingdom

70685049R00224